W9-AEJ-195

THE LIBRARY
ST. MARY'S COLLEGE OF MARYLAND
ST. MARY'S CITY, MARYLAND 20686

Congress and the Fall of South Vietnam and Cambodia

Congress and the Fall of South Vietnam and Cambodia

P. Edward Haley

Rutherford • Madison • Teaneck
Fairleigh Dickinson University Press
London and Toronto: Associated University Presses

© 1982 by Associated University Presses, Inc.

Associated University Presses, Inc.
4 Cornwall Drive
East Brunswick, N.J. 08816

Associated University Presses Ltd
27 Chancery Lane
London WC2A 1NF, England

Associated University Presses
Toronto M5E 1A7, Canada

Library of Congress Cataloging in Publication Data

Haley, P. Edward.
Congress and the fall of South Vietnam and Cambodia.

Bibliography: p.
Includes index.
1. Vietnamese Conflict, 1961–1975—United States.
2. Cambodia—History—Civil War, 1970–1975. 3. United States—Politics and government—1974–1977. 4. United States. Congress. I. Title.
DS558.H32 959.704′33′73 81-65871
ISBN 0-8386-3099-5 AACR2

PRINTED IN THE UNITED STATES OF AMERICA

Contents

To Elaine

Oh, I have picked up magic in her nearness . . .

—from Ezra Pound, "A Virginal"

Preface

At the present stage in the continuing debate over the proper roles of Congress and president in foreign-policy making, all sides appear to agree that Congress, having acquired new powers, is playing a new and more influential role vis-à-vis the executive in the foreign-policy process. There is far less agreement, of course, over whether or not Congress *should* play such a role. If the first assumption is valid and Congress indeed possesses new and greater influence over U. S. foreign policy, it follows that considerable importance attends the goals for which that influence is exercised, the means used to obtain these goals, and the procedures and people and organizations involved in their attainment. One way to help reveal what is to be known about the newly significant ends and means of congressional foreign-policy making is to examine specific instances in which Congress decisively affected the foreign policy of the United States by its actions. A pair of such instances occurred during the Ford administration from January to May 1975, the last months of the existence of the pro-American regimes in Cambodia and South Vietnam. The purpose of this book is to describe and analyze the effect of congressional influence on American policy as the governments of those two countries were defeated and overthrown by the Khmer Rouge and Vietnamese Communists.

The fall of Vietnam and Cambodia was chosen for this study of legislative-executive relations for two reasons. The first derives from the political and emotional significance of "the war"—as the Vietnamese conflict was known—to millions of people around the world, and not least to those Americans, of all ages who were politically conscious in the mid-1960s and early 1970s when the American combat role became an important one. They will recognize the passion and intensity of the debates, for they recall another time, already strangely distant, when it seemed no one could escape taking sides for or against the war in Indochina. Those who have come of age since that time will find in this study part of the story of the remarkable politics of that period in the history of the United States. For all readers, lay and expert alike, the book offers a thorough, sometimes startling glimpse of the workings of a representative democracy, of Congress and president, bureaucracy, press, and people, in the fashioning of foreign policy in a particularly interesting, important, and difficult period of American and world history.

Although the actions of the Senate are examined in this study, special attention is given to the House of Representatives and to its Committee on Foreign Affairs.* The House is at the center of this book, in part because less is known of its foreign-policy role than is known of the role of the constitutionally favored Senate. It is also given most prominence because the House and its Foreign Affairs Committee played an extremely important part in the formation of American policy in the last years of the Vietnam conflict, from the passage of the War Powers Resolution and the prohibition of combat in Indochina in 1973, to the fall of Phnom Penh and Saigon in the early spring of 1975. Finally, throughout 1975 I worked in the House of Representatives as an International Affairs Fellow of the Council on Foreign Relations, serving for a time on the staff of a member of the Foreign Affairs Committee. I was thus able to observe developments and to conduct extensive interviews for nearly twelve months from a kind of "outside inside" position among the Congressmen and committee staff most intimately involved in dealing with the fall of Cambodia and Vietnam. My position as a Fellow working in a congressional office also aided my quest for interviews in the State Department, White House, and Pentagon, as well.

It is a pleasure to acknowledge the assistance of two members of the staff of the House Committee on Foreign Affairs: Jack Sullivan, now assistant administrator for Asia in the Agency for International Development, and Jack Brady, now chief of staff of the committee. They made time in their hectic schedules to answer my many questions, not only while I was working on the Hill, but during repeated follow-up interviews since my return to Claremont. Of the dozens of people I interviewed in the executive branch, I particularly wish to thank Les Janka, on the staff of the National Security Council in 1975 and later deputy assistant secretary of defense, General Brent Scowcroft, and Peter Rodman. They generously answered my questions. The views expressed in this book are, of course, the responsibility of the author.

Without the support of the Council on Foreign Relations it would have been impossible for me to conduct the research essential to the

*Early in 1975 the committee changed its name from *Foreign Affairs* to *International Relations*. In April 1979, it took back the old name and became once again the Foreign Affairs Committee. To avoid confusion the name *Foreign Affairs* is used throughout the book.

book. I would also have been denied the remarkable firsthand experiences of my year in the Congress, a time when my knowledge of foreign-policy making and executive-legislative relations was broadened and deepened in ways invaluable to me personally and of tangible benefit to my students. The director of the International Affairs Fellows Program at the council is Alton Frye, and I wish here to express my thanks to Alton for his kindness and for support he has shown for my work. Toward the end of my fellowship year, in particular, Alton arranged a seminar at which I presented a preliminary report on my work. The occasion, like my fellowship itself, undoubtedly yielded more to me, by pushing me beyond the known and the obvious, than to my listeners. It sparked initiative and that precious element of hope which alone, on some occasions, sustained my efforts. An outstanding student of Congress himself, Alton has that rarest of human abilities, the capacity to encourage and facilitate the work of others. I also wish to thank Marjorie Pacitti, then at the council, for her help and friendliness toward me and my work.

Claremont, California

1
Introduction

We were learning again—although we hardly needed to—what everyone in the executive branch since Washington's day had learned, that to advise and consult with Congress is next to impossible. One can learn its uninformed opinion or one can try to inform the opinion of a few key members by long, patient, secret talks, as Lovett had done with Vandenberg leading up to the Vandenberg Resolution of 1948; but to devise a joint approach to a complicated and delicate matter of foreign policy is not within the range of normally available time and people. Here the separation of powers really separates.

—Dean Acheson

Proponents of a more active or even a dominant Congress sometimes argue that the legislative branch has declined so far in power and prestige that the chief task in American government has become to check presidential dominance rather than, as it was in the past, to curb congressional initiative and caprice.[1] Others have detected a kind of historical imperative operating to thrust Congress to the fore and to shrink presidential influence. Since Congress is destined to gain influence, they suggest, the sensible course is not to buck the trend but to exert ourselves to make certain that Congress contributes sensibly to the making of policy.[2]

The notion that presidential aggrandizement is responsible for the nation's errors and difficulties, both foreign and domestic, is attractive. It shifts the blame for Vietnam and all other mistakes to "the enemy within"—to the president and an overweening executive branch. It is also an analysis much favored by liberals and those on the not-so-radical left of American politics.[3] One would have thought that liberals, burned by McCarthyism, would be shy of a new "enemy within" and more inclined to regard the country's difficulties as resulting as much from the fallibility of human judgment and the tyranny of circumstances at home and abroad, as from the hunger for power of president and bureaucrats.[4]

Doubtless there are a few liberals who embraced the argument chiefly as a means of discrediting a Republican opposition that, under Nixon, needed little help in that department, as things turned out. Others, less genteel, may have chosen it instrumentally, as a way of disparaging an administration they detested. A more plausible explanation of the motive of most liberals might be that by blaming the president, or the office of the president, or Defense and State, the CIA, the Chiefs of Staff, the Army, or even the upbringing and career patterns of top bureaucrats, an actor on the national scene need not face himself to assess the degree of his own responsibility for the mistakes and failures.[5] That most of the significant American decisions to intervene in Vietnam, not to mention much of the combat and bombing, took place during the tenure of Democrats John Kennedy and Lyndon Johnson, along with many of the abuses committed by the CIA and FBI, only serves to augment the force of this explanation. Whatever their actual motives, it is the left in the United States rather than the right who have "found" enemies in the White House and the other executive agencies, the left who have used this rationale to justify an attack on a branch seen as having grown dangerously powerful and immoral. It was not always so.

A number of scholars and politicians in the 1950s and 1960s emphasized the desirability of the expansion and use of presidential power.[6] The policies they commended and their approach to presidential power, adopted during the Kennedy and Johnson administrations, went smash in the late 1960s. The war in Southeast Asia could not be won and urban decline in the United States could not be overcome by activists for either a "New Frontier" or a "Great Society." The same people served both administrations. Recognizing failure, they were then obliged to change the generalities to support their new policies. As long as unilateral initiatives by the president promised to realize the kinds of foreign and domestic changes they desired, by a marvelous ingenuity they discovered the constitutional and practical justification for such boldness. When the outcome was found wanting and the horrors that came in the presidential baggage were examined, overboard the president went and out came arguments in favor of poor, slighted Congress, or at least against the abuse of presidential power and executive authority.

Late in the Vietnam War, it is true, one could still find those willing to extol the untrammeled use of presidential power. Such a one was James M. Burns. A proper president for the nation in 1972, Burns suggested, was one who understood he must preside over the decade of the 1970s, "ruling in partnership with Congress if national goals can thus be met, but *acting without Congress if the national legislature is unable to come to grips with the job ahead.*" At its best, he argued, "the presidency . . . seeks *to liberate American society from whatever binds it* [and] to extend the theory and practice of equality."[7] It was hard to discover from Burns's argument just how a president acting in this way could be kept from becoming a tyrant. Burns offered little help. The only restraints a president needed, Burns alleged, came not from his "political enemies in Congress" or from the opposition party but from a "small party council" of persons committed to party goals and able to sustain and challenge the president as "allies in a common cause."[8] One's natural reaction is that these are no restraints at all, particularly if the president should have a strong will and be even slightly intolerant of criticism from dependent subordinate advisers. This would not have troubled Burns, for he plainly desired to impose no effective restraints of any kind on presidential action. Rather, he chose to entrust his liberties and well-being, along with those of his countrymen, to the splendid personal qualities of individual leaders, the "giants," as he called them, who were ready to spring from the earth if it were not for the institutions, opportunism, and false idealism that thwarted and crushed their abilities.[9]

Instead of a handbook for future presidents, Burns's arguments may have represented a high-water mark for theories and theorists of presidential power. In the years immediately after these arguments were published the nation experienced Watergate, the revelation of a seemingly unending stream of abuse of authority by CIA and FBI, and the total defeat of American policy in Indochina. Drastic inflation and high unemployment contributed to a widespread realization that the achievement of "social justice" might be the painful undertaking of generations. It certainly was not easily to be won or readily to be measured in the four-year span of a presidential term.

For good or ill, these failures, scandals, and disappointments tarnished the presidency. The response of many liberals was to argue for the restraint of presidential prerogative in foreign affairs. As Emmet John Hughes has observed, "the more or less liberal-Democratic and the more or less conservative-Republican beliefs and attitudes on national policy managed to achieve an almost complete reversal. . . . The new attitudes struck at partisan images of the Presidency that had been cherished for a generation, since the first bold initiative of Franklin Roosevelt's New Deal."[10] Those who sought to reduce presidential influence found a sympathetic audience in the legislature, and with the support of most liberals and some conservatives, Congress passed a number of important laws limiting the discretionary authority of the president to decide foreign policy. These acts included the War Powers Resolution, the prohibition of combat by American forces in Indochina, the establishment of political and humanitarian criteria for the granting of foreign aid, the refusal to permit further clandestine intervention in Angola, the increase of congressional supervision of arms sales, and the elimination of most military grants.

Important as they were, the demands for control of presidential power in foreign affairs were not repeated in regard to the domestic field. To be sure, there was talk within the Democratic party and among Democratic presidential candidates of a need to make government responsive to the people and more efficient, to streamline bureaucratic organization and to eliminate wasteful and foolish spending. Such talk was not always disingenuous. But these propositions had to coexist with equally serious commitments to advance "social justice," to aid the poor, to succor the aged and handicapped, and to establish equal treatment of minorities. All these cost money and require more rather than less action by the central government. Jimmy Carter, the Democratic nominee in 1976, campaigned against Washington, but once he entered the White House he hardly undertook to dismantle the federal bureaucracy or abandon the quest for "social justice." There is a contradiction here, of form if not of substance. No longer would the Democrats know the bliss of consistency in foreign and domestic methods: frequent intervention and heavy expenditures were acceptable domestically; they were increasingly suspect internationally.

There is more consistency in the conservative than in the liberal reaction to the debacle in Vietnam, to Watergate, to scandal and abuse of authority in the executive branch, and to high inflation and unemployment. Opposed by taste and preference to the use of the federal government to correct social and economic problems, conservatives distrusted the Democratic conversion to the anti-Washington camp, sought to exploit the contradiction inherent in the new liberal and Democratic views, and opposed restraining the president or cutting the budget in foreign operations. Conservatives generally reversed the liberal preference. The president's ability to wage war, to dispense aid, and to engage in clandestine activities cannot be reduced, they avowed, without endangering national security. At home, on the other hand, the president and in particular the "creeping bureaucracy" must be kept on a short leash. If they were not, they would enslave and ruin the American people by constant meddling in their private lives and by draining them of money and the spirit and opportunity for commercial enterprise.

There is sense to the liberal denial of a contradiction. Do not be misled, their argument ran, by the apparent inconsistency of method. A larger consistency is sought between goals within the United States and the ends of American foreign policy. This consistency of ends obviously, and even naturally, requires different methods at home and abroad. The international goals analogous to a decent, just society at home are peace and social and political progress. They are not served by presidentially inspired armed intervention, support of dictators, arms races, and subversion. Moreover, times have changed. The threat of war with the USSR has lessened, China and the Soviet Union have replaced their alliance with hostility, the questions of resources and population have gained in importance, and rather serious economic adjustments ought to be made, both among the industrial nations and between them and most of Africa and Asia. Besides, the abilities of the United States or any single government, however powerful, to accomplish good in the world are rather more limited than we thought.

The conservative rejoinder is straightforward and compelling: prudence knows no such easy political boundaries. If there is reason to doubt the efficiency of governmental action in foreign affairs, there is every reason to doubt it in domestic affairs, as well. There may be even more reason to oppose the expansion of government authority within the nation's boundaries than in our dealings with other countries. After all, we must live in this country and suffer the loss of freedom that inevitably accompanies the growth of government. Abroad, we deal with other governments, some of whom are our enemies or wish us ill. The watchwords, then, are vigilance and preparedness internationally and restraint at home.

It is not necessary here to decide in favor of one or the other approach to foreign and domestic policy. It is important, however, to note the centrality of the role of Congress in foreign-policy making whether one prefers the liberal or the conservative response to the difficulties that confronted the United States at home or abroad from the late 1960s to the mid-1970s. Liberals have turned to Congress as a refuge, finding there both an institution capable of challenging the president's hold on foreign policy and, in the power of the purse, a means of winning a major, and perhaps, decisive voice in policymaking. Conservatives have found Congress to be a nemesis, not a refuge, and have looked to the presidency and the executive branch generally for salvation. They fear Congressional meddling in foreign affairs and have sought to prevent and reduce it.

Both sides have argued their case over the years, and it is interesting as well as useful to survey the briefs. Dean Acheson probably put the case against a large role for Congress as well as anyone. Congress alone, or Congress dominant, he argued, is unsuited by nature to conduct a sensible, effective foreign policy for the nation. Congressional government must result in "a negative and vacillating foreign policy, the impairment of our world position, and danger to our national safety." In his experience, congressional foreign policy was "formed by slogans and emotion; decisions represented the lowest common denominator of the groups in the legislative assembly."[11] All too often, action on vital problems was postponed and evaded in Congress until events decided the issue.

What of the internal structure of the House and Senate? Are the members of these bodies so divided by faction and parochial interests that they are incapable, by themselves, of comprehending the collisions of power and interest beyond the nation's shores and of fashioning a consistent policy for dealing with them composed, as it must inevitably be, of costly and distasteful sacrifices? Is it this inherent disability that makes the president "the pivotal point, the critical element in reaching decisions on foreign policy"?[12]

Acheson believed this to be true. He went further and challenged the very idea that the presidency had grown so great that the chief task in American politics was to check presidential aggrandizement. Admitting that presidential power, prestige, and, above all, responsibilities had increased, he suggested this had not been a steady growth, but a response to national emergency and war. Whenever the nation begins to believe itself secure, whether that belief is well founded or not, he argued, "the power of the office as a means of accomplishment, diminishes in competition with the multitudinous and often inconsistent appeals of congressional leaders."[13]

If this is a valid interpretation, it is both interesting and ironic. It is interesting because it follows that the present sorry state of congressional-executive relations arises, in part at least, out of a perceived absence of threat and emergency. The fervent engagement of Congress in a multitude of accusations and investigations directed at the executive represents not the restoration of congressional powers—the powers were never lost—but the exercise of those powers in an atmosphere free from a shared perception of threat. Acheson regarded the power of Congress over foreign affairs as a kind of evil genie in a bottle: one had to hope the stopper stayed firmly in place. There was not a Constitutional or practical mismatch in favor of the president over Congress. Even in the realm of foreign affairs Congress held many high cards: "Today nearly all programs require funds, authority, and men, which Congress may grant, skimp, or withhold."[14]

Acheson's judgment is ironic because détente—the keystone of the foreign policy of the Ford and Nixon administrations—depended on fostering a widespread public impression that all of foreign affairs, and particularly great power relations, have entered an especially benevolent and peaceful era—a time when important negotiations may go forward, when there is, in fact, nothing that cannot be negotiated, and when old and bitter ideological enmities are muted. The era of crusades was over and, according to this view, foreign policy might safely be left in the hands of a few experts dealing in a secret and complicated fashion. If Acheson was right, the foundation of Kissinger's diplomacy was also the source of his downfall with the Congress. The more successfully he negotiated with the Russians and Chinese the more recalcitrant and assertive Congress became.

It may be that this is a dilemma forced on the nation by the need to conduct foreign policy within the limits set by democratic political practices, a dilemma that can not be made to disappear, but whose harmful effects can be ameliorated. Kissinger recognized the dilemma and publicly answered the criticism that his conciliatory diplomacy hurt the nation's ability to maintain the initiative in foreign affairs and keep strong armed forces in existence. Would you, he has asked in so many words, have the government of the United States fabricate emergencies and hypocritically spread a sense of alarm and danger among the people? A great nation like the United States should be able to maintain strength and purpose on the basis of reality, without illusion. Kissinger would not, or so he said, make a policy that depended on crying wolf. The problem of maintaining a sense of unity, discipline, and vigilance in a democracy has preoccupied American leaders for the last four decades and has troubled men as different as Truman and Kennedy, Acheson and Kissinger. All would perhaps have agreed that a diplomacy that relies primarily on conciliation, negotiation, and secrecy, however mature, responsible, and appropriate it might be, surrenders important advantages in maintaining presidential leadership of Congress in foreign affairs.

A final aspect of Acheson's outlook on legislative-executive relations merits examination. He believed and argued persuasively that to ask whether Congress or the president was the dominant actor in the foreign-policy process utterly and even dangerously confused the issue. "The question," he suggested,

> is whether the checking and balancing prescribed by the Constitution is so conducted as to permit a continuity of policy, involving over a period of years, the maintenance of distasteful measures. For this is essential if we and our friends are to maintain our position and safety

in competition with powers of unmistakable capacity for consistent and sustained effort. I believe that it is possible to do this only if the presidential office is made and maintained strong and resolute.

The central question is not whether the Congress should be stronger than the Presidency, or vice versa; but, how the Congress and the Presidency can both be strengthened to do the pressing work that falls to each to do, and to both to do together.[15]

Acheson's viewpoint, summarized in these two paragraphs, depends on a number of prior judgments. The president must take the lead in making foreign policy. Acheson would not have regarded this as "domination." The conduct of foreign relations requires above all else perseverance in courses of action that, inevitably, will seem distasteful and wrongly burdensome to Congress and the people, but whose success hangs on the ability of the nation as a whole to choose and maintain the uncomfortable, unpopular course. In a system of government based on the separation of powers it is possible to define policy—or to limit it—by exploiting the obstacles to unity and decisive, timely action inherent in this kind of regime. This would seem to be the approach chosen by the Ford and Nixon administrations. Instead of this, Acheson asked, considering the intractable nature of foreign problems and the strengths and weaknesses of both branches, wouldn't it be wise to discover ways to take the best from both Congress and president?

Three years after leaving office, Acheson sought to discover the manner and circumstances in which Congress and executive acting together made creative contributions either in the origination or development of policy. To Acheson the process was "individual," "elusive," and "secreted in the qualities of men." He had discussed the subject at length with Senator Vandenberg, reflected on it, observed the process in operation, and participated in it. "What then," he asked, "are the qualities in men and the posture of circumstances which make for the creative process when policy is moved forward to a new phase?"[16] His answer is both revealing and, surprisingly enough, naive—not an adjective one ordinarily applies to Acheson. Characteristically, Acheson chose to make the congressional participant a senator and the chairman of the Foreign Relations Committee as well. The senator should be widely respected and trusted in his own party. He must have a vigorous intellect, but not necessarily an original one. He must be an adept politician, able to assure that what is done in foreign affairs neither injures his party (or himself) nor aids its opponent. He must not be tricky and must state frankly what his conditions of support are. Before the measures come to a vote he must have made certain his colleagues will agree with what he has chosen to support.

But above all, he must temper the proposals of the executive with what he knows the legislature will permit. "His great function," Acheson wrote, "is to bring the suggestions within the realm of the possible, to use method as a means of molding a proposal to make it politically feasible."[17]

The executive participant in the creative process must be able to speak for the administration because he is trusted by it. He must not lose touch with his colleagues and principals, and he must pursue the main objective frankly and without trickery. The two from Congress and executive must have confidence in one another. They must be unusually gifted people, for they must inspire trust, command the facts, and have a mastery of maneuver and advocacy. Together, Acheson suggested, two such individuals will be able to achieve "what neither could have accomplished separately."[18] The example he cites is the collaboration in 1948 between Senator Vandenberg, chairman of the Foreign Relations Committee, and Robert Lovett, under secretary of state. Together they gained passage of the Vandenberg Resolution, paving the way for the North Atlantic Treaty, a striking innovation in American history and diplomacy.[19]

Naive may be the wrong term to describe Acheson's analysis of Congress and president joined in creative and novel endeavor. It may only seem naive because it appears to come from a different and somehow simpler time. In 1948 it was generally believed that the Soviet Union threatened American security, and perhaps this common perception of threat lay behind Acheson's words and united Congress and executive far more readily than the personal qualities and institutional arrangements he described. Whatever the true explanation may be, Acheson described what must be recognized, in the end, as a rare coincidence of gifted individuals and favorable international circumstances.

The approach described by Acheson and followed by General Marshall, Lovett, and Acheson himself inspired criticism as well as praise. One high official, able to observe the approach in operation and forced to participate in it, objected strenuously. The official was George Kennan, who, in addition to his responsibilities as head of the Policy Planning Council, served as chairman of the international working group drafting the North Atlantic Treaty. Even twenty years later the memory irked him, and he recorded his objections in his memoirs:

> I disliked, in particular, being placed in the position of spokesman for the views of unnamed figures in the legislative branch of our government . . . views which I could only relay in the most laconic

> form and the rationale of which I could neither explain, nor, to tell the truth, myself accept. If senators were to constitute the final and unchallengeable arbiters of such proceedings, then, it seemed to me, they ought to conduct the negotiations themselves. I can recall an occasion, during one of the main plenary meetings, when some sort of suggestion made by one of the European representatives was crushed, properly and unavoidably, by Mr. Lovett, who said he could assure the gathering that anything in the nature of what had been suggested would be quite unacceptable to the Senate. The objection was final. It produced only a moment of glum silence. I could not help but wish, though, that one of our European friends had stood up at that point and said: "Mr. Lovett, if you and your colleagues in the State Department cannot speak responsibly for American policy in this matter, will you kindly introduce us to the people who can?" Our European friends had a right, it seemed to me, to deal with someone who had some latitude of decision, whose reflections and appreciations were relevant to the process of decision, and with whom it therefore paid to engage in rational discussion and argument.[20]

Whatever one's opinion of Marshall's method of dealing with Congress, it is clear that it was not Kissinger's approach, and by such a margin that it sometimes seems that Kissinger designed his own method of dealing with Congress to be the exact opposite. If Watergate had not occurred and there had been no Vietnam War, no illegalities and excesses committed by FBI and CIA, no loss of trust in government, Secretary Kissinger's attempt to impose foreign policy on Congress by accomplished fact might not have resulted in the defeats and upsets he faced. To say this is to make a point of abstract interest alone, of course, for those things happened, policy had to be made in their gloomy shadow, and to fail to take them into account invited the very downward spiral of failure that it is the duty of policymakers to avoid. The Kissinger approach is not without merit, as Kennan's observations show. It is a great advantage for a government to speak with one voice when dealing with other governments, and it is a blessing for foreign governments as well, although a number of them understood and quite handily took advantage of the diffuse and decentralized character of American decision making in foreign affairs. The British during the Lend-Lease period enjoyed quite remarkable success playing one part of the bureaucracy and government against another, and others as different as Israel and the Soviet Union have played the same game.

An additional advantage of the Kissinger approach is that it reduces the sheer physical effort needed for consultation with Congress. The committee chairmen and formal leadership are informed after a decision has been reached within the executive branch itself, or after delicate negotiations are brought to a conclusion. There is only notification after the fact, not consultation and mutual accommodation in advance. In the "reformed" Congress of the early 1970s, of course, the chairmen and leadership were far less able to "deliver" Congress than they had been in the past. It did not matter as much as it once might have, for Kissinger sought only tolerance, not support. The trouble begins when even a limited tolerance is not granted by Congress, as was the case, for example, with arms for Turkey or money to support covert American involvement in Angola.[21] The approach fails when it becomes necessary to lobby virtually every member of both houses—something the executive repeatedly vows it will never and can never accomplish, but which it undertakes when the stakes are sufficiently important, as they were in the case of Turkey. Eventually, the administration and the committee were able to win approval for a partial lifting of the embargo, but not before the strengths and weaknesses of the administration's approach to Congress had been revealed.

The limit on Kissinger's foreign policy was what people and Congress would oppose forcefully and effectively. Since he did not seek to win support but only to avoid the withdrawal of tolerance, Kissinger was able to withstand many kinds of congressional sanctions that were originally intended, after all, to be effective only against an administration seeking support from Congress. Briefly stated, this is the manipulation of congressional and domestic opinion by the manipulation of events abroad.

Through secret decisions and personal negotiations brought to detailed, complex, and interdependent conclusions without consultation with Congress, the secretary of state sought to create international situations that accorded with his view of what was necessary and beneficial to the United States and, in the process, so to prejudice American policy that Congress could refuse to agree only at the risk of seeing the entire baroque edifice come tumbling down, bringing to ruin its good as well as its bad elements.[22] In theory, of course, either response was possible, but in practice the manner of presentation made it far more difficult to refuse than to acquiesce. Congress was presented with accomplished facts, and this alone would cause members to balk, even if they agreed with the substance of the undertakings, which many did not. It would be wrong to say that the administration ignored Congress. The goals of Congress and congressional opinion were taken into account in fashioning the agreement or negotiation or policy at issue, but they were considered *in camera,* within the executive branch, by bureaucrats. Congressmen were not allowed to bring their influence to bear on the course of deliberations within the executive or on negotiations in process with other countries. Kissinger and Marshall both sought to make it possible for Congress to reject their policies, but Marshall's approach was quite different from Kissinger's. Marshall chose to involve influential congressmen so deeply in ongoing negotiations that, believing they had influenced every stage of the process, the congressmen became parties to the final settlement and used their prestige and power in Congress to effect its approval.

How to obtain the "consent of the governed" is a problem central to democratic governments, and, indeed, to modern government itself. Locke and Rousseau, the principal theorists of social contract, posed the problem in an acute form and were forced to deal with the logical and practical difficulties of founding political society on consent. How was this consent to be obtained, after all? What would happen if measures were adopted that were repugnant both to reason and to the public good? Above all, how and why should later generations be bound by the "consent" of their forebears? Answers to these questions were not easily found, but they included the notions of "general will" and the rights of revolution and unfettered emigration.

A certain vagueness in the meanings of consent has been the doorway through which modern government has escaped some of the dilemmas of the theorists. Hidden in the term *consent* are two meanings. Consent can mean passive acquiescence, best expressed, perhaps, by the words "endure without opposition," "bear with," "put up with," or "tolerate." "Silence gives consent" is one example of this meaning. Its importance in a modern democratic government is easily seen. It allows the state considerable latitude in decision making and policy. Without seeming to violate the spirit of democracy, rulers may assume that in the absence of forceful effective opposition they act with the consent of the governed. This approach, which I call the politics of acquiescence, in extreme version, is the one Kissinger and the administrations he served followed in making American foreign policy.

The chief characteristic of the politics of acquiescence was the determination to do what the Nixon and Ford administrations believed right in foreign affairs regardless of opposition from Congress. It was an approach born of weakness, not evil motives. The weakness was both partisan and national: partisan because of the declining electoral and congressional position of the Republican party,* and national because

*In his book about legislative-executive relations in the Nixon and Ford administrations, John Lehman, who served in the Nixon White House, observed that the Nixon administration was the first in 120 years during which the opposition controlled both houses of Congress: 57–43 in the Senate and 243–192 in the House. See *The Executive, Congress, and Foreign Policy: Studies of the Nixon Administration* (New York: Praeger, 1976), p. 215.

the entire country was confused and uncertain after a decade of civil disobedience, violent dissent, failure, and scandal. It is as an effort to tap what Sidney Hook called "unsuspected potential resources" of will and matter that one should understand the foreign policy of Henry Kissinger and the presidents he served. The potential may not have existed. Mind and body may simply have been too tired, too disgusted to respond after Vietnam and Watergate. In any event, success is never certain. "We may lose," Hook observed, "even after we have chosen intelligently and fought bravely. In that case regret is always vain."[23] One may doubt that Kissinger's choices were always wise or good, but one must not confuse his policies with his past thought and experience or underestimate the complexity and audacity of what he attempted.

There is another meaning of consent. To consent can also mean to support a course of action, to strengthen the position of a person or community or policy by one's assistance. Obviously this kind of consent is far more difficult to obtain than the other, for it requires a substantial unanimity of view and agreement on both ends and means of policy. This approach, which I call the politics of support, was in general terms the one followed by Secretary Kissinger's predecessors, particularly George Marshall, Robert Lovett, Dean Acheson, and John Foster Dulles. They would undertake only policies that would be widely and positively supported. Kissinger, by contrast, attempted projects that fell within a much broader realm. The limits on his power in foreign policy were the boundaries of popular and congressional acquiescence. He sought to know not what people and Congress would support enthusiastically but what they would not oppose or, even more precisely, what they would not forcefully and effectively oppose. Both approaches—the politics of acquiescence and the politics of support—are truly distinct in analysis only. Elements of both methods are sometimes present in differing degrees in a single policy encounter. One may think of them as opposite poles of a continuum along which executive policymakers move, seeking acquiescence when they can and support when they must.

2

Nixon, Kissinger, and the Politics of Acquiescence

The Nixon administration resorted to the politics of acquiescence on many occasions. It was their preferred style of operation in foreign affairs. Examples of the politics of acquiescence in operation would include the Paris Agreements on Vietnam, the negotiations and agreements on strategic arms limitation, the Sinai agreement between Egypt, Israel, and the United States, and, in a sense, the opening to China. A brief discussion of the resort to the politics of acquiescence as practiced in regard to Cambodia will give the reader important background information and will also establish the distinction I have identified between foreign policy based on support and that based on acquiescense.

As a rule, when the Nixon administration touched controversial problems or by their actions entered a gray area of uncertain legality or dubious constitutionality, Kissinger and Nixon frequently withheld the information about foreign initiatives the Congress required in order to make the granting of consent informed and meaningful rather than misinformed and meaningless. The Nixon administration, for example, kept secret from Congress and the American people the extent of the intensive bombing of Cambodia from 1969 to 1973. In their concern for secrecy the administration even required pilots, crews, officers, and men right up the chain of command to falsify their official reports about the air raids flown against Cambodian targets.[1] In early 1971 Secretary of Defense Melvin Laird warned his staff of the need to maintain perfect secrecy: "The roof would come flying off the Capitol if [Congress] knew we were seriously considering flying large numbers of sorties [all over Indochina] in 1973 and 1974. We must keep some considerations very quiet."[2]

Nor was this the extent of the concern with secrecy. Nixon and Kissinger also encouraged the Joint Chiefs of Staff (JCS) to deal with the National Security Council (NSC) behind the back of Secretary of

Defense Laird, who favored more openness toward Congress. The channel around Laird was a Liaison Office established to promote cooperation between the JCS and NSC. Operating through this channel Kissinger and the JCS could exclude Laird altogether from many important policy deliberations and allow him to learn of others only after Kissinger and the Chiefs had concerted their positions. This happened often in regard to Cambodia and Vietnam.

What is sauce for the goose is sauce for the gander. Realizing they were being excluded from other important matters, the Joint Chiefs refused to be as patient or scrupulous as Laird. They penetrated Kissinger's armor by ordering an enlisted man attached to the Liaison Office to spy on Kissinger by taking notes and copying documents and passing them to the JCS. The JCS agent, Navy Yeoman Charles Radford, was energetic and imaginative in carrying out his duties, even to the point of rifling the briefcase of Kissinger after his first secret trip to Peking and that of General Alexander Haig, soon to be Kissinger's deputy on the NSC, during one of Haig's visits to Cambodia.[3]

Nor did the pursuit of secrecy end within the bureaucracy in Washington. The embassy consciously interfered with the work of American journalists in Cambodia by advising the Khmer government to withhold transportation on military aircraft and even, at one point, asking the Cambodian government to expel an American reporter. Congress got the same treatment: "When the House Foreign Affairs Committee or the Senate Foreign Relations Committee sent teams to report on the war, the embassy was encouraged by Washington to make their work as difficult as possible and to withhold all information they could possibly manage."[4]

The United States began to bomb Cambodia secretly on March 17, 1969. A year later, on April 30, 1970, a few weeks after the overthrow of Prince Norodom Sihanouk, large U.S. and South Vietnamese combat units invaded Cambodia. The secret bombing, the invasion, and the initial support of the successors to Sihanouk, led by Lon Nol in Cambodia, were all justified by the administration as necessary to disrupt enemy communications and to destroy supply depots in order to protect American troops in South Vietnam and to hasten their withdrawal from the country. The public outcry against the invasion was fierce and widespread and shocked the administration. The Senate soon passed the Cooper-Church Amendment to the Foreign Military Sales Act, a provision that appeared to bar all forms of direct military action or assistance by United States forces in Cambodia. By the terms of the amendment, U.S. forces could not stay in Cambodia, the United States could not send its own advisers to that country nor could it hire others to teach or fight there, and, last, the United States could not provide combat support for the Cambodian government.

The first problem for the administration was to retain the ability to strike North Vietnamese forces in Cambodia because of the threat they posed to Vietnam and to the withdrawal of American troops from Vietnam. This difficulty was overcome through an amendment proposed by Senator Robert Byrd that put into Cooper-Church recognition and approval of the "constitutional power" of the president "to protect the lives of United States armed forces wherever deployed."[5] Fighting Cooper-Church "with every means at its disposal," the Nixon administration organized a filibuster against the Foreign Military Sales Bill until the troops came out of Cambodia, and then arranged for the bill to be bottled up in conference until the second problem could be solved. This was to fashion some sort of legal basis for providing direct American combat support to the Lon Nol regime, especially by air attacks.[6] The vehicle for this—the "presidential loophole" as it became known—was not found until a defense appropriations bill was passed by Congress in November 1970, after much of the turmoil in Washington and around the country had subsided.

The American war in Vietnam was undeclared and rested on uncertain treaty obligations to South Vietnam. Because of this, Presidents Johnson and Nixon had emphasized that repeated congressional appropriations of funds for the conduct of the war assured its legitimacy under the law and the Constitution. Problems arose, however, when Congress began to tie the appropriations. In Cooper-Church and every military appropriation bill from 1970 on, Congress prohibited direct American combat support of the Lon Nol government unless such support was coincidental with action taken to protect the withdrawal of U.S. forces from Indochina and the return of all prisoners of war.[7] The Nixon administration defied the Congress and systematically provided direct American combat support to the Cambodian government even after the withdrawal of all American troops from Indochina.[8] In part, this was accomplished through secrecy and the falsification of after-action reports. It was also based on the loophole carefully built into the law by the Nixon administration and its supporters in Congress.

After the overthrow of Sihanouk, the amount of assistance the Nixon administration wished to supply Cambodia quickly reached hundreds of millions of dollars and made an approach to Congress unavoidable.[9] Winning congressional consent to this supplemental request became, in the words of a member of the Nixon White House, "the highest priority matter of foreign policy in the Administration."[10] A large, high-ranking coordinating group was assembled and set to work, a presidential message and aid package were prepared with great care, information teams were assigned to targeted legislators, and an elaborate program of briefings was prepared to be presented to select groups of Senators. President Nixon met personally with the congressional leadership on November 18 and 19 to plead the case for the Cambodian assistance, which had been joined to requests for Israel, Jordan, Lebanon, and South Vietnam. He asked for $155 million for Cambodia ($90 million had already been transferred to Cambodia from other Defense Department funds) and an additional $65 million for South Vietnam.

Working closely with Senators Cooper and Church, the administration maneuvered the supplemental through a tangle of parliamentary and political problems. The outcome was a revised Cooper-Church amendment to the aid request that prohibited the introduction of U.S. ground troops or advisers into Cambodia—omitting any explicit limit on U.S. air power— and, in a crucial reservation, went on to warn that the supply of military and economic aid could not be understood as a commitment of the United States to the defense of Cambodia. A ceiling of two hundred was later fixed on the number of U.S. personnel who could help in the delivery of the military equipment. The original, much more restrictive, Cooper-Church amendment to the Military Sales Bill was dropped altogether in conference on that bill on December 31.

As the dust settled, there was no doubt that the administration had won a substantial, if not a total, victory. Nixon and Kissinger were free to order bombing in Cambodia in support of Lon Nol not because Congress had agreed to such a policy but because Congress had not expressly forbidden it. As one eyewitness put it:

> In the course of interplay, and compromise, the prohibition on direct air support that passed as part of the Cooper-Church Amendment on the Foreign Military Sales Bill was especially dropped. This was taken by executive supporters in the Senate, by the House leadership, and by the White House to be an explicit authorization of such air support. U.S. close air support to Cambodian forces began in earnest shortly after Cooper-Church became law.[11]

The victory had not been without costs. Congress had put severe limits on the use of American troops in Cambodia, even against North Vietnamese sanctuaries. Here the public outcry against the Cambodian invasion was probably as important as Congressional restraint in causing President Nixon to keep American ground troops out of later forays along the borders of Cambodia and, in particular, Laos. A more important cost was the accumulation of added mistrust of the administration in the Congress. The administration began to bomb in Cambodia and to tie that country to the United States in defiance of the opposition of one-third of the Senate and despite the express agreement of both chambers that the United States should not make a commitment to the defense of Cambodia.[12] This was the politics of acquiescence in its strongest and purest form.

For the short term the administration had its way, but as the air war in Cambodia expanded and more and more evidence accumulated of the misconduct of the "military equipment" teams in Cambodia, the reputation of the administration for honesty and frankness sank lower and lower. Congress reacted against the unwillingness of the administration to deal openly, and began slowly but surely to close the loopholes that allowed military action in Indochina. When the end came in Cambodia and Vietnam, the administration had lost virtually all its freedom of maneuver, while Congress feared to loosen any of the knots so laboriously tied for fear that the administration would lash out against the North Vietnamese and Khmer Communists. Many congressional opponents of the war regarded the drastic military response of the Ford administration to the seizure of the *Mayaguez* by Cambodia's new Communist government as proof of what might have happened if the president had been allowed to use force during the evacuation of Americans and their friends from South Vietnam. The president, needless to say, viewed the matter as an appropriate way of rescuing the ship and its crew and perhaps of reasserting his power to take decisive action without the consent of Congress. "Credibility on both sides was at an absolute nadir."[13]

As the example makes clear, the risks of the politics of acquiescence are two. The essence of democratic government is all too easily lost, for decision is reserved not to the representatives of the people but to a handful of policymakers. The elite may utterly fail to bring the country along behind them, and discover eventually that no one is willing to make the sacrifices and pay the bills that cannot be avoided even by a balance of power diplomacy conducted among the cabinets of the world's governments. Fundamentally uninterested in popular and congressional support—regarding it as a nuisance, as merely one of a number of factors to take into account—the policymaking elite may overestimate public support for its actions and blunder in this way. The second risk is equally likely: they or their successors will turn shy after a few close scrapes and underestimate their popular base, an error that would lead them to act with excessive pessimism and caution and to accept unnecessary compromises. The contrast between the two approaches may be briefly stated. The politics of support seeks the ability to shape events abroad by the manipulation of congressional and domestic opinion. The politics of acquiescence seeks instead to shape congressional and domestic opinion by the ability to manipulate events abroad.[14]

Since the politics of acquiescence was not adopted in a vacuum, it is appropriate to consider what led two successive Republican administrations to embrace this as their approach to Congress and the nation. Much use has been made of the past experiences and even of the personalities of Nixon and Kissinger to explain their approach to foreign policy.[15] While the best of these interpretations are, no doubt, valid and helpful, there is a limit to the uses of the past to explain the present. Should we suddenly be given power to influence events on a large scale, what we do is influenced by more than what we are and have been.

There are institutional, intellectual, and political bounds on what is possible in the present that are at least as decisive for policy as the personality and experience of leaders, and that are far more potent than distant and even unknown acts of other decades or centuries. In evaluating political accomplishment one begins by learning what there is to know about the lives and thoughts of politicians and diplomats. Except in rare cases this is not particularly interesting. One must then ask what were the possible courses of development. Which objectives lay within the scope of human achievement and which were truly impossible to realize?

The political, institutional, and intellectual context that greeted the new administration in January 1969 must have seemed profoundly unappealing and restrictive, however much they as individuals liked a challenge. By this time the institutional weaknesses of American foreign-policy making had become onerous. There was widespread agreement in government and the universities that, in John Franklin Campbell's words, "the machines [had] indeed come out of control."[16] The ills, frequently studied and consistently diagnosed, were thought to be "excessive size and fragmented authority," coupled with a harmful displacement of the State Department from its proper role "in charge" of American foreign policy.[17] A feeling had spread in Congress, the bureaucracy, and the nation as a whole that anti-Communism and the bipolar system it necessitated were an unsatisfactory intellectual base for contemporary American foreign policy. In essays written in the several years before he joined the first Nixon administration, Kissinger added his voice to the rising din of criticism on both the institutional and intellectual fronts. He found the bureaucracy sterile, "increasingly absorbed in its own internal problems," and judged the foreign policy elite in America unsuited to their task by their training in law and business. The chief problems for American policy-makers were, in Kissinger's eyes, to overcome the inertia and awkwardness of the bureaucracy and to develop a philosophically profound concept of world order that would suit the changes that had occurred in world politics. The old concepts and organization just would not do.[18] The mirror held to the nation's face by these critics revealed little of beauty and promise. It showed ugliness, war, oppression, irrelevance, decline, unmitigated confusion, and organizational chaos.

Political circumstances gave no relief. The Vietnam War had divided and bewildered the country. "The coherence of American policy and the public consensus backing it had broken down to a catastrophic extent," as Anthony Hartley observed.[19] It was, above all, a collapse of domestic willingness to continue as before in foreign affairs with which the administration had to deal if it was to have any diplomacy at all. To the corrosion of authority that had followed unavoidably from massive civil disobedience during the civil rights movement, to the first recent stirrings, however primitive and inarticulate, of ideologically based rejection of existing political economy had been added the catalyst of opposition to the government for conducting a massive costly war in a strange and distant place under extremely adverse conditions. "The War" became so abhorrent to some Americans that they found in opposition to it justification for jail, exile, the betrayal of the trust and confidence of friends and colleagues, and even murder and terrorism.

For the nation and the incumbent Republican administration these circumstances spelled weakness. What to do about that weakness was the central question. The Nixon and Ford administrations believed a great deal turned on the United States acting responsibly and consistently in world affairs, avoiding the swings of the past between overengagement and isolation. Whatever else they wished to accomplish, the administrations had first to deal with this weakness, to discover ways, if they could, to make weakness work for them and become strength. The remedies they adopted were coherent, imaginative, and purposeful. But one must not underestimate the tyranny of the circumstances that awaited them. In assessing the Nixon and Ford administrations, one is above all assessing an attempt to cope with weakness.

Ironically, even Nixon's landslide victory in 1972 could not uncover the answers to the specific, recurring, frightening question: how could the government be made strong and be made to appear strong when the public consensus on foreign policy had cracked wide open? The nation's diplomacy had backed it into a corner and surrendered much of its freedom of action. Congress was increasingly hostile to established policy and in the hands of an aggresive, swollen opposition. No president, no administration for at least three decades had ever been at such a disadvantage, had ever been confined within such excruciatingly narrow margins. Even Lyndon Johnson had been able to draw on clear, if diminishing, nuclear superiority and on the strength of a Democratic majority in Congress, although in the end he had been driven from office.

The natural response would have been to slow down at home and abroad, to do less rather than more until the nation could recover its poise and become of one mind again, at peace at least with itself. Overseas this would mean an immediate end to the Vietnam War and a significant, worldwide retrenchment. Not only should old conflicts be ended, but a low profile should be adopted in all the other danger spots, in the Middle East, in Africa, in Latin America, in East Asia. At home, the instinctive reaction would have been to allow the American people to catch their breath and to assess the value and accomplishments of the vast expansion of social welfare programs accomplished during the Johnson administration. This would have been the time as well to undertake a careful, thorough reform of those agencies involved in foreign-policy making.

As it turned out, no major candidate in 1968 or 1972 would accept both domestic and foreign retrenchment. George McGovern and Hubert Humphrey promised a modified version of foreign disengagement, but both favored an expansion of welfare at home. Richard Nixon, the winner on both occasions, rejected the natural and the Democratic reactions to the national difficulties. He stood the Democratic program on its head and ignored the wisdom of instinct, choosing to dismantle welfare at home and expand responsibilities overseas. The Vietnam War was to be brought to an end (at least American troops would no longer fight on the ground), and limited reductions in troop strength elsewhere were to be made, but these steps were not to lead to a time of relative calm and inactivity in foreign policy. Incredibly, the United States, even while still fighting in Vietnam, was to assume the task of constructing an entirely new world order.

There was to be a new "creation," to borrow Acheson's term, and present at this creation would be President Nixon and his Special Assistant, Henry Kissinger, the new and more skillful midwives to history. The new world was to be significantly improved over the old, particularly in the elimination of moralistic cant from American policy and the reduction of the role of ideology in international politics itself. Nor was that all. The nation's new foreign role must assume important domestic responsibilities as well. Nixon and Kissinger plainly intended to use the vision of the United States as the principal source of moderation and peace in the world to restore harmony and concord to domestic American politics. By showing the people an administration apparently engaged in an admirable foreign policy, they would bring a renewal of faith in government and an increase in public support for their policies.

These considerations suggest that in no sense did Nixon and Kissinger attempt less in foreign affairs than any of their predecessors. Quite the contrary; their conceptions and ambitions are on the same scale as those of Wilson, both Roosevelts, and Truman. The logic of their diplomacy led to a continuation and even an expansion of global engagement, not to the reduction in American responsibilities. This is now irrefutably clear in the Middle East. The United States is more deeply engaged in that region than ever before. Its technicians now play a role on the ground in the Sinai peninsula to preserve peace between Arab and Jew; Kissinger himself was a ubiquitous, perhaps irreplaceable, catalyst of negotiation and settlement; every new agreement is, apparently, to be underwritten by more American money and promises and commitments.

One suspects that a similar enlargement of American responsibility for events has also occurred in East Asia, despite and perhaps because of the withdrawal from Vietnam. Rather than attempting to maintain the independence of the small nations on the periphery of the Asian mainland, a vast and thankless task itself, the United States now finds she is the major support of the Chinese in their conflict with the Russians. The new role in Asia is potentially far more dangerous and costly (and important, one must add) than any undertaken in that part of the world since the support of republican China against Japan during the Second World War. The wonder is not in the new commitments and novel responsibilities, but in how successful their initiators have been in fashioning them despite their extraordinary handicaps at the outset.

Instead of a pause and gentle assessment at home, the natural response to adversity, the Nixon and Ford administrations decided on a contraction and dismantling of the burgeoning Democratically inspired welfare state. Their assault on welfare programs lies outside the scope of this essay, with two exceptions: those of method and consequence. The consequences of domestic and foreign strategy were similar. Both heightened bitterness and divisiveness in the country on these matters and, at the same time, prevented the emergence of a new consensus favorable to either foreign or domestic policy. As regards the Nixon administration's domestic strategy, one is tempted to observe that an attempt was made to create an entirely new domestic political alignment, an undertaking as ambitious in the national sphere as the Nixon-Kissinger efforts on the world scene. The "Southern strategy," the appeal to the working-class "hard-hat" opinion, the general appearance of "Tory politics" in operation—all suggested an attempt to turn the tables on the Democratic party.[20]

In their public discussions of foreign policy, Nixon, Ford, and Kissinger spoke yearningly of a strategy based on balance of power diplomacy, and in practice they went a considerable way toward adopting it outright: the constant talk of an emerging multipolar international system, the determination to eliminate the external role of ideology, the casualness toward Japan and the willingness to shift alignments—shown most spectacularly in the opposition to India's dismemberment of Pakistan, a policy adopted in part to signal America's willingness to side with China in important international conflicts. Their failure to seek and to encourage the fashioning of a new domestic consensus on foreign policy was not an accident, but a logical consequence of a balance of power strategy.[21] Its practitioners, like the Nixon and Ford administrations, "not only did not worry about getting their acrobatics approved and supported by a wide public, but felt that the existence of a broad and active foreign affairs constituency might actually be a burden, because the game was so subtle and demanded such concentration as to rule out unprofessional kibitzers."[22] Moreover, the very peripatetic virtuosity of Nixon and Kissinger tended to hypnotize and to discourage, not to excite, wider public and even governmental involvement in foreign questions.

Method as well as consequence were the same in domestic and international affairs. The method chosen was the expansion of executive power beyond all precedent and in disregard of what lay at the very heart of the American political system. It was not so much what was done as how it was done that distinguished the Nixon administration from its predecessors. It was, as Louis Fisher has argued, a matter of

> restraint . . . replaced by abandon, precedent stretched past the breaking point, and statutory authority pushed beyond legislative intent. For all its trappings of conservatism and "strict constructionism," the Nixon Administration never demonstrated an understanding of what lies at the heart of the political system: a respect for procedure, a sense of comity and trust between the branches, an appreciation of limits and boundaries. Without good-faith efforts and integrity on the part of the administrative officials, the delicate system of nonstatutory controls, informal understandings, and discre-

> tionary authority could not last. At a time when public programs could have benefited from flexibility and executive judgment, Congress was forced to pass legislation with mandatory language and greater rigidities.[23]

The same exaggeration is the identifying trait of the politics of acquiescence. In domestic affairs Nixon and Ford governed by veto and impoundment, defying the Congress to override repeated presidential attempts to dismantle the welfare program. The application of this concept to foreign policy was more difficult, in a sense, because abroad the president wished to accomplish the new, while at home he wished to abolish the recent and the established. Abroad he needed more money and supplies, if not necessarily more troops, rather than fewer and less, as at home. The politics of acquiescence as practiced by Nixon, Kissinger, and Ford toward Congress thus required a bureaucratic aspect: the imposition on foreign-policy making of the strictest possible central and, necessarily, secret control.[24] The reorganization of the National Security Council and, above all else, the attempt to create procedures that led all debate and information to Henry Kissinger first and last not only reduced the State Department to ignorance and impotence and decreased the influence of the military on policy but diminished even further an already slight congressional role in policymaking. So complete was this control that in the eyes of one insider: "Nothing of consequence was permitted to be done by State or Defense without clearance from NSC."[25] The imposition of central control and secrecy denied erstwhile opponents in Congress and the bureaucracy their customary weapons of influence and, in last resort, of sabotage. In the past, policy deliberations had been marked by diffuseness of authority and an extraordinary amount of publicity. These were the traditional openings in the American system through which advocates, foreign and domestic, could gain approval for their plans and ideas, even in the face of explicit rejection the first or second time around. The Nixon administration meant to close these openings and succeeded, to a remarkable degree, until Watergate and the subsequent inquiry into the intelligence establishment made it impossible to preserve either centralization or secrecy.

It is clear from the preceeding discussion that the use of the politics of acquiescence in dealing with Congress went deep into the fundamental nature of the Nixon and Ford administrations—their goals and domestic political weakness—and represented a response to the difficulties of contemporary international politics. The politics of acquiescence, therefore, transcend any notion of "human relations" or "consultation" with members of Congress, not to mention any question of how sweet are the personalities of the main actors in the foreign policy process. It may be that the Nixon and Ford administrations, by design or default, made a fetish of centralization and secrecy in the bureaucracy and resorted to the politics of acquiescence in dealing with Congress in order to create the domestic circumstances in which a balance of power strategy could succeed. These conditions are alien to the traditional manner of formulating American foreign policy—a manner which has been, often to the detriment of coherence and efficacy, far more plural and public than in any other major government. The effort to establish these conditions, and their repudiation by the American people and Congress, seriously damaged the presidency itself.[26] One would expect those on the "outside" of the Nixon-Kissinger-Ford system to resort to the old pluralism and publicity to reassert themselves and, in the existing domestic circumstances, it was natural that Congress would be in the vanguard.

3
The Fall of Cambodia

Mais où sont les neiges d'antan?

—François Villon

Prologue to Impasse

The period from Richard Nixon's second inaugural until the beginning of 1975 was a time of unprecedented and momentous developments both overseas and within the United States. Abroad, the Paris Agreements brought to a close yet another phase of the Vietnam War. Egypt and Syria won a political victory against Israel in the Yom Kippur war, the Organization of Petroleum Exporting Countries overnight caused a spectacular redistribution of world income in their favor, the government of Portugal was overthrown, Greece intervened in Cyprus and in response Turkey invaded and partitioned the island. In the United States the nation was transfixed and horrified by the scandals and revelations known as Watergate, which had ended with the resignation of Richard Nixon to avoid impeachment and the succession of Gerald Ford.

Although they certainly affected the pattern of congressional-executive relations, these spectacular domestic and foreign events also tended to overshadow all other thought and action. Perhaps this is why one is surprised to learn how many times in the previous two years Congress had not only defeated or blocked the president on specific issues but had also increased its involvement in the formulation and management of foreign policy by laying claim to prerogatives that, over the past three decades, at least, had been recognized as uniquely presidential.[1] The defeats suffered by the Ford administration in 1975 must be seen in light of two previous years of encroachment. If it is an exaggeration to say that the defeats were the logical or necessary outcome of the events of 1973 and 1974, it is correct to see them as consistent with what had gone before. The Ford administration might have avoided the setbacks of 1975 if, sometime along the way, Secretary Kissinger had fallen in love with Congress, the North Vietnamese had forgotten how to fight and the Arabs how to figure, and Watergate had never happened. Needless to say, none of these ever materialized. Instead, domestic and foreign crises combined in 1973 and 1974 in such a way as to deny the Ford administration room to maneuver and set it up for defeat after defeat in Congress.

There is an air of tragic necessity about congressional-executive relations in the first year of Gerald Ford's term as president, a genuine sense in which men and institutions were driven by events beyond their control. Understandably, Secretary Kissinger emphasized the compulsion of circumstances and regarded inescapable domestic setbacks as the main reasons his policies failed. It is important, nonetheless, to take the examination further and to ask questions about the nature of the political forces at work that defeated the administration, and to understand the manner in which the administration dealt with Congress, and especially the House Foreign Affairs Committee.

"Tied Appropriations" and the War Powers Resolution

In the summer of 1973 the Congress stopped all American participation in combat anywhere in Indochina and enacted severe and unique restrictions on presidential war powers, one of the most important tools of foreign policy. Taken together these two different kinds of restraints, expressed in Public Laws 93-50 and 93-52, and House Joint Resolution 542 (P.L. 93-148), took the Congress a giant step into the arena of foreign policy.[2] They also decisively affected the willingness of the Congress and the ability of the executive to treat the fall of Vietnam and Cambodia as a crisis requiring drastic military response by the United States in a few hours at the most.

Stopping American participation in combat in Indochina amounted to an assumption by Congress of the power to dictate in certain crucial areas of American policy. At a stroke, Congress had prevented any outcome of the conflicts in Vietnam, Laos, and Cambodia that required the use or threat of American military force for its realization. Less than two years later, when the South Vietnamese government was about to fall, it became clear that the threat of renewed American military intervention had probably been decisive in persuading both North and South Vietnam to accept the Paris Agreements. As usual, little is known about North Vietnamese calculations, but a secret exchange of letters became public in April 1975 in which, two years earlier, President Nixon had promised President Thieu to use American military power if the North Vietnamese violated the Paris Accords.[3] This promise, or threat, was more than the "price" of South Vietnamese acquiescence; fear of U. S. intervention must have been intended to cause the North Vietnamese, as well, to abide by the terms of the agreements.

By refusing to allow the use of public funds for combat by American military forces anywhere in Indochina at any time, present or future, Congress struck a devastating blow at the Paris Agreements and the South Vietnamese government long before the North Vietnamese finally rolled both up, along with the remnants of the army of the Republic of South Vietnam. President Nixon vetoed the first prohibition of combat in Indochina by Americans and the House sustained the veto. The administration was, nonetheless, compelled to accept the ban. Congress simply refused to pass any supplemental appropriations for the operation of the government that did not contain the prohibition on combat in Indochina.[4] Forced to choose between the paralysis of the government and the defeat of his Indochina policy, President Nixon chose to sacrifice the foreign policy. He obtained a few weeks grace as a "compromise," but a specific cutoff date had been named. All bombing and combat activities for Americans anywhere in Indochina stopped by act of Congress on August 15, 1973. While Americans were engaged in actual military operations in Laos and Cambodia right up to the deadline, they had not been involved in fighting anywhere in Vietnam since the signature of the Paris Agreements the previous January. What was fatal to the Nixon administration's Indochina policy, in addition to the weakness of the governments of Cambodia and South Vietnam, was that after August 15 the president could intervene in Vietnam only by explicitly violating an act he had signed into law. It was not a happy prospect for a man who would soon be trying desperately to avoid impeachment.

The restrictions on presidential war power enacted into law over a veto were even more effective than the "tied" appropriations acts in preventing the administration from honoring its promises to intervene in case North Vietnam flagrantly violated the 1973 cease-fire. Under the War Powers Resolution the president may send troops into battle only in response to a congressional declaration of war, or specific statutory authorization, and in case of attack on the United States, its territories, possessions, or armed forces.[5] There are, in addition, requirements for consultation between president and Congress, and for reporting to Congress, a time limit of sixty days for military action unless Congress authorizes an extension, and procedures for Congress to follow in case American forces become involved in hostilities.

The "tied" appropriations and the War Powers Resolution helped to determine the outcome of the wars in Vietnam, Cambodia, and Laos. The effect of the War Powers Resolution continues to be felt, of course, while the narrowly written appropriation, full of directives, ideological tests, time limits, and reporting requirements, has become a standard means for Congress to use in influencing foreign policy.[6]

Although it is true that Congress dealt a series of heavy and ultimately fatal blows to the Paris Agreements and to the existence of the friendly governments of South Vietnam, Cambodia, and Laos, few members of Congress wanted either of these things to happen. This was surely not what most of them intended when they cast their votes to prohibit combat by American forces in Indochina and to limit the prerogatives of the president to involve the country in war. What they sought was to end American participation in the fighting in Indochina and to keep the president from sending the country to war in the future without explicit authorization by Congress. Neither Congress nor the nation was told by the executive that the Paris Agreements and the survival of South Vietnam and Cambodia depended on the use, and the threat to use, American military force. Congress was told by the president and secretary of state that Vietnam would require substantial economic and material aid for an indefinite period, and during the next two years Congress voted assistance funds that, although in successively smaller quantities, amounted to more than several billion dollars. Meanwhile, the South Vietnamese and, probably, the North Vietnamese were told to count on American military intervention if it were needed to save South Vietnam from defeat. The leaders and members of Congress must have thought they had struck a bargain with the executive: no Americans in combat and substantial economic and material aid for Cambodia and Vietnam. The executive, acting in secret, had concluded an important international agreement that depended on the very thing—American military force—that Congress had denied a few months after the signatories completed the agreement.

It will not do to say that the Paris Agreements were not important or amounted to nothing more than a screen for American defeat. They were important in every sense: they involved the life and death of friendly governments and tens of thousands of people; they touched a crucial issue in domestic and foreign policy, one as divisive as any in American life since the Great Depression, and perhaps even the Civil War; and an issue bearing heavily on U. S. relations with China and the USSR. Last, the Paris Agreements consumed an extraordinary amount of the time and energy of the highest officials in the American government. Clearly, the agreements were important, and they were based on totally inadequate support and understanding in Congress. Within six months Congress had destroyed the foundation of the Paris Agreements; another two years passed before the house built on that foundation fell down in Saigon and Phnom Penh.

It is difficult to avoid the impression that the Nixon administration concluded the Paris Agreements over the heads of the leaders and members of Congress. Either because they thought it unnecessary or because they believed they could not obtain it, neither Nixon nor Kissinger made sure Congress would allow continued bombing in Cambodia and a resumption of bombing in Vietnam. This, in turn, suggests that the administration believed that if it became necessary to intervene in Vietnam it could obtain the support it needed in Congress and the nation as a result of dramatic and adverse developments overseas. In short, it counted on being able to conduct foreign policy in a crisis atmosphere. The picture is one of an administration more confident of its ability to control foreign governments than of its ability to win popular approval for its policies at home. To give the analysis an even finer point, the administration was confident of its ability to win domestic support by *its manipulation* of foreign governments. It was, in short, the politics of acquiescence.

The events of 1973 suggest that there is a pattern to executive-congressional relations during the Nixon administration: Nixon and Kissinger believed they could take extremely important actions based on deterrence without first making sure of their support in Congress; if deterrence failed, they could rely on a foreign enemy to frighten or anger the American people and Congress into acquiescing in a drastic military response formulated by the president and a few of his close advisors. In the end this approach failed.

Dogs of War . . . and Peace

In 1974 Congress moved still farther away from administration policy on Vietnam, even as the North Vietnamese and Vietcong increased their military and political pressure on the Thieu regime. Throughout the year these two developments worked in what must have seemed nightmarish tandem to officials in Saigon and Washington. Two examples will illustrate this deadly coincidence. In mid-May, North Vietnamese forces attacking with tanks captured three government outposts and threatened Bencat, a district capital only two dozen miles from Saigon. During these battles, the Senate Armed Services Committee reduced the administration's request for military assistance for South Vietnam by $700 million, cutting it from $1.6 billion to $900 million. Five days later, on May 22, a House-Senate Conference Committee agreed to hold the ceiling on military aid for Saigon in fiscal year 1974, which had been established at $1.126 billion. That same day, the House approved an identical military ceiling for the year ahead.

A second round of political and military setbacks for Saigon and Washington began in mid-June 1974 when the Vietcong delegations quit the two-and four-party military committees established after the Paris Accords. On July 29 North Vietnamese forces took seven government outposts south of Danang. The same day, the House passed a Senate-House conference authorization for military procurement in 1975 that lowered military assistance for Saigon from $1.126 billion to $1 billion. Less than a week later, communist forces captured ten South Vietnamese positions in Quang Ngai Province, seventy-five miles south of Danang. The next day President Nixon signed the authorization that included the reduced military assistance for Saigon, and twenty-four hours later the North Vietnamese took the district town of Thuong Duc, thirty miles northwest of Danang. Virtually during the battle for Thuong Duc, the House reduced even further the military assistance to be allowed South Vietnam in the coming year by setting the appropriation for military aid at $700 million and requiring a 10 percent reduction in American personnel stationed in South Vietnam.[7] This bill passed both houses of Congress on September 23–24 and became law on October 8, 1974.[8] Two days later the Vietcong escalated the political struggle against Saigon by declaring that the Provisional Revolutionary Government would continue negotiation only after the overthrow of President Thieu.

The bad news from Washington continued. The outcome of the debate on aid for Vietnam, Laos, and Cambodia was affected not only by growing antiwar sentiment in Congress and the country but also by a major effort by both foreign affairs committees to reform the foreign aid program as a whole. The Senate Foreign Relations Committee described its authorization bill, S. 3394, as an "overall effort to restore congressional control over the foreign aid program and retract major grants of discretionary authority over foreign aid matters which have been given to the president in the past."[9]

Administration supporters defeated this controversial approach on October 2, voting 41 to 39 to recommit S. 3394 to the Foreign Relations Committee. Some weeks later, nonetheless, a quite similar bill passed the Senate by one vote 46 to 45. Like its counterpart in the House, H.R. 17234, the revised Senate foreign aid bill cut off all military aid to Turkey. Both houses approved the conference report on foreign assistance in mid-December, and the Foreign Assistance Act of 1974 became law on December 30, too late in the session for passage of an appropriations bill.[10] Both houses approved a continuing resolution to fund foreign aid through February 28, 1975.[11]

The provisions of the Foreign Assistance Act for 1974 revealed that Congress was determined to reduce drastically the United States involvement in Indochina. At the beginning of the session the administration had requested $1.6 billion in military assistance for South Vietnam alone. Congress first slashed military aid to $700 million, as noted earlier, and then placed a ceiling on total aid to South Vietnam—military and economic—of $1.26 billion. In addition, a ceiling on economic aid for Indochina was set at $617 million, with subceilings of $339.9 million for South Vietnam, $100 million for Cambodia, and $40 million for Laos.[12] Aid ceilings were also placed on total assistance to Cambodia of $377 million, with no more than $200 million in military aid in fiscal year 1975, and on total assistance to Laos of $70 million, with no more than $30 million in military aid. In addition to this massive cut, the act prohibited the president from transferring military aid from one country to another, prohibited the purchase of material without prior authorization, and required that the number of Americans in Vietnam be reduced to four thousand within six months and to three thousand within a year. The act also called on the executive to begin planning for economic reconstruction and development of Indochina, using both bilateral and multilateral sources of international assistance.

Nor was the foreign aid program the only means used by Congress to signal its determination to reduce and change the American role in Indochina. The State Department/USIA authorization act for 1974–75 gave the sense of the Congress that the secretary of state should prepare a detailed plan for the gradual reduction of aid to South Vietnam until a level was reached at which the United States was no longer the principal outside source of assistance for the security and economic development of that country.[13] Even credit sales of food under Public Law 480 were "tied." To prevent the diversion to military purposes of large amounts of money from the food program, Congress declared that no single country could receive more than ten percent of the total food credits available under the Food for Peace program.[14] In a related action the Foreign Assistance Act and its continuing appropriations resolutions prohibited the purchase of fertilizer for South Vietnam in fiscal year 1975.

The Year of Decision: 1975

The new year began with an attack by a large North Vietnamese force on Phuoc Binh, the provincial capital of Phuoc Long. The city fell to the North Vietnamese within a week.[15] It was the first provincial capital to be captured by the Communists since 1972. Initially, the Communist offensive appeared to be intended to drive government forces out of the area along Vietnam's northern and western frontiers, both as a means of weakening South Vietnam politically and of making it possible to launch even more dangerous military campaigns in the next dry season. The early attacks were successful, however, and apparently threw the South Vietnamese government into confusion. Events moved even more swiftly in neighboring Cambodia. In late January 1975 the last convoy carrying food and ammunition up the Mekong from South Vietnam reached Phnom Penh. The Khmer Rouge committed 5,000 troops to close the river, and the Cambodian government, whose Seventh Division fielded 130-man battalions, was unable to stop them. By February 17, Cambodian troops had abandoned their attempt to keep the Mekong River open for supply convoys to Phnom Penh. "The river was never reopened, and the city began to starve."[16] The government and many of the people of Cambodia now depended for their survival on an American airlift of food and ammunition into the capital. The Communists soon brought Phnom Penh and its airport under artillery fire and threatened to cut the last source of nourishment for the thousands of refugees who had fled the war and the Khmer Rouge. In the first two months of the bombardment over 1,000 rockets and artillery rounds hit the city, killing 150 people and wounding 900.[17]

Prevented by law from using force to protect South Vietnam and Cambodia, the Ford administration turned to diplomacy and what deterrent gestures remained open to them. On January 11, for example, the United States addressed the countries that had guaranteed the Paris Accords, the most important of which was the USSR, and accused North Vietnam of seeking military victory. The administration asked the signatories for their aid in renewing military and political negotiations between North and South Vietnam.[18] On the deterrent side, the United States conducted unarmed reconaissance flights over Vietnam and Cambodia.[19] While the United States gave South Vietnam the information collected during the flights, the North Vietnamese must have wondered if the B-52s would follow the camera planes, as they once had. In addition, the United States warned vaguely and ominously that Hanoi "must accept the full consequences of its actions."[20]

On January 14 the State Department made a different kind of attempt to deter the North Vietnamese from seeking military victory. The department spokesman announced that because of North Vietnam's violation of the cease-fire the United States was entitled to suspend fulfillment of some or all of the obligations it had accepted in the Paris Accords. While this threat applied immediately to continued observance of the ceilings on military and economic assistance for South Vietnam, it must also have been intended to remind the North Vietnamese that if they continued their offensive they would lose all hope of obtaining aid from the United States for postwar reconstruction—as in fact happened—and might even precipitate renewed American bombing.

The administration was bluffing about the use of force, but it was not bluffing about the denial of aid. Although the Paris Accords probably depended more on the threat of renewed bombing than on the promise of American economic aid, Kissinger had obviously promised the aid in the first place both to create an incentive for the North Vietnamese to respect the cease-fire and to obtain a means of punishing them if they started fighting again. He did not hesitate to deny the aid when South Vietnam fell. Although the prospect of losing U. S. aid failed to prevent the final military campaign, the Communists felt the loss keenly, and repeatedly appealed to the United States to give postwar assistance. Kissinger was adamant, and the aid was doomed without the support of the administration, for there was no widespread sentiment in the Congress or the country in favor of giving aid.

The Appeals to Congress

The motives of the leading members of the administration in asking for large supplemental aid for Cambodia and Vietnam are still unclear. The president and secretary of state, for example, might actually have believed that South Vietnam and Cambodia could survive if only the Congress would appropriate the additional military and economic aid required to cope with the heavy fighting. They might have regarded the additional aid as a kind of political stiffening needed not so much for the immediate fighting, for South Vietnam had large military stockpiles, but as a signal to the Communists of another military stalemate in the making. They might also have doubted the importance of the aid for Vietnam and Cambodia one way or another and have sought congressional approval because of its effect on the perceptions of the United States held by the Russians, Chinese, Israelis, and Egyptians, among others. Whatever the exact motives for the aid requests, and they might have been combinations of these and still others, it is not necessary to identify their actual content in order to analyze the part played by Congress and the House Foreign Affairs Committee in the making of American policy during the last months of American involvement in Cambodia and Vietnam.

The First Supplemental Request

In a special message to Congress on January 28, 1975, President Ford requested supplemental appropriations for military assistance of $300 million for South Vietnam and $222 million for Cambodia.[21] As early as October 9, 1974, while signing the Defense Appropriations Act with its reduced military aid for South Vietnam, President Ford had said he would have to ask Congress for additional aid if North Vietnamese attacks continued.[22] On December 30, when signing the Foreign Assistance Act with its reductions and ceilings on aid to Indochina, he had described the amounts of economic and military assistance for Cambodia as "clearly inadequate to meet basic needs," and expressed concern that the funds provided for Vietnam made "less likely the achievement of our objectives and significantly [prolonged] the period needed for essential development."[23]

The president linked the additional funds not only to the defense of South Vietnam against the Communists but to the relations of the United States with its allies and with the USSR as well. Referring to North Vietnam's violation of the Parris Accords, for example, he said: "It cannot be in the interests of the United States to let other nations believe that we are prepared to look the other way when agreements that have been painstakingly negotiated are contemptuously violated. It cannot be in our interest to cause our friends all over the world to wonder whether we will support them if they comply with agreements that others violate."[24] The $300 million supplement would restore assistance to the $1 billion level originally authorized and supply the "minimum needed to prevent serious reversals."[25] "Withholding additional aid from Cambodia," he argued, "would endanger the very survival of that republic and undermine peace and stability in the area." His request for $222 million in additional military aid for Cambodia required him to ask Congress to eliminate the $200 million ceiling on military aid and the $377 million overall ceiling on assistance to that country. The hope for the governments of both countries, according to the president, was to achieve a new military stalemate that would lead to a renewal of negotiations.[26]

The Significance of Legislative Reform

Established legislative practice sent the Cambodian request to the foreign relations committees in both chambers as part of the foreign aid program. Requests for military aid to Vietnam had been treated as defense appropriations since fiscal year 1967 and went for authorization in this case to the armed services committees.[27] Because Congress had already authorized more for military aid to Vietnam than it had appropriated, no authorization hearings were needed, and the Vietnam request went, as intended, directly to the House Defense Appropriations Subcommittee, whose chairman was George Mahon (D., Texas).

President Ford made his request just as the House was completing the organization of the new Ninety-fourth Congress. It proved to be a difficult and controversial task. When it ended, three sitting committee chairmen had been ousted by the Democratic caucus. F. Edward Hebert (La.) lost his place at the head of the Armed Services Committee, as did W. R. Poage (Texas) of Agriculture, and Wright Patman (Texas) of Banking and Currency. A fourth committee chairman, Wayne Hays (Ohio) of House Administration, was not nominated for the first ballot by the newly powerful Steering and Policy Committee of the caucus.[28] Hays retained his chair by defeating the Steering Committee's nominee, Frank Thompson (N.J.), and winning election on the floor of the caucus. The defeat of the committee chairmen broke with sixty years of tradition in the House, and it was symbolic of the hopes of the seventy-five new freshmen Democrats elected the previous November to break the old rules and patterns and make their influence felt both within the Congress and on national policymaking as well. Their success had already made the House in the Ninety-fourth Congress more than two-thirds Democratic.[29]

The departing Ninety-third Congress had eased the way by shaking up the House rules. On March 19, 1974 a bipartisan select committee, led by Richard Bolling (D., Mo.), had presented to Congress an ambitious plan for the reorganization of the committees of the House. Bolling's proposal attempted to order committee responsibilities according to broad policy areas and to limit members of Congress to membership on one major "exclusive" committee and one narrower "nonexclusive" committee. Inevitably, this approach took jurisdiction away from certain committees and gave it to others. The plan would also have abolished several committees and proposed to split Education and Labor into two major committees. The predictable result was to arouse the opposition of many of those members of Congress who stood to lose control of policy areas and to stir into action those interest groups who benefited from the established dispensation.[30] Labor unions, for example, vehemently opposed the division of Labor and Education.

After delaying adoption of the proposal for six months, opponents of the reforms defeated the Bolling plan and adopted a substitute plan developed by a committee of the Democratic caucus led by Julia Butler Hansen (D., Wash.).[31] The Hansen substitute drew enough Republican support (53 of 151 voting) to pass 203 to 165. It left essentially untouched the distribution of committee responsibilities established by the Legislative Reorganization Act of 1946. Though refusing Bolling's drastic remedy, the House nonetheless had agreed to a number of significant reforms. In what was perhaps the most important provision of the plan, the House required all committees with more than fifteen members to have at least four subcommittees.[32] Other provisions of the Hansen substitute allowed the speaker more freedom in deciding how to refer bills to committees and allowed the majority and minority leaders to call their parties into caucus to organize themselves between December 1 and December 20.

Both the Democrats and Republicans in the House took advantage of the organizational caucus idea and met in early December. The Republicans took only four hours to reelect John Rhodes (Ariz.) minority leader, and to choose Robert Michel (Ill.) to be minority whip and John B. Anderson (Ill.) to be the House Republican Conference chairman. All eyes were on the Democrats who, with their huge majority, were organizing the Congress as well as their own party. One way to look at the accomplishments of the caucus is to conclude that the House Democrats voted to "consolidate their prior reforms within the House Democratic Party and to assert the new power of the party caucus."[33] The reporters covering the early caucus for *Congressional Quarterly* suggested that the House Democrats had strengthened "their elected leadership at the expense of committee chairmen, especially [Wilbur] Mills."[34] Certainly both views are consistent with what the caucus decided. By a vote of 146 to 122, for example, the caucus denied Democrats on Ways and Means their power to assign other Democrats to committees and gave it instead to the party Steering and Policy Committee.[35] The Speaker gained the power to appoint all Democratic members of the important Rules Committee, with the approval of the caucus. The caucus stipulated that all nominations for subcommittee chairmen of the Appropriations Committee must be approved by the caucus.

In addition to curtailing the power of committee chairmen and strengthening the Speaker and the Steering Committee, the caucus also knocked still more power from the hands of a few senior members at the center into the arms of junior members throughout the House. In 1971 the caucus had held that no Democrat could be chairman of more than one subcommittee. By adopting a resolution proposed by David Obey (Wis.) on December 3, 1974, the caucus allowed senior Democrats to keep only two of their subcommittee memberships. Once the senior members on a committee had chosen their assignments, the junior members were to make their choices among the remaining slots. This change obviously provided a remarkable opportunity for the seventy-five entering freshmen members of Congress to play a significant part in committee politics right from the start. The change was especially important to legislative-executive relations in general, and to the debate on Vietnam and Cambodia in particular, because the new members were much more liberal than Congress as a whole.[36]

Taken together, the diffusion of power, the rising importance of the caucus, and the decline in the influence of committee chairmen amounted to a substantial change in the structure of Congress—one that was especially important for foreign-policy making, particularly if one includes the shift to the left in the politics of the 1974 freshmen members and the trend toward less frequent use of closed rules (prohibiting amendments on the floor of the House). It is hard to avoid the impression that the cumulative reforms had gone far to remove the old skeleton and nervous system of the Congress: that small group of senior, often southern members able to punish and reward, able to conduct business with the executive and "deliver" the Congress when compromises were struck, able to "speak for" Congress. From the executive viewpoint, consultation with the unreformed Congress was rewarding and feasible. In contrast, the reformed Congress must have appeared invertebrate—or perhaps multi-vertebrate, with too many candidates for the roles of the bones and brains of the legislature. For the executive, the fruits of consultation became much less certain and increasingly difficult, since consultation could now mean dealing with several hundred or even all 535 members in both houses, as the executive was forced to do in the attempt to repeal the embargo of arms sales for Turkey.[37] Needless to say, the view on Capitol Hill was that congressional reform had allowed democracy at long last to be felt in foreign-policy making and that its effect was a welcome antidote to the arrogant blundering of the executive branch.[38]

On top of the reforms enacted by the Democratic caucus in December 1974 and January 1975, the House Foreign Affairs Committee spent part of February changing its name and subcommittee organization. The new name was to be Committee on International Relations.[39] The new subcommittees, discussed in committee caucus on February 3 and approved at an organizational meeting on February 20, were established according to functional topics in international affairs rather than by geography. Among the new subcommittees were the Committee Chairman's Subcommittee on Oversight (Thomas E. Morgan), International Security and Scientific Affairs (Clement Zablocki), International Political and Military Affairs (Dante Fascell), and Special Subcommittee on Investigations (Lee Hamilton).[40] With sixty-year-old precedents being broken and major reforms adopted, with almost one member in five new to the House, and with a significant committee reorganization underway, it was mid-March—nearly six weeks after the president's special request—before Congressman Lee Hamilton's Special Subcommittee on Investigations of the Committee on Foreign Affairs (International Relations) opened hearings on additional aid for Cambodia.[41]

What Happened to February?

At the time President Ford asked Congress to give supplemental military aid to Cambodia and Vietnam, the U.S. officials responsible for analyzing Hanoi's political and military intentions viewed the Communist offensive as important but limited, definitely not an all-out offensive aimed at total victory.[42] The administration clung to this view of the fighting in Vietnam well into March, although they were more pessimistic about the situation in Cambodia.[43] This apparent lack of concern about the military situation in Vietnam probably explains President Ford's decision to allow the secretary of state to go twice to the Middle East in the weeks ahead, as well as Kissinger's willingness to leave the country.

The day after he sent the special request to Congress, President Ford discussed the proposal with congressional leaders. Any hopes for easy passage vanished. After talking with Mr. Ford, Senate Majority Leader Mike Mansfield (D., Mont.) said the aid request was already "in trouble." Although he favored the president's plan, Senator John Tower (R., Tex.) called its chances "pretty dim." Two other powerful members of the Senate promptly opposed the proposal: Senator Edward Kennedy (D., Mass.) accused the administration of using "scare tactics," while Senate Majority whip Robert Byrd (D., Va.) invited South Vietnam and Cambodia to buy more military equipment if they wanted it.[44]

The administration was to use four lines of argument in pressing its case. Two were already in evidence. The additional military supplies would assure a stalemate in both countries; this would mean the difference between survival and defeat and would bring an early resumption of negotiations (if no aid were given, the enemy would have no reason to negotiate); and, an effective foreign policy for the United States would be achieved only by bipartisan cooperation between the legislature and executive in a spirit of mutual trust and faith in each other.[45] The third argument, one especially favored by Henry Kissinger, was that the denial of aid to Vietnam and Cambodia would have the most serious consequences for American credibility everywhere in the world.[46] The fourth argument—blaming Congress for the failure of American policy in Indochina—surfaced after Congress rejected the aid requests and the Cambodian and South Vietnamese governments went from defeat to defeat.

Undaunted by the cool reception Congress had given his request, the president tried again. On February 3 he met again with the formal leadership and suggested that Congress send a delegation to South Vietnam and Cambodia for an on-the-spot appraisal of the need for more military aid.[47] According to one report, the room filled with "oppressive silence" after the president made the suggestion.[48] It was not that anyone objected to the idea in itself—members of Congress frequently flew just about everywhere at taxpayer's expense, and sometimes for legitimate reasons—but the delegation wouldn't take the "right" shape. No key committee members accepted the invitations being given by Assistant Secretary of State Philip Habib, and without their seniority the list failed to attract any other senior members of either House.

Two days after the meeting at the White House, the newly appointed commander in chief of North Vietnam's offensive, General Van Tien Dung, crossed the border into Military Region 1 to begin setting up a field headquarters for an assault in the highlands. Within a fortnight three North Vietnamese divisions were ready to attack Ban Me Thuot. North Vietnam had achieved local numerical superiority of five to one.[49] In Cambodia, starvation took its toll in the shrinking areas under government control. At the beginning of the airlift, only 440 tons of rice a day arrived in Phnom Penh. In 1973, before the flood of refugees had started to fill the city, daily rice consumption had been 770 tons a day. Eventually the rice tonnage brought by air was increased to 700 tons a day, still pitifully less than was needed.[50]

With his secretary of state off to the Middle East, President Ford tried still another idea. On a trip to Chicago a few days later, the president told several representatives of the *Chicago Tribune* he was prepared to stop military aid to South Vietnam within three years if the Congress would just give enough aid during that time. The new budget allotted $1.3 billion in military aid to Vietnam and $497 million to Cambodia. Mr. Ford quoted the U.S. ambassador in Saigon, Graham Martin, that two more years of high levels of aid would be enough. "I would be willing," he added, "to take sufficiently large amounts over a three-year period and say, 'This is it'—if the Congress will appropriate it, I would agree not to ask any more."[51] An early answer came from Congress. Within twenty-four hours, eighty-two of the bipartisan Members of Congress for Peace through Law wrote Mr. Ford and asked him to stop U.S. aid to South Vietnam and Cambodia. They saw no "humanitarian or national interest" to justify continued aid.

That nearly one-sixth of the membership of both Houses opposed all aid was an ominous signal for the administration, even if most members of Congress didn't share the views of the group in Peace through Law. To be sure, a few members took the opposite view and urged immediate and continuing large-scale assistance. By far the largest number found themselves between these extremes, and were ready to grant aid only if they were satisfied it would be used to end the fighting in Vietnam and Cambodia. Their skepticism of stalemate as a route to peace was compounded by the deteriorating military situation in Cambodia and Vietnam. The administration presented these setbacks as the reason to give more aid. There was thus a curious mirror-image quality to the showdown between president and Congress: the two increasingly drew opposite conclusions from the same horrifying evidence. The *Washington Post* expressed the congressional view on Cambodia in an editorial on March 4: "To provide aid in a context that does not offer some reasonable prospect of peace is, in our judgment, insupportable."[52]

Eventually, a delegation formed to visit South Vietnam and Cambodia. Making the trip from the House were Bella Abzug (D., N.Y.), Bill Chappell (D., Fla.), Millicent Fenwick (R., N.J.), John Flynt (D., Ga.), Donald Fraser (D., Minn.), Jack Kemp (R., N.Y.), Paul McCloskey (R., Calif.), John Murtha (D., Pa.), and Samuel Stratton (D., N.Y.). Senator Dewey Bartlett (D., Okla.) left with Congressman McCloskey on February 21, and the remainder of the group followed on February 25.[53] The delegation stayed barely a week in Indochina. What they saw made a profound impression on them personally. On their return, most of them agreed to recommend additional military assistance, although considerably less than Mr. Ford had requested. They also urged the administration to use every possible diplomatic channel to renew negotiations.[54]

While the delegation was away, the administration stressed the importance of the aid to the survival of the Cambodian government. The president and secretary of state deliberately likened the giving of aid to Cambodia to U.S. aid for Israel and other countries dependent on the United States, and maintained that a refusal would undermine the ability of the United States to conduct an effective foreign policy.[55] Leading members of the Senate Foreign Relations Committee remained unconvinced.[56] Weary of the human costs of the war, the crucial foreign affairs committees in the Senate and House were determined to use their power over the purse to force a change in U.S. policy. As a result, the administration attempted an end run to get around the foreign affairs committees.

The plan was complicated and dubious from the beginning and was probably most useful as an indicator of how little hope the administration already had of winning approval of the aid. The idea was that Congressman Otto Passman (D., La.) would add the $222 million for Cambodia to the regular foreign aid bill for 1975 in his House Appropriations Subcommittee, thus circumventing the authorizing committees on foreign affairs in both the House and the Senate. For the plan to have worked, however, Passman would have had to obtain a special exemption from the Rules Committee blocking objections to the bill on the House floor as an appropriation without an authorization.[57] Four days after he started Passman dropped the effort, in his words, "as a courtesy to the House and Senate foreign affairs committees." Apparently he couldn't find the votes he needed to sidestep the foreign affairs committees.[58] The same day, Henry Kissinger departed on his second trip to the Middle East.

The most adamant opposition to Mr. Ford's proposal for aid to Cambodia came from the House of Representatives rather than the Senate. Within the House, the members of the Foreign Affairs Committee also refused to yield to administration policy when their counterparts in the Senate passed a compromise measure which, though it authorized smaller amounts than requested, was generally congruent with the position of the executive branch. For this reason, and because more is known about the Senate committee, the following discussion centers on developments in the House. A few words are necessary at the outset to describe the compromise aid proposal passed by Senator Humphrey's Foreign Relations Subcommittee, and much admired at the White House.

On March 12, after hearing various members of the administration and the congressional Indochina delegation, the Humphrey subcommittee went against its chairman and voted 4 to 3 to give Cambodia $125 million in military aid, $73 million in food, and $15 million in medical supplies, with no strings attached. The vote was completely partisan, with the subcommittees's three Republican members, Jacob Javits (N.Y.), Clifford Case (N.J.), and Hugh Scott (Pa.), joined by a conservative Democrat Gale McGee (Wyo.) to oppose the three Democrats, Humphrey (Minn.), Frank Church (Idaho), and George McGovern (S.Dak.). The military aid was to be taken from existing stocks and repaid later with foreign aid funds. Apparently this was done to avoid having to authorize new expenditures.[59]

The vote in the Senate came during a tumultuous two weeks on Capitol Hill. "Dear Colleague" letters poured into the offices of members of the House as Congressmen attempted to make their views heard and to win support from their fellow legislators.[60] At the high point of deliberations on aid for Cambodia, a crucial vote was taken in the House Democratic caucus and the administration appeared to nail its colors to the mast of a sinking policy.

Cambodia and the House Foreign Affairs Committee

The House Foreign Affairs Committee opened hearings on supplementary aid for Cambodia on March 6. Its Special Subcommittee on Investigations, chaired by Lee Hamilton of Indiana, heard testimony from Philip Habib, assistant secretary of state for East Asian and Pacific affairs; from Lt. Gen. Howard Fish, director of the Defense Security Assistance Agency; and from Garnett Zimmerly, a high-ranking official in the Agency for International Development.

Most of the questions on that first Thursday's hearings went to Assistant Secretary Habib. The day before Habib met with the subcommittee, President Ford had urged the Congress to grant the funds for Cambodia and Vietnam and had declared he would not send U.S. forces back to Vietnam. Habib advanced one of the four administration approaches to the aid issue by accusing Congress of thwarting what had promised to be successful negotiations in Cambodia when it had ordered a halt to bombing in August 1973.[61] Habib made his comments at a news conference. One of the main items he discussed with the newsmen was a "Summary of Negotiating Efforts on Cambodia" distributed by the Department of State to a few members of Congress in early March.[62] The department stressed what it termed repeated efforts of the United States to establish an independent, neutral Cambodia "through negotiations and not through a battlefield victory."

Congressman Hamilton's voice and manner are gentle and understated, but he opened with a series of razor-edged questions challenging Habib to say exactly what he had meant by blaming Congress for the failure of negotiations. Methodically, he forced Habib to say that the congressional ban on bombing was not a hindrance to negotiations. Habib was trapped neatly, for if he had said anything else he would have appeared to be advocating a resumption of the bombing, something few Americans wished to see.[63]

In his responses to the other questions, Habib repeated the standard description of administration policy in Cambodia: the United States sought a military stalemate that would create the conditions necessary for peace negotiations to succeed. Neither the United States nor the Cambodian government wished to win a military victory. It is impossible to say precisely how long the United States will have to give aid to Cambodia; so far, the Communists aren't interested in a compromise settlement. The amounts requested by the administration probably will enable the Cambodian government to survive until June, when the present dry season ends. By September the Mekong River will be spread wide in full flood, Communist mines and ambushes will be much less effective, and the Cambodian government will be able to use the river once again to bring ammunition, weapons, and food to the soldiers and civilians in areas still under its control. In Habib's view, by providing aid to Cambodia over the preceding four years the United States had incurred an implicit responsibility for the fate of the existing Cambodian regime. A "historical relationship and a historical dependency" has been built, he argued, and the United States should not turn its back on that obligation. The obligation was all the more demanding, Habib added, because there would certainly be a bloodbath if the Khmer Rouge were allowed to win a military victory.[64]

The congressional delegation that had visited Vietnam met the Hamilton subcommittee on Thursday morning, March 11. In their minds and the minds of those who participated in the hearing was the knowledge that the Cambodian army had dwindled to a strength of 60,000 men in the foxholes out of a paper-strength of 230,000. In Vietnam the vital outpost of Ban Me Thuot had just fallen and the North Vietnamese had closed all major roads in the highlands, cutting off the South Vietnamese troops in position there.[65] Members of the delegation had testified a few days earlier before a Senate Foreign Relations Subcommittee chaired by Senator Hubert Humphrey. Just after the delegation's appearance in the Senate, the results of a Gallup poll on the question of aid for Vietnam and Cambodia were published. According to the poll, 78 percent of Americans opposed giving further assistance to Vietnam and Cambodia: eight out of ten Democrats and 72 percent of Republicans.[66] On March 9, thirty-six freshmen Democrats released the text of a letter to President Ford saying they would vote against additional aid.[67] On March 10, thirty-eight representatives sent a similar letter to their colleagues.

The delegation's visits to the two countries had obviously touched them deeply, and their vivid stories evoked scenes of death and hunger and loss. Congressman John Flynt (D., Ga.) chairman of the delegation, spoke briefly, followed by Don Fraser. Fraser told the subcommittee "the war in Cambodia is lost." The attempt by the United States government to achieve a negotiated settlement was an attempt to achieve something that had been beyond its reach and that of the established Cambodian government for several years. Even if Congress voted the full administration request, there was no hope for a military stalemate and a negotiated settlement. Accordingly, the United States should attempt to bring the war "to an orderly end with as little bloodshed as possible."[68] The only way out, in Fraser's view, was for the United States to contact the French government or the secretary general of the United Nations and ask them to find out on what terms the Khmer Communists would finish the war. Fraser also advised the subcommittee to meet with the acting secretary of state. If the State Department would agree to a policy of seeking a "negotiated surrender"—an orderly transfer of power to a government that included Khmer Communists—then Fraser believed Congress should vote additional money in support of that objective.[69] In order to persuade the Communists to start negotiations for an orderly transfer, the Cambodian government would have to keep fighting. It would be permissible for the United States to help them in this "provided the Department of State had changed its negotiation objective."[70] In this context alone, Fraser indicated, he would support giving additional economic and military assistance to Cambodia. Because it would be extremely difficult to write this all in a suitable piece of legislation, he advised getting a commitment from the administration rather than trying to write it into law.[71]

Representative DuPont asked the obvious question. How can the United States, he inquired, go to another government and say: "We are going to volunteer to help dismember your government and we want you to help us"? Fraser answered in two ways: first, that the United States could simply stop its aid, but if it did it would lose the chance to meet certain humanitarian obligations in Cambodia such as evacuating those who would be killed when the takeover occurred; second, that more aid would merely continue the war to the last Cambodian in pursuit of unachievable objectives. There was no choice but to "work it out with the Lon Nol government" and focus American influence to persuade them to agree to "an orderly transfer of power" to the Communist insurgents.[72]

Although one may agree or disagree with Fraser's reasoning and his recommended course of action, there is no disagreeing over the attractiveness of both to a majority on the subcommittee. Fraser had outlined the path Chairman Hamilton and the staff would follow. It was an ambitious approach. They would use their control over aid funds to try to change the policy of the United States government toward Cambodia. There would be food and ammunition for Cambodia if—and only if—the administration would abandon its effort to help the Lon Nol government achieve a military stalemate as a prelude to negotiations and, instead, begin to compel the Cambodians to surrender, with suitable humanitarian guarantees for the Cambodian people. As will be seen, the subcommittee chose to try to write a bill that would make this complicated maneuver the law of the land rather than to settle for a commitment to a new policy from the administration. In fact, so many members of Congress distrusted the good faith of the administration so gravely that it is unlikely a majority would have supported a grant of military aid in exchange for a verbal promise from the State Department.

After Bella Abzug (D., N.Y.) stated her opposition to any further military aid, Paul McCloskey (R., Calif.) described a basis for calculating how much military and economic aid to give to Cambodia, linking his presentation to Fraser's intention to compel the State Department to change its policy. The United States Embassy in Phnom Penh had told him that the Cambodian government used an average of 450 tons of ammunition a day. McCloskey said that if the United States provided that much ammunition for seventy-five days—lasting roughly until the end of June and the beginning of the rainy season—it would cost $84 million. The Defense Department estimated that shipping and transportation charges for a continued airlift would add $19.6 million. The military had asked for $6.7 million in spare parts, and McCloskey said an approximate figure for medical assistance was $6.4 million. The total he supported was, therefore, $116.7 million in military supplies—about half the requested $222 million. In addition, he said, the entire delegation favored an increase in the supply of food for Cambodia. This would mean raising the ceiling on Public Law 480 assistance and, if this were done, raising by twelve the number of Americans allowed to work in Cambodia in order to assure the proper distribution of the food.[73]

McCloskey closed with several personal observations. He had left for Cambodia, he said, opposed to giving any further aid, but two things had changed his mind. Both sides were executing prisoners, and if the Cambodian government simply ran out of ammunition there would be brutal reprisals by the winners. Second, the refugees he spoke to had described large numbers of summary executions by the Khmer Communists when they took over villages. McCloskey thought the Khmer Communists would continue to act this way and for this reason the United States ought to "continue the limited military aid to get the Cambodian Government into the wet season."[74] He ended by saying that the delegation had asked the secretary of state about the possibility of American diplomatic initiatives to end the fighting. Kissinger had answered that he had been within a few days of a settlement in June 1973 when Congress had scuttled his efforts by stopping the bombing; he had no interest in negotiating from weakness.

Subcommittee Markup

The Hamilton subcommittee reconvened Thursday afternoon in a "markup" session, that is, a meeting in which they would try to agree on the outline of a piece of legislation most of them could support. Chairman Hamilton began by saying he had asked a member of the staff, Michael Van Dusen, to put in writing the options available to them. As will be seen, Van Dusen's early part in the subcommittee's work indicated the staff would play a substantial part in the entire Cambodian issue. There were four options:

1. to reject the entire supplemental aid request;
2. to provide additional food aid with no additional military assistance;
3. to provide both food and military aid, but make it conditional upon initiatives to end the war;
4. to provide the executive branch with all or a substantial part of the funds requested without conditions.[75]

Hamilton recommended trying to agree on an option and then on the wording of a bill. Personally, he favored option 1—rejection of all further military aid—and would support option 3 only if the bill would lead toward a peace settlement.

At this point the subcommittee had three documents before it. The first, H.R. 2704, was the president's request for an additional $222 million in military assistance and $15 million in "draw-down" funds, used for unexpected expenses (see Appendix 1). In place of this bill Congressman Fraser and another member of the staff, Dr. John Sullivan, had drafted a complicated substitute that offered to provide funds amounting to 10 percent of existing ceilings on all aid for Cambodia, renewable every thirty days, only if the president certified every month that the United States and the Cambodian government were seeking an end to the conflict, and that peace initiatives had been taken toward the other side that would allow those Cambodians who wished to leave to get out of the country. Congress could deny the aid if it disapproved the report by concurrent resolution within ten calendar days of receiving it (see Appendix 2). Given the existing ceilings on Cambodian aid, the amounts would have been $20 million in military aid, $7.5 million in draw-down authority, and $17.7 million in food under Public Law 480, renewable every month for three months, or a total of $82.5 million in military aid and $53.1 million in food.[76]

Congressman DuPont, the most active Republican throughout these deliberations, wished to make the conditions imposed on the administration and Cambodia even clearer. His draft substitute allowed the percentage formula and thirty-day renewable grants but stated that additional aid was to be given only to relieve human suffering "by ceasing military action," that military aid would be given only until the Khmer Communists assured the United States it would treat noncombatants and prisoners in accord with the Geneva Convention (see Appendix 2). DuPont omitted any reference to obtaining the departure of Cambodians from their country.

In taking such a severe line with the administration in regard to Cambodia the members of the Foreign Affairs Committee could rely on the eyewitness reporting of two senior members of the staff, John Brady and John Sullivan. The two had visited Vietnam, Thailand, and Cambodia from February 21 to March 3. On their return they immediately briefed the entire committee, meeting behind closed doors, and a version of their findings about Cambodia was immediately published as a confidential committee print.[77] In addition to this report, the committee also could examine the report of another of its survey teams sent to Cambodia just eight months before, in July 1974, and could question the two staff members on the situation in South Vietnam, which they had studied closely and systematically.[78] Also available to the committee was Senator Sam Nunn's report on his survey visit to Vietnam in early February 1975.[79]

In the July 1974 report, the Foreign Affairs Committee survey team had found the Lon Nol government in Cambodia able to survive only because of American assistance. "Its once-large reserves now all but depleted," the team observed, "its exports earnings low, and its economy wrecked by the war, Cambodia exists from day to day largely on American aid. If that aid were removed, the present government would fall and the Khmer Communists could well prevail within a short time."[80] Much of the countryside and about 40 percent of the population had been lost to the Khmer Communists. Many provincial capitals were surrounded; some could be resupplied only by air. Airdrops by the United States were essential to preserve these towns. In fiscal year 1974 the United States had flown an average of 693 sorties each month, delivering 9,900 tons of cargo by C-130 aircraft. "Phnom Penh itself is an enclave," the team observed, "with all major roads leading to it interdicted." The Mekong River was the only remaining supply route open to government convoys. "Should the river be cut," the team concluded, "Phnom Penh also would require supply by air."[81] Despite its truly desperate situation, the Cambodian government showed little sense of urgency and had not required equitable sharing of the sacrifices of the war.

In the report on their visit the following February, Brady and Sullivan could only document the worsening of the trends identified by the previous survey. The Communists had closed the Mekong River to government convoys. Phnom Penh lived by the "largest airlift since Berlin 1948."[82] The Cambodian military command was weak, corrupt, and incapable of inspiring confidence. The army had suffered losses that cut into combat effectiveness, and no experienced replacements were available. Foxhole strength was as low as 20 to 30 percent in most fighting units, and higher commanders were unable to mass their troops to hold key areas. The morale of the soldiers was low. Three hundred men were lost each day—a battalion a day—dead, wounded, or missing. The troops were underpaid and received too little food to feed their families, who usually accompanied them into the fighting.

The deteriorating military situation made the economic prospects gloomy for 1975. Rice production had fallen to 20 percent of the average annual production in the 1960s. Industrial production was down to 42 percent of the 1969 level. Prices had risen 254 percent in 1975. The value of exports had fallen from $88.5 million in 1968 to an expected $7 million in 1975. Insecurity and war had created large numbers of refugees, and the totals were rising: from 866,000 in March 1974 to 1.27 million in January 1975. There appeared to be an additional 900,000 to one million displaced persons living rough or with relatives and not registered with the government.[83]

The survey team thought they detected some indication of a change in U.S. policy as a result of the deepening crisis in Cambodia. In the past the United States had sought a stalemate on the battlefield as a way of establishing a "Laos-type" solution: a coalition government in which the Communists would play a major role. The American ambassador in Phnom Penh now spoke of a "controlled" solution as the American goal in Cambodia, instead of an "uncontrolled" solution. Conceivably, a "controlled" solution would be a negotiated transfer of power. Americans and Cambodian officials and their families would be allowed to leave the country in safety, safeguards would be established to protect the civilian and military officials who remained behind. The team advised the committee to try to discover if a "controlled" solution was in fact the goal of the president and secretary of state.[84]

Additional American aid would not guarantee the survival of the Lon Nol regime; if aid were withheld the government would fall. The denial of aid would set in motion a series of grave and dangerous events, the team warned. Cambodians once allied with the United States might turn on the Americans still in the country. The Khmer Communists would quickly begin their assault on Phnom Penh. The U.S. government would be responsible for the safety of the American citizens in Cambodia, and the use of troops in an evacuation would trigger the War Powers resolution and its procedures. Prophetically, Brady and Sullivan warned that once in power the Khmer Communists could treat their country men savagely. A bloodbath might well occur after a Communist victory. Thousands of refugees might flee persecution and attempt to escape to neighboring countries. The U.S. embassy at least, saw this as an "uncontrolled" outcome, one to be avoided at all costs.[85]

The notion of a "controlled solution" in Cambodia underlay the subcommittee draft. The idea of restraint of any kind seems so out of keeping with the murderous ruthlessness of the Khmer Rouge, even before they took over Cambodia, that it is worth considering whether the idea was a pipe dream or actually might have prevented the slaughter that occurred in Cambodia after the Khmer Rouge had succeeded in outlasting all other centers of power in the country.

Soon after he arrived in Phnom Penh in the late spring of 1974 the new U.S. ambassador, John Gunther Dean, realized that the regime could not survive and attempted to persuade the State Department to recognize this and deal with it. He began to try to move Lon Nol and Henry Kissinger toward a "controlled solution." Kissinger balked, but Dean was able to persuade Lon Nol to issue several appeals for unconditional negotiations with the other side. Ambassador Dean's definition of a "controlled solution" was "a nonmilitary solution which would take account of the realities," allow the Cambodians to stop fighting, and permit a dignified American withdrawal.[86] Dean's views were published in the House Foreign Affairs Committee staff report of July 1974. The views of the ambassador were thus known to the committee well in advance of the crisis of March and April 1975. They were obviously persuasive. Dean took advantage of a trip to Washington in August 1974 discreetly to inform a handful of powerful senators and congressmen of his fears of a defeat in Cambodia and of the corresponding need to attempt to fashion a negotiated end to the war in Cambodia. Congressman Fraser was among those who spoke to Dean during the visit.

It remained, of course, to give flesh to the skeleton of the idea of a "controlled solution" achieved through negotiations. One of the most imaginative models sprang from the mind of the French ambassador to Peking, Etienne Manac'h. The plan called for the United States to depose Lon Nol and allow the return of Prince Sihanouk. Once he had regained his throne, Sihanouk would take charge of a coalition government of which the Khmer Rouge would form only a part. By rallying the army and bureaucracy to him, Sihanouk could hope to counterbalance the strength of the Communists and restore peace to his people. Even if Washington could be persuaded to abandon Lon Nol and a four-year commitment, the plan still depended on the willingness of Peking and Hanoi to restrain the Khmer Rouge. Moreover, if too much time elapsed, a victory for the Khmer Rouge alone would become unavoidable.

The plan was a hothouse specimen, complex and risky at best. It was far from certain, for example, that Sihanouk could have restrained the Khmer Rouge in any significant way even if all the other conditions had been fulfiilled and cooperation between Hanoi and Peking had held firm. While all these developments were hypothetically to occur in the future, the United States was required to oust Lon Nol immediately, an irrevocable practical step in the present that would have been fatal to the U.S. position in Cambodia. That position, it must be said, grew less hopeful every day and eventually collapsed. In short, a case could be made on behalf of a "controlled solution," and as late as mid-December the idea was very much alive in the foreign ministries in Peking and Paris, if not in Washington.[87]

If timing doesn't mean everything in diplomacy it means a great deal. What might have been possible in mid-1974 or even in the fall of 1974 was clearly impossible in March 1975 with the Mekong closed and Phnom Penh surrounded and starving. Thus, in proposing a "controlled solution" as Cambodia foundered, the committee had chosen an idea whose time had come—and gone. It is hard to discover what group or coalition on the government side still possessed the power and coherence to survive the onslaught of the Khmer Rouge, let alone negotiate a division of authority with them. If renewing military and economic aid every thirty days would hardly give the Cambodian government a feeling of confidence, it was equally foolish to throw money at the problem and coax the Cambodian government into the wet season. Without some fundamental change in the military situation this was a waste of lives and money. In short, a dialogue of might-have-beens was about to begin. The committee championed a negotiated surrender that might have been a "controlled solution" if the administration had acted wisely and early enough. The administration demanded a large-scale provision of aid, which it recognized would not make any difference, although in its view the same money might have been enough if only it had been provided earlier. Now the money would not save Cambodia, but it must be given in order that no one could blame the United States for the fall of the regime. In this way U.S. policy in the Middle East and elsewhere would not be harmed by the appearance of having abandoned an ally. In the bargain, if Congress refused to appropriate the money—even though it was without value to Cambodia—then the administration could (and would) blame Congress for the disaster that was certain to follow.[88] Meanwhile, on the ground in Cambodia the units assigned to defend Phnom Penh melted away and government ammunition supplies dwindled.[89] In Washington on March 10 the director of the CIA, William Colby, had told the Hamilton subcommittee he doubted Cambodia could survive, even with additional U.S. assistance. Hamilton described Colby to reporters as "deeply pessimistic" about the ability of the Lon Nol government to survive.[90]

As discussion continued in the markup session of the Hamilton subcommittee, it was clear that there was no support for the administration's strategy or for their request and that the congressmen and the staff were split into two camps: (1) no aid at all, or (2) small amounts of aid conditional on a reversal of U.S. policy, a negotiated surrender to the Khmer Communists, an "orderly transfer of power," and an attempt to save as many Cambodian lives as possible within the limits of an unarmed diplomacy. Michael Harrington (D., Mass.) spoke in favor of giving no further military aid. This was option 1. His view was that however carefully the bill would be written, the grant of any military aid would simply prolong the war, and he opposed it for that reason. Don Bonker (D., Wash.) opposed additional aid, as well, on the clear-sighted ground that there was no possibility for compromise because the Khmer Communists were not interested in compromise. "I just don't see the assurances and the commitments on the other side to find an area of conditional assistance. . . . I just don't see the middle ground."[91] Hamilton's answer to this sensible observation was based on hope and reason. By granting limited support to the Cambodian government the United States would prevent a sudden collapse and create an incentive for the Khmer Rouge to accept a negotiated transfer of power. This would minimize their problems and create a "controlled situation" that would help reduce violence and loss of life in Cambodia.

An agreed draft, incorporating the Hamilton and DuPont viewpoints, was worked out by the subcommittee that first afternoon.[92] Michael Harrington then moved to table this draft and reject all further military aid. Some fast maneuvering followed. DuPont said he would support Harrington's motion because he still disliked the wording of the bill he had helped perfect. Larry Winn (R., Kans.) then moved to table Harrington's motion. The motion failed in a tie, 3 to 3, with Harrington, Bonker, and DuPont in favor of Harrington's motion, and Winn, Hamilton, and L. H. Fountain (D., N.C.) voting to table. The subcommittee next voted on Harrington's motion to table the compromise bill and it, too, failed with an identical vote. At an impasse, the subcommittee adjourned. Chairman Hamilton said he would report to Chairman Morgan and reconvene the subcommittee the following afternoon.

The Democratic Caucus Opposes Further Assistance

On the morning of March 12 the Democratic members of the House of Representatives met in caucus to vote on a resolution sponsored by Robert Carr (Mich.), Bella Abzug (N.Y.), Thomas Harkin (Iowa), Toby Moffett (Conn.), and Edward Pattison (N.Y.), giving the sense of the caucus being opposed to "any further military assistance to South Vietnam or to Cambodia in Fiscal Year 1975." In Vietnam, heavy fighting continued throughout the country. The main thrust of the North Vietnamese again was felt in the highlands and had as its apparent objective the opening of a supply corridor ending just north of Saigon.[93] All the sponsors of the caucus proposal were freshmen except Abzug. The resolution carried, 189 to 49 with four voting present. Before the caucus voted on the Carr resolution, they rejected by 151 to 98 a motion put by David Obey (Wisc.) to scotch the Carr proposal by sending it to the House Steering and Policy Committee.

Even if one judges the Obey motion to be a more accurate assessment of members' views, three Democrats in five opposed additional aid. Opponents of the aid proposal preferred to speak of the vote on the Carr motion, of course, and the margin there was overwhelming. The vote of the freshmen was nearly unanimous against further aid. Thirteen of fifteen first-term southern Democrats supported Carr and broke with their senior colleagues from the South who opposed Carr (favored aid) 32 to 22. Of 71 first-term Democrats, 68 voted against further aid, while 121 of 167 who had served more than one term opposed the aid requests. The next day the Senate Democratic caucus opposed further aid to Cambodia 38 to 5 and all additional military aid in fiscal year 1975 by 34 to 6.

The votes in caucus do not bind Democrats, not in the sense that the party punishes members who later reverse their position. The caucus tallies are made public, however, and there would be little reason for senators or representatives to reverse themselves during voting on the floor. By revealing the striking absence of support in the dominant party for aid to Cambodia and South Vietnam, the caucus votes undoubtedly shaped the expectations of supporters and opponents of the president's request in both houses.

The Hamilton-DuPont Compromise

The day before the vote in the House Democratic caucus, the Senate Foreign Relations Subcommittee on Foreign Assistance and Economic Policy approved 4 to 3 the transfer to Cambodia of ammunition and matériel worth $125 million from U.S. supplies.[94] Senator Javits said after the vote that he supported the proposal as the best way to bring an orderly transition to a new government in Cambodia.[95] The Senate recommendation also provided $73 million more for food, and $15 million in medical supplies, or $213 million altogether.

The Hamilton subcommittee met Wednesday afternoon, a few hours after the House caucus vote, to try to find agreement on a recommendation for the full committee. In the interval the staff had talked with legislative counsel who advised that exact amounts be specified for each category of aid. The revised draft worked out by Hamilton and DuPont incorporated this change and some more important additions (see Appendix 3). Congress would now direct the United States government to end the Cambodian conflict by June 30, 1975. The thirty-day installments of aid would be granted if the United States were making efforts to end all military assistance by June 30; if the Cambodian government were actively pursuing specific measures to reach a political and military accommodation with the other side; and if initiatives had been taken to achieve a peaceful and orderly end to the conflict, to allow people to leave if they wished to, and to obtain assurances that the rest of the Cambodians would not be massacred.[96] To this had been added a requirement that the United States ask the secretary general of the United Nations to assist in achieving peace, including the use of a UN peacekeeping force, in accordance with General Assembly Resolution 3238.[97]

Direct evidence of the bargaining undertaken by Chairman Hamilton to win DuPont's vote emerged during an exchange with Harrington. The administration, Harrington said, had requested $400 million for Cambodia in the coming year. Would DuPont, as the senior Republican on the subcommittee, say that the administration would agree to the termination of all military aid on June 30? DuPont answered that he had "informed" the administration that he wanted a bill like the one before them to pass. He could not promise the administration would give up its request for the $400 million, but he intended to oppose "every penny" both in committee and on the floor of the House. Apparently, the administration agreed to the cutoff.[98] Hamilton then revealed he had agreed with DuPont to oppose any further military aid if the subcommittee bill passed. When Harrington asked if the chairman had told that to the administration, Hamilton replied that he had told only chairman Morgan, the ranking minority member, William Broomfield (R., Mass.), and several other members of the committee.

With Hamilton and DuPont reconciled, the division in the group was now simply between those who favored giving economic and military aid to assist in ending the conflict and preventing a massacre and those who opposed all further military aid. Bonker praised Hamilton and DuPont for their success in finding an area of compromise. He opposed the bill but, in the interest of strengthening it, proposed an amendment. In addition to directing the United States to end the war by June 30, Bonker wished Congress to require that all U.S. involvement be ended by the same date. The staff (Van Dusen and Sullivan) quickly suggested a more precise term—to end all U.S. military assistance rather than involvement—and the subcommittee approved the Bonker amendment by voice vote. When Fountain and Winn each took a turn and said they would support the revised bill, Hamilton knew he had enough votes to win in the subcommittee.

In offering his alternative, Congressman Harrington first challenged the idea that Cambodia needed military assistance.[99] He then introduced a substitute for the Hamilton-DuPont compromise. He proposed that Congress reject the request for supplementary aid and instead direct that it would be the new policy of the United States "to secure an immediate cease-fire in Cambodia and to facilitate whatever change in governmental arrangements [in Cambodia] is required to achieve and maintain that cease-fire." Once a cease-fire had been arranged Congress would give special attention to any request by the administration for humanitarian assistance for Cambodia. To Harrington this was the only proposal that was consistent with the political facts, with the Democratic caucus vote and the views of the American people on further military aid. Harrington said that his original idea had been amended by Congressman Don Riegle (D., Mich.), and that he had shown an outline of the proposal to both Hamilton and DuPont before the markup began.[100] Congressman Winn objected that this amounted to saying: "When the Communists take over we will help them in every way we can." Representative Fountain added that this approach denied the administration the influence it needed to end the war and disregarded the chance of a bloodbath. The subcommittee was ready to vote.

The Harrington proposal allowed the subcommittee a clear choice between a complicated effort to try to achieve an orderly transition in Phnom Penh, on the one hand, and a simple stop to all further military aid on the other. In the terms set by Chairman Hamilton, this was a choice between options 1 and 3. Although the choice was clear, its clarity should not obscure the remarkable agreement between them. They were alike in the importance given to Congress, in the reversal of American policy, in the determination to end the war in Cambodia and the U.S. participation in it, and in the concern for saving lives. In both proposals Congress directed that the United States reverse its policy, abandon the hope for a military stalemate in Cambodia, and end the war and U.S. military assistance. The Hamilton-DuPont plan went farther than the Harrington approach. Hamilton-DuPont offered to barter three months of military aid in exchange for the administration's acceptance of the policy reversal, eventual termination of aid, the rescue of Cambodians who might lose their lives if the Communists won, and the participation of the UN. The obvious meaning of the two proposals was that no one on the subcommittee thought the administration proposal worth talking about. The markup had not even begun with the administration bill, H.R. 2704, but with a totally different substitute.

On reflection, a less obvious meaning appears. No one on the subcommittee or staff could have expected the administration to accept even the Hamilton-DuPont compromise, let alone the Harrington plan. Why all the bother, then? Why spend all the time in markup? The answer seems to be that the congressional counterpart of the maneuvering by the executive branch had already begun. The administration appeared to expect Cambodia, and eventually Vietnam, to fall. Although they held out hope of stalemate and negotiations, in fact what the Ford administration wished was for Congress to appropriate the additional money and, when the end came, the United States could say its allies lost because of their own weakness and not because the United States had pulled the rug from under them. But this wasn't all.

The additional money might make a military and political difference in Indochina. Wasn't it worth a try? And if the Democratic Congress reneged and the worst happened in Cambodia and Vietnam, wouldn't the blame fall on Congress, especially if the president and secretary of state blamed Congress repeatedly and publicly?

The first concern of the congressional leadership and particularly of chairmen Morgan and Hamilton was to remain true to their own assessment of the situation in Indochina.[101] But they could not ignore the political high-pressure hose the administration was using to undermine their position. Their task was not easy. It was to find a legislative path consistent with their own views and the wishes of their constituents, as revealed on March 9 by the Gallup poll.

Thus while the executive branch operated on two levels the Congress answered in kind. It was this that led to the Hamilton-Dupont compromise. If, against all expectations, the administration actually accepted the plan, the Foreign Affairs Committee would have its way. For the next ninety days the United States would work for a cease-fire and an orderly transfer of power to the Khmer Communists and, in any case, would stop all military assistance on June 30, thus ending all American influence and involvement in Cambodia. The war would end soon afterward in a Communist victory; on this all agreed. No one on the Foreign Affairs Committee wished this to occur, but they were prepared for it to happen rather than prolong the war in what they saw as an obviously vain effort to establish a military stalemate in Cambodia. A second benefit would accrue to the Congress as a whole in its struggle with the president over control of foreign policy. The Hamilton-DuPont bill directed the executive branch to reverse American policy. If the Ford administration accepted this kind of dictation not only in goals but in tactics, Congress would have gained substantial influence in the foreign-policy making process.

Last, even if the administration rejected the bill the committee stood to gain in the opinion of their constituents and the many Americans who despised "the war," and in the view of their colleagues in the House. As the Gallup poll had revealed nearly 80 percent of the American people were unwilling to give supplementary assistance to Vietnam and Cambodia because they were afraid the United States would somehow end up back in "the war" again. By rejecting the committee's plan to end the war in Cambodia and American military assistance to that country, the administration would have to take on its shoulders again at least part of the blame they were so eagerly thrusting on Congress.

In addition to these political considerations the Foreign Affairs Committee also had to be aware of the expectations of the House as a whole and the risk that control of the aid issue could be taken away from it on the House floor both because the committee was deeply divided and because of the way other members of Congress regard foreign affairs. House members expect their Foreign Affairs Committee to lead them in legislation about international questions, but they seldom accord the committee's bills the respect they grant recommendations from the Appropriations or Ways and Means committee.[102]

On an issue as controversial as military aid to Cambodia, and given the sentiments of House Democrats as revealed in the caucus vote, any bill less unyielding than Hamilton-DuPont would surely raise a swarm of amendments. Even Hamilton-DuPont might be altered beyond recognition or rejected, as sometimes happened to the committee's recommendations on foreign aid. To make matters worse, the committee was sharply divided over Cambodia and Vietnam, which made the bill even more vulnerable on the floor of the House. Representatives Harrington and Bonker, or perhaps Abzug or Philip Burton (D., Calif.), might introduce their own substitutes on the floor and take control away from the committee. Their bills might be better or they might be worse, but the committee leaders would hardly enjoy losing control of an issue so squarely in their charge, nor would they let it slip away without making an effort to keep the lead.

With these considerations in mind the Hamilton subcommittee began to vote. First the Harrington amendment was defeated 3 to 4. Then the Hamilton-DuPont amendment passed 4 to 3. In both votes the four were Hamilton, DuPont, Fraser, and Winn; the three were Harrington, Yatron, and Bonker.

Last Act for Cambodia

The Hamilton subcommittee was thus able to make a recommendation to the full committee at its meeting the next day. If the terms of the bill were cast far too high for the executive to accept, they were congruent to the political realities within the committee and the House and answered the double game of the Ford administration with a congressional twin. Hamilton and DuPont spoke first as authors of the bill and gave a brief introduction summarizing the work of the subcommittee and the major points in the bill. Wayne Hays (D., Ohio) interrupted to ask that nagging question first raised by Bonker in the markup session: What happens if the other side won't negotiate?[103] Chairman Morgan intervened and gave the floor to the acting secretary of state, Robert Ingersoll.

Ingersoll made the now-familiar arguments: additional aid was urgently needed; with it the Cambodian government might survive, without it they would collapse; the Cambodians themselves ought to judge when to stop fighting; the United States should not abandon a people still willing to fight. As Ingersoll spoke it became clear that no one would have to answer Hays's question. The administration was adamant. They would accept the Senate Foreign Relations Subcommittee bill, but they would not agree to stopping military aid on June 30.[104] With that admission, support within the committee for Hamilton-DuPont began to vanish. One by one, the committee members registered their astonishment and disappointment at the administration. Secretary Ingersoll is not a flamboyant man. His testimony and his rebuttals read better than he presented them orally that day. Disbelief and anger and disappointment came from the congressmen behind the huge, brown, tiered desks. They were met by the dogged attention of a slender, graying man who seemed tired as he spoke in a faint voice for the Ford administration in that cavernous, still room. The audience was critical. His lines were bleak. Don Fraser was the first to desert Hamilton-DuPont. Reddening, his voice filled with emotion, Fraser addressed Ingersoll:

> FRASER: I was prepared to vote for the Hamilton recommendation today if I thought that the Department was willing to change course and actually to seek to close out the war in as orderly a way as possible in order to save the most lives, permit the Cambodians, who need to get out, to get out, to continue humanitarian aid under as peaceful conditions as possible.
>
> But so long as you continue to pursue this war to the last Cambodian to achieve an unattainable stalemate, I am forced to vote "no" today, and I tell you this in the hope that there might be some indication that the Department was prepared to change course.
>
> INGERSOLL: I am not sure what your indication of changing course would mean, Mr. Fraser, because the Department has been pursuing a constant effort to negotiate with the other side. . . .
>
> FRASER: Mr. Secretary, the basis on which I would understand the requirements to be met would be the assumption that the war is lost, not that it either is or can be stalemated. If I am not speaking clearly enough, I will spell it out even more clearly.
>
> INGERSOLL: You are asking for a surrender then, Mr. Fraser?
>
> FRASER: Yes; under controlled circumstances to minimize the loss of life. . . . If you are not prepared to move in that direction, then I am not prepared to vote any more money.
>
> INGERSOLL: I think it is difficult for the U. S. Government to ask another sovereign government to seek surrender. I think that must be their decision.[105]

After several other questions Congressman DuPont's turn came. In a mocking tone he lectured Secretary Ingersoll. Did he know he had only two choices: either Hamilton-DuPont or no aid at all?

Back came the answer: Why not another choice? Why not amend the Hamilton resolution so that it did not have a cutoff? Sarcastically, DuPont tried again:

> DuPont: Mr. Secretary, you just are not coming to grips with the problem and I don't know whether you don't want to see it or whether you have been instructed not to see it, but there is no other choice. There is going to be no aid or there is going to be some humanitarian help for the refugees, for the combatants, and we will try to wind the thing down with as little bloodshed as possible.
> Ingersoll: Mr. Chairman, is it not legal to amend the Hamilton resolution?
> DuPont: Mr. Secretary, we have worked for four days to put this together . . . [O]ne of two events is going to happen and your response is you would prefer a third course. Maybe you would prefer a third course, but you are not going to get that choice.
> Ingersoll: I believe the Committee as a whole, in its wisdom, would determine that.
> DuPont: You betcha it will.[106]

The chairman then intervened to say that time was short and there were several amendments to consider. Congressman Zablocki moved to cut off questioning at eleven o'clock; the motion was approved by acclamation. That left five minutes. In that interval Congressman Lagomarsino established that the administration was prepared to accept Hamilton-DuPont if the cutoff date were removed. Stephen Solarz (D., N.Y.) drew the response he wanted from the secretary. Yes, Ingersoll said, if the Lon Nol government survived the present fighting the United States would have to continue sending military assistance. Question time expired after Ingersoll's answer to Solarz's question. The clerk then read H.R. 2704 and the Hamilton-DuPont bill, and debate began on these with each speaker limited to five minutes.

Congressman Charles Whalen (R., Ohio) put the first amendment by reintroducing the Harrington proposal that had been defeated in subcommittee. Speaking for Harrington and Riegle as well as himself, Whalen urged the committee to recommend to the House that it reject the request for additional aid, direct the United States to secure a cease-fire in Cambodia, and welcome a request for humanitarian assistance after a cease-fire had been established. Whalen scored a debating point by using the testimony of former Secretary of State William Rogers to the committee. Rogers had said the United States had no legal commitment to Cambodia and had invaded that country and then aided it only as part of its plan to turn the Vietnam war over to the South Vietnamese and to protect the withdrawal of American forces from Vietnam.[107] Whalen changed no minds.

Congressman Winn repeated his view of the folly of promising to help a Communist government after their victory as a means of persuading them to be moderate. The United States had tried the method with North Vietnam in the Paris Accords, and it hadn't worked. "Besides that," he added, "the American people raised all kinds of hell when they thought they were going to give aid to North Vietnam."[108] Lee Hamilton repeated that the Whalen-Harrington-Riegle plan ignored the need to prevent the violence that was sure to accompany the "uncontrolled and unorderly" situation in Cambodia when the Lon Nol government ran out of ammunition. It gave no one an incentive to try to end the conflict, from the Khmer Rouge to the U.S. State Department, and it even endangered the six-hundred Americans still in Phnom Penh.

Congressman Paul Findley (R., Ill.) proposed a simpler idea: let Congress reject the administration request for military and economic assistance and promise sympathetic consideration of humanitarian aid if a sustained ceasefire occurred promptly. To him, this offered a remedy for the shortcomings of both the Whalen and Hamilton proposals. The Whalen bill would put the United States in the middle of arranging a settlement in Cambodia; the United States didn't belong there and his bill kept it out. As for the Hamilton proposal, why wouldn't it encourage the Khmer Rouge simply to wait ninety days and then collect their victory? If the bill was meant to prevent a bloodbath in April, what about a massacre in July, or whenever the new installment of aid ran out? Let the Congress say what the United States would do; that alone was America's responsibility. Let the Congress terminate military aid and show the nation's humanitarian concern for the region. What right had the United States "to be telling the Lon Nol government to quit fighting for survival? Why should we sit in judgment over whether the Lon Nol government has a right to continue its effort to sustain itself?"[109]

Clement Zablocki then added the missing element by proposing to delete the cutoff date of June 30. He spoke only a few words on behalf of the amendment because everyone knew the rationale for it. Here, as repeatedly during the months of controversy over the aid requests, the brevity and silences of the formal record reveal the sophistication of the proceding. Everyone present understood that the cutoff meant the end of the Lon Nol government and that its deletion would enable the administration to continue the policy of military stalemate. Accordingly, Zablocki said only that neither side was going to cease fire or negotiate before June 30, and if the Congress kept the date in the bill both were unlikely any time afterward.

All sides had spoken, and it was time to vote. No one could be absolutely certain of the outcome and several committee members used parliamentary inquiries to protect their positions in case the vote went against them. Representative Edward Derwinski, the second-ranking Republican, used the device to ask if he could try to amend the Hamilton substitute bill even after it had passed. Chairman Morgan assured him he could. Don Fraser sought still further time to persuade the State Department to change its policy. What if all the amendments were defeated, he asked the chair, and the committee then rejected the administration request. (Congressman DuPont had already promised to move disapproval if the compromise bill failed.) Could the committee hold its report until the first of the week "in order that we might get some further response from the Department of State"?[110] The chairman replied that if the committee defeated all the amendments and rejected as well the proposal to disapprove the administration request, the committee would have nothing to report unless it took further action of some other kind to deal with the aid question.

The committee then began to vote. The Zablocki proposal to delete the cutoff and the Findley substitute were defeated by voice vote. Don Riegle asked for a record vote on the Whalen proposal, and the necessary four others agreed. Marian Cznarnecki, the committee chief of staff, then called the roll, and the Whalen substitute lost 9 to 24.

A record vote was also requested on the Hamilton-DuPont proposal, which was then defeated 15 to 18. The vote on Hamilton-DuPont was very close. A shift in only two votes would have made the difference. Presumably, these votes would have had to come from those who opposed both bills, for those in favor of Whalen's flat termination of aid would not logically support the elaborate installment mechanism contained in Hamilton-DuPont. Of the thirty-three committee members voting, eight opposed both bills: Fascell, Diggs, Nix, Fraser, Taylor, Collins, Findley, and Burke. Three of these had made their views known before the vote: Fascell, Fraser, and Findley. Congressman Fraser would have supported the Hamilton bill only if the administration had been willing to agree to reverse its policy. Findley thought the United States had no business meddling in Cambodia any longer and opposed both plans on this ground. Fascell had said that in his mind both the Whalen and the Hamilton plans missed the point. Congress had imposed a ceiling on aid to Cambodia in the existing foreign aid act. Only the Zablocki plan to delete the cutoff date put the question in its proper light by proposing, in effect, to establish a new, higher ceiling. Whether or not there should be a new ceiling was the central issue. He could not vote for either bill.

After the voting, Congressman Solarz's amendment to arrange for the evacuation of Cambodians was conscientious but anticlimactic.[111] Debate was short and the amendment lost by a voice vote. Wayne Hays then moved to adjourn, a motion that cannot be debated or deferred. Although the committee then voted to adjourn by 18 to 15, there is no clear pattern to the ballot. Nine of the eighteen who voted for adjournment had opposed Hamilton-DuPont and nine had supported it. Nor does support for Whalen give a much better clue about the reasons for adjournment. Five of the nine supporters of the Whalen bill opposed adjournment (Rosenthal, Harrington, Riegle, Solarz, and Whalen), but the other four voted to adjourn (Bingham, Yatron, Meyner, and Bonker). Apparently the reasons for adjourning were personal and obviously varied widely, from those of Don Fraser who wished to allow the administration one last chance to reverse U.S. policy to those of William Broomfield, a friend of the Ford administration.

An analysis of the voting by party is somewhat more revealing. The Democrats held twenty-two of the thirty-three votes cast that Thursday. The vote to defeat the Whalen bill was decidely nonpartisan and included fourteen of twenty-two Democratic votes and ten of eleven Republican votes. The votes on Hamilton-DuPont and adjournment were partisan (a majority of Democrats opposed a majority of Republicans). The split on the Hamilton bill was: *Yes:* 15 (7D, 8R); *No:* 18 (15D, 3R). On adjournment the vote was: *Yes:* 18 (14D, 4R); *No:* 15 (8D, 7R). In both cases Republican votes were needed to establish a majority. In this sense, the opposition to U.S. policy in Cambodia of Findley and Whalen—both Republicans—becomes as important as that of Fraser, a Democrat. The votes had gone against the Ford administration, which found itself separated from Congress by a profound distrust and grave disagreements on policy.

The Foreign Affairs Committee had adjourned without even voting on the administration request after defeating by a very narrow margin a bill that called for a reversal of U.S. policy in terms bound to humiliate and even insult the president and his cabinet. The vote had also gone against the established Cambodian government. There was now little chance they would receive the ammunition, food, and fuel their regime depended on for survival. As the committee members and administration witnesses stood to leave the hearing room, one had a sickening feeling that fateful decisions had been taken, and that there was no going back on them. It was as if one were watching a large ship leave the pier: a feeling of something forever lost. The official record of the session shows that the committee adjourned at five minutes past noon.

4
Vietnam: The Next Step

I claim not to have controlled events, but confess plainly that events have controlled me.
—*Abraham Lincoln*

The first reaction of the Ford administration after the defeat over aid for Cambodia was to move back a step, offer a compromise in the form of a delayed cutoff, and try to win enough votes in this way to pass its aid requests. On March 15 the *Washington Post* reported that President Ford would accept a cutoff date on military aid to Cambodia if Congress would immediately approve $82.5 million in military supplies for that country. The White House officials interviewed by the *Post* carefully distinguished President Ford's position from that of Secretary Ingersoll. "Nobody should think that it's all or nothing," one White House official said. "We're willing to take what we can get."[1] Another official suggested Mr. Ford wanted to go "considerably beyond" what Ingersoll had told the Foreign Affairs Committee.

The belief at the White House was that the president's willingness to compromise would lead to a delayed cutoff—perhaps after a few months rather than on June 30—and this alteration would win enough votes to enable the committee to report a limited aid bill to the House. White House officials thought a bill of this kind would have "a fighting chance" before the full House. They were dismayed by Ingersoll's statement and thought it revealed "a surprising lack of realism about the situation in Congress." Events in the next few days made it hard to tell that there was much greater realism about Congress or Indochina at the White House.

On March 15 South Vietnamese forces began to withdraw from the Central Highlands along Route 7b from Pleiku through Cheo Reo city toward the coast. President Thieu's plan was to sacrifice the provinces of Pleiku and Phu Bon in order to strengthen the defense of the coast and to free troops for the attempt to recapture Ban Me Thuot.[2] Two days later Acting Secretary of State Charles Robinson wrote the Foreign Affairs Committee and asked it to report the Hamilton bill.

Although the administration, he wrote, has "serious objections" to the plan, "we view it as the only legislative vehicle to bring this issue before the House." Finally aware that they might lose everything without a vote, the administration thought that if they could just get the bill to the floor of the House, they might find the votes to pass the military aid and kill the cutoff date.[3] It was not to happen. Meanwhile, in Vietnam Cheo Reo city fell to the North Vietnamese 320th Division, cutting the evacuating ARVN units in half, and threatening their very survival.

That same Monday, the full Senate Foreign Relations Committee by a vote of 9 to 7 approved $82.5 million in military aid to Cambodia, and added a provision, sponsored by Republican Senators Charles Percy (Ill.) and Jacob Javits, terminating all military supplies after June 30.[4] The Senate plan was based on the Hamilton bill and contained the same wording: that it was U.S. policy to end the war in Cambodia and stop all U.S. military assistance on June 30, and that the Congress would require monthly reports about efforts to achieve these goals. Before voting against the bill, Senator Humphrey had stiffened the prohibition of military aid by winning approval of an amendment forbidding every imaginable kind of military transaction: grants, loans, sales, credits, and shipments of excess military articles. The Senate committee bill allocated $58 million in food aid and $15 million in general economic aid. Like the Hamilton bill, the Senate measure would stop only military aid on June 30. Economic aid could continue as in the House package.

Then from the State Department came the announcement that the United States had "found" an additional $21.5 million in funds for military aid for Cambodia.[5] Senator Mathias pounced on the various discrepancies.[6] Apparently the money was found by recalculating the prices for ammunition and other supplies charged to the Cambodia account. It was a small matter, but opponents of the administration policy seized it and used it to damage the administration's already weakened reputation for straight dealing with the Congress. The administration had been saying for some time that all funds for Cambodia had been spent.

At a meeting at the White House on Tuesday, Mr. Ford told Republican congressional leaders he opposed the cutoff because it interfered with his ability to conduct an effective foreign policy. The Republican leaders answered that unless the president agreed to a cutoff there was no chance that Congress would allow any emergency military assistance. Senator John Tower (Tex.), chairman of the Senate Republican Policy Committee, said later that they had told Mr. Ford: "This is the best you can get—if you can get that. This is a take-it-or-leave-it proposition and even this has limited chance for success."[7] Representative Broomfield left the White House meeting convinced that the president had rejected the June 30 cutoff.[8] On learning this from Broomfield, Congressman Morgan, Chairman of the House Foreign Affairs Committee, decided to delay the next committee meeting a full week, saying "We don't have the votes." Morgan also said a postponement would allow the Senate to act, and if the Senate rejected the request, there would be no need for the House to consider it. He thought the newly discovered $21.5 million had eased the pressure on the administration although it had damaged their credibility, as well.[9] The South Vietnamese chose this moment to abandon An Loc, a city in northern Military Region 3, in which Saigon was located. Tay Ninh province now lay open to unchecked North Vietnamese assault. The North Vietnamese also seized a village seventy miles east of Saigon and cut the main road to Dalat in southern Military Region 2.

Apparently, the administration had already begun to look beyond the Cambodian request and even beyond the immediate request for emergency military aid for Vietnam. Several signs pointed to this change in tactics. Representative Mahan on Tuesday told Leslie Gelb, a reporter for the *New York Times,* that the administration wasn't pushing the Vietnam aid request, although "no one in the White House or Pentagon has told me that they would not like to have it."[10] White House officials told Gelb in other interviews that the administration had designed a three-year $6.4 billion package of military and economic grant assistance for South Vietnam. This large amount was thought to be enough, officials said, to enable the United States to stop all grant aid to South Vietnam at the end of three years, although military and economic loans would still be possible.[11] Two senators, Frank Church (D., Idaho) and James Pearson (R., Kans.), had approached the president after he first mentioned a phaseout several weeks earlier. The senators had suggested a figure of $1.6 billion for three years, and the two sums were so far apart that they and the administration hadn't gotten anywhere.[12]

Blaming Congress

Nor were the administration's difficulties easing in the House. On March 19, fifty representatives wrote Mr. Ford and condemned the Cambodian aid proposal. "This is the time to spend that $222 million on our own people," they told Mr. Ford.[13] The administration, apparently under pressure from congressional Republicans, began to answer in kind. Also on March 19, General George Brown, chairman of the Joint Chiefs of Staff, blamed the reversals in South Vietnam on congressional reductions in assistance.[14] Secretary of Defense James Schlesinger repeated the allegation the next day, saying that the South Vietnamese would not have had to abandon the Central Highlands and northern provinces "if Congress had supplied more military aid over the past two years."[15] Secretary Kissinger chimed in to blame Congress in his unique and cataclysmic global manner. Reporters traveling with him en route to Riyadh, Saudi Arabia, from Israel were given "the most pessimistic appraisal of the overall world situation in some time." Spreading a sense "of almost fatalistic gloom," Kissinger told newsmen that Congress had caused the major North Vietnamese attack by cutting aid to South Vietnam. If he had known in 1972 and 1973 that Congress would reduce aid to Saigon so drastically, he said, he would never have negotiated the Paris Agreements. Moreover, the dire situation in Cambodia and South Vietnam had already harmed his diplomatic campaign in the Middle East: Israel had grown afraid to trust the United States and Syria had been encouraged to be intransigent in hopes that the United States would soon abandon Israel, as Cambodia and Taiwan had been abandoned. In fact, around the world, American diplomatic influence was declining.[16]

In Vietnam, by the evening of March 19, four days after the start of the withdrawal from the highlands the South Vietnamese commander, General Pham Van Phu, had ordered his men to abandon their heavy weapons and supplies and to flee to Phu Bon province. Troops and refugees—two hundred thousand of them—from Kontum and Pleiku were stuck near Tuy Hoa City on the central coast. The troops, indeed all South Vietnamese units except the Marine and Airborne Divisions, moved with their dependents, and this responsibility had preyed on the minds of the men and had greatly complicated their efforts to conduct a fighting withdrawal.[17] Nor was this the end of the dislocations: sixty thousand people had fled the fighting at Ban Me Thuot and were making their way toward the coast while to the north more than two million people had become displaced persons in Military Region 1 as a result of attacks and withdrawals. On March 19 the *Post* carried a report that the South Vietnamese government had abandoned Pleiku, Kontum, and Darlac and that the North Vietnamese offensive was becoming a countrywide assault. On Thursday, the *Post* added that South Vietnam had abandoned Quangtri and Hue in the far north of the country. At least two of Hanoi's strategic reserve divisions were fighting in the South, the article said, and one and perhaps two others as well.[18]

In Washington, Mr. Ford took up the theme of congressional responsibility for the defeats in Vietnam. The calamitous defeats in Vietnam made him sad, he told a reporter from the *Washington Post,* and it was all because "the Congress won't appropriate $300 million, plus a commitment for the next fiscal year."[19] He saw no chance for a diplomatic settlement in Cambodia because the enemy was winning, and they surely would not respond to the needs of the side they were beating. Meanwhile, the administration was showing documents on Capitol Hill that were intended to prove that China and the USSR had given far more aid to North Vietnam than Congress had allowed to go to South Vietnam.[20]

In *Decent Interval,* Frank Snepp argued that this analysis had been bungled because, leaving the numbers aside, it failed to reveal how much more Hanoi had gained from the Chinese and Soviet aid it had received than had Saigon from the reduced American aid it had obtained.[21] In fact, two documents were being circulated by the administration: one from the Embassy in Saigon dated March 1 and the other, prepared by the Central Intelligence Agency, the Defense Intelligence Agency, and the Bureau of Intelligence and Research of the Department of State, dated March 5. The document from the Intelligence Community is the most complete, but it leaves an ambiguous impression and this supports Snepp's view. It failed to indicate that Saigon was facing an urgent, let alone desperate, situation. It demonstrated only that Communist countries had nearly doubled the military and economic aid they supplied North Vietnam in 1974 ($400 million in military aid, $1,295 million in economic) as compared to 1970 ($205 million in military aid, $635 million in economic aid). The United States supplied $700 million in military aid to South Vietnam and $500 million in economic aid in fiscal year 1975. By this tabulation, Saigon appeared to have received twice as much military aid as Hanoi in the past year.

The document also stated that the North Vietnamese possessed "record stockpiles" of military supplies and would "sharply increase the tempo of the fighting" in the next few months. Buried in the numbers is equality and perhaps even an edge for the North over the South in the crucial category of military equipment and ammunition delivered in 1974–1975 ($275 million to Hanoi and $268 million to Saigon) especially since inflated U.S. prices would have significantly reduced the supplies bought for Saigon with that sum. But this is mentioned only in passing. Although nothing in their tables appeared to justify the observation, the authors concluded that the expected higher levels of fighting would put the Communists "in a position of significant advantage over the South Vietnamese forces in subsequent fighting."

Against this unsupported generalization a reader on Capitol Hill would have had to weigh the document's own significantly larger figure for U.S. military aid to South Vietnam ($700 million compared to $400 million for the North) and the assurance—again unsupported by any evidence in the document—that "Given the present military balance in the South, the GSV's [Government of South Vietnam's] forces will not be decisively defeated during the current dry season." No doubt an expert intelligence analyst, deeply versed in the esoteric study of foreign military assistance, could have detected warning signs in all this, particularly in the extremely difficult area of assigning dollar values to Soviet military aid. If a member of the House or the Senate or (more likely) someone on their staffs had read the document they surely would have concluded that South Vietnam had been well supplied and had even received more military aid than the enemy. The United States, they would have added, could not be blamed if the North used its apparently smaller supplies more efficiently than the South. In short, far from a brief for more aid, the document came close to an indictment of the government of South Vietnam for inefficiency. Since that surely was not the intention of those who authorized its release, one concludes that the document was a political and intelligence blunder and that South Vietnam's weaknesses did not stem from a shortage of ammunition.[22]

On March 22, Senate Majority Leader Mansfield said there was no chance the Senate would vote on the Cambodian aid plan before the Easter recess. Unnamed officials in the administration admitted to reporters that there would be no aid for South Vietnam unless the request were drastically cut and a cutoff of some kind were set for the funding. The next day, Kissinger returned from the Middle East without a new agreement between Israel and Egypt. The same front pages that reported Kissinger's return also reported the fall of two more South Vietnamese towns and the intention of the Thai government to stop the supply airlift to Cambodia.[23]

On March 27 Congress began a twelve-day Easter recess. During the recess the administration attempted to find an approach that would not be made irrelevant by the steadily worsening military situation in Cambodia and South Vietnam or the declining political support in Congress for any further aid to either country. Secretary Kissinger decided to try to revive the three-year phaseout of aid to Vietnam, and the president ordered Army Chief of Staff General Frederick Weyand to Vietnam to examine the situation there and report to him on it. For the next ten days the president and secretary of state repeatedly blamed Congress for the defeats in Indochina. When the Easter congressional recess ended, the administration had formulated a plan to reequip and reorganize the regional reserves in South Vietnam along with those few regular units still intact and to try for a military stalemate as a prelude to negotiations.

Neither blaming Congress nor formulating billion-dollar plans stopped the Communists in Vietnam. As early as March 25, the military correspondent for the *New York Times* wrote that the North's remarkable week of victories had created "a situation that favors an attempt to put an early end to the war." The Communists had overrun Khiem Hanh, thirty-five miles northwest of Saigon, and at the opposite end of the country had won spectacular gains. Danang, a port city and the main military base in the north, was isolated. The only exit was by sea or air. Phu Loc, between Danang and Hue, was under heavy attack. Hue was besieged. The Communists had cut the coastal road, forty miles south of Danang, by taking Tam Ky. Another city on the coast, Quang Ngai—a provincial capital—was under attack. American sources said the position in the north was hopeless.[24]

A week later Secretary of Defense Schlesinger announced that Saigon could be attacked in the current dry season. All depended, he said, on whether the Saigon government could stabilize the military situation. The defeats in the north had shaken the morale of the South Vietnamese army, and the North Vietnamese had exploited the demoralization and disintegration and made important gains all over the country.[25]

At a news conference on March 27, apparently in an attempt to break the stalemate in discussions with members of Congress about the three-year phaseout, Kissinger likened a refusal to give aid to South Vietnam to a refusal to help any country that depended on United States resources. If that were to become the national policy of the United States—to compel countries dependent on the United States to rely entirely on their own resources—"then we will have brought about a massive change in the international environment that in time will fundamentally threaten the security of the United States."[26] At the time of the Paris Agreements the United States told the South Vietnamese government that if they would cooperate in the withdrawal of American troops and the recovery of U.S. prisoners, then, in the opinion of the administration, the Congress would grant the military and economic assistance necessary to sustain South Vietnam. "We're not talking here of a legal American commitment; we are talking here of a moral commitment."[27]

A reporter asked specifically if the administration had obtained any assurances that Congress would continue the assistance. He answered, "We had no assurances."[28] That was not the point, he insisted. First of all, the domestic controversy was over withdrawal of *American* soldiers, the saving of *American* lives. There was never any suggestion from 1969 to 1973 that the United States would stop giving military and economic aid to South Vietnam. Second, his own public assertions that aid would continue had never been challenged. Accordingly, he had told Saigon that if they cooperated in permitting the United States to withdraw its forces and recover its prisoners, Congress would, in his judgment, provide the aid needed to sustain South Vietnam militarily and economically. In his own words, Kissinger thus revealed the extent to which he relied on the politics of acquiescence in conducting foreign policy. Faced with the collapse of his policy, it was to the silences of Congress—about Americans in the fighting, about U.S. assistance after the Paris Agreements were signed—to which he had to turn to justify his course. He could not point to explicit assurances of legislative support, for there had been none. He had never allowed an occasion to arise in which he might have sought such support, had not even submitted the Paris Agreements for congressional approval.

There wasn't a difference of principle about aid in the current year, Kissinger added, for the original authorization for South Vietnam had passed with little controversy. The administration was asking only for money that had already been authorized. Moreover, voting now for a three-year phaseout would "take Vietnam out of the national debate . . . in order to avoid what we think would be a very grievous blow to the United States."

In Kissinger's mind these points were important, but he put greatest emphasis on a more philosophical point: "The problem we face in Indochina today is an elementary question of what kind of a people we are."[29] The United States had fought for fifteen years in Vietnam and had lost fifty thousand lives. Now the question was "whether [the United States] will deliberately destroy an ally by withholding aid from it in its moment of extremity." This was "a fundamental question of how we are viewed by all other people, and it has nothing to do with the question of whether we should ever have gotten involved there in the first place."[30]

If this was an attempt to bring pressure on Congress, it failed. Senator Pearson, who with Senator Church had been trying for three weeks to agree with the president on a three-year phaseout, thought the two sides were still "miles apart." The administration's proposals were "not realistic when one considers the political attitudes in the

Senate." There was little support there for the plan, according to Senator Pearson, even among Republicans. "I think it will be damn hard to get anything through the House," he observed, and added:

> The problem is that the State Department is dealing in facts and figures, and they don't seem to understand that we have had facts and figures for 10 years [and] . . . these terms don't have credibility any more . . . [The problem is] not how you measure needs, but what is politically feasible in the Senate and in the House—and maybe nothing is.[31]

In Vietnam and Cambodia, meanwhile, the situation worsened. U.S. officials announced a chartered airlift of three hundred thousand Vietnamese refugees from Danang to Camranh Bay. Three days later, on March 29, 1975, the North Vietnamese captured Danang. General Weyand arrived in South Vietnam the same day. The fall of Danang and with it of Military Region 1 was a terrible defeat for the South Vietnamese government. Of the three million people who had been under government control, less than seventy thousand escaped, most by sea. Four divisions had been lost. Only sixteen thousand troops were evacuated. On April 1, Lon Nol left Cambodia, with a half-million dollars as an incentive to his going. That evening, the town of Neak Luong on the Mekong fell in hand-to-hand combat, freeing six thousand more troops for the assault on Phnom Penh.[32] On April 3, as government troops deserted the defenses of Phnom Penh, Ambassador Dean was allowed to evacuate the first part of the embassy staff.

On a golfing vacation in Palm Springs, California, President Ford continued to blame Congress for the defeats suffered in Indochina. The ruinous decision to abandon the Central Highlands, Mr. Ford said, had been caused by North Vietnamese violations of the Paris Agreements and, in the words of a White House spokesman, "by the effect on South Vietnamese morale of the prospect that the United States Congress would not approve any more aid in the way of ammunition and equipment that would enable them to fight for their own survival."[33]

On April 2 the North Vietnamese captured the major base cities of Nhatrang and Camranh Bay. U.S. analysts were now quoted to fear a total collapse in Vietnam. In less than a month one-hundred-fifty thousand South Vietnamese troops and militia in the northern half of the country had been killed or lost. Only one Marine brigade had escaped Military Region 1 intact. Of the two divisions in Military Region 2, only two regiments and one airborne brigade were capable of combat. At least $1 billion in equipment had been destroyed or left behind. Six infantry divisions, two brigades, a few ranger groups—

ninety thousand in all—were all that remained of the South Vietnamese army. They faced three-hundred thousand North Vietnamese organized in eighteen divisions in the South. Five more divisions waited ready to help beyond the Demilitarized Zone (DMZ).[34]

At a news conference in San Diego on April 3, the President repeatedly blamed Congress for the defeats in Vietnam. First, he indicated he was "frustrated" by the failure of Congress to provide economic and military aid to South Vietnam and by the limitations imposed by Congress on the chief executive since 1973. Baited by a reporter who asked if "the whole thing has come to nothing in South Vietnam," Mr. Ford said that U.S. policy had been correct; only the failure to honor the promises made to South Vietnam at Paris had been wrong. "Are you blaming the Congress?" came the inevitable follow-up question. No, he was not blaming the Congress, Mr. Ford said, and then proceeded to put all the blame entirely on Congress.

> I am not assessing blame on anyone. The facts are that in fiscal year 1974, there was a substantial reduction made by the Congress in the amount of military equipment requested for South Vietnam.
>
> In fiscal year 1975, the current fiscal year, the Administration asked for $1,400 million in military assistance for South Vietnam. Congress put a ceiling of $1 billion on it and actually appropriated only $700 million.
>
> Those are the facts. I think it is up to the American people to pass judgment on who was at fault or where the blame may rest. That is a current judgment.
>
> I think historians in the future will write who was to blame in this tragic situation. But the American people ought to know the facts. And the facts are as I have indicated.
>
> I think it is a great tragedy, what we are seeing in Vietnam today. I think it could have been avoided. But I am not going to point a finger.

What about the fifty-five thousand Americans who were killed, he was asked; did they die in vain? Their lives would not have been wasted, he answered, if the United States had only carried out the commitments it made to South Vietnam when the Paris Accords were signed. "If we had carried out the commitments that were made at the time, the tragic sacrifices that were made by many—those who were killed, those who were wounded—would not have been in vain. But when I see us not carrying through, then it raises a quite different question."[35]

The president used the news conference to announce the steps the United States was taking to help relieve the plight of the hundreds of thousands of refugees in South Vietnam: American naval vessels would help; appeals had been sent to the UN and to North Vietnam; the United States would fly two thousand Vietnamese orphans to Travis Air Force Base and arrange for their adoption by American families; he was going to ask Congress for more humanitarian aid and possibly more military aid as well.[36]

Mr. Ford also used the conference to indicate to all his listeners—foreign and domestic—that the United States had no intention of intervening again in the war in Vietnam.[37] The president said unequivocally that he would abide by the War Powers Act. At the same time, he said, he believed the president had "certain limited authority" to use force to protect American lives during their evacuation from South Vietnam, if that became necessary.[38]

This reasonable assertion of a constitutional and statutory power became increasingly important in the debate over what to do to help South Vietnam. Many in the House and Senate so distrusted the executive branch that they feared the president would treat the provision of funds and permission to spend them for military protection of an evacuation of Americans as a pretext for starting up once again American participation in the war. With the passage of time, this fear seems groundless and even unworthy. At the time it did not seem unwarranted by many patriotic, sensible members of the House and Senate. It is commentary enough, of course, that the mutual lack of confidence should have reached these proportions.

In defense of the congressional skeptics, one should recall that one of the initial pretexts given by President Johnson for the invasion of the Dominican Republic was his constitutional authority and obligation to protect American lives. That intervention quickly evolved into the massive use of American power to hold the two Dominican combatants apart and compel them to negotiate. If it was farfetched to imagine the United States acting in this way in the South Vietnam of April 1975, it was not unprecedented, and was perhaps possible given the extraordinary invasion, bombardments, and blockades undertaken by the Nixon administration from 1970 to 1973. In defense of President Ford, he never permitted action of this kind to occur, whatever contingency plans might have been discussed in secret.[39]

While President Ford seems to have consistently acted as he said he would, a number of officials and observers in Washington already doubted that he and his administration had been very skillful in handling the aid requests. In his article in the *Washington Post* on the San Diego press conference, for example, Michael Getler wrote that "a number of experienced officials" believed the campaign for more aid had been poorly conceived and badly executed. Although they had known early in the fall that more aid would be needed, Getler reported, the administration had intentionally waited until after the November elections and the convening of the new Congress before sending the requests to Capitol Hill. Cambodia and Vietnam were lumped together and, as the situation worsened around Phnom Penh, the administration concentrated its efforts on Cambodia and blamed the Congress for the defeats there and in South Vietnam. When South Vietnam began to fall apart, "the Administration had little good will to exploit on Capitol Hill to try and help the South Vietnamese."[40] Several days earlier, Murrey Marder had commented on the peculiar and self-defeating tactics of the administration: on alternate days the administration appealed to Congress to cooperate in restoring national unity and a bipartisan foreign policy and indicted it for undermining U.S. policy in Indochina, Turkey, Greece, the Middle East, and just about everywhere else.[41]

In addition to its dilatory and fuddled character, the campaign for more Indochina aid lacked the strong public support of the highest officials in the administration. Before his news conference in San Diego the president had made only one televised statement on Indochina, and that had dealt with Cambodia. As mentioned earlier, Secretary Kissinger had spent much of this period out of the country. This had left the effort to obtain aid in the hands of a White House press secretary new to his job, to middle-level officials in the State Department, and to the Pentagon.[42]

A number of senators and representatives reacted angrily to Mr. Ford's indictment of Congress. Representative George Mahon, Chairman of the House Appropriations Committee said "I never did have any special appeals from anybody" in the administration to rush the $700 million through the Congress. "Pentagon officials told me," he added, "they would rather not expend their fire [to get a supplement] but would concentrate on getting a sizable appropriation in 1976." Mahon's counterpart in the Senate, John McClelland (D., Ark.) also said he had received no emergency appeals before the latest North Vietnamese offensive began.[43] On their return from the Easter recess a number of other senators and representatives denied that Congress was to blame for the deterioration in Indochina. Representative G. V. Montgomery (D., Miss.), long a supporter of the war in Vietnam, said the South Vietnamese had only themselves to blame for their present difficulties. In the Senate, Democrats Robert Byrd (W.Va.), John Pastore (R.I.), Jennings Randolph (W.Va.), and Russell Long (La.) criticized the blaming of Congress and stated their opposition and that of their constituents to further military aid for Cambodia and Vietnam.[44]

Something else in Mr. Ford's statements had begun to raise a controversy. In a series of sentences that seemed to link unrelated ideas, Mr. Ford had said that the fifty-five thousand American dead in Vietnam were lives wasted because the Congress now refused to honor the commitments made to South Vietnam in Paris.[45] What commitments was the president talking about? "Sometimes commitments are invented where no commitments exist," Senator Byrd observed, "and then Congress is blamed for not living up to those commitments."[46] An editorial in the *Washington Post* asked about the commitments in much stronger language. President Nixon and Mr. Kissinger had never told the American public they had promised South Vietnam open-ended, continuing military assistance. Above all, neither Congress nor the people had been informed of an American promise to resume bombing and other military action if North Vietnam attacked the South. "What the administration seems to be arguing," the *Post* writers continued,

> is that the possibility of open-ended military aid and the potential reentry of American forces were in fact crucial to enforcement of the Paris accords as they were drawn and that this was our clear understanding with the South Vietnamese at the time. From this comes the judgment that the Congress made the cease-fire unsustainable and the defense of South Vietnam impossible by cutting back aid and passing the 1973 War Powers Act which strictly limited the administration's ability to hold up the threat of more forceful action against the North. And the best that can be said for that judgment is that it could only have some measure of validity if the Nixon Administration had told Congress what kind of "peace" it really had negotiated. Instead, Mr. Nixon was congratulating himself for averting a settlement that "would have ended the war for us but continued it for the 50 million people of Indochina."
>
> Mr. Nixon, in short, did not level with the public then; in the hoariest tradition of the American government's Vietnam performance. . . . And now, in his efforts to transfer the blame for the misfortunes of Cambodia and South Vietnam to the Congress, President Ford is confounding his own hopes for some measure of bipartisan cooperation in foreign policy by falling into the same old game.[47]

On Saturday, April 5, Secretary Kissinger held a news conference at Palm Springs. As he spoke, Communist units had launched their attack on the Mekong Delta. Kissinger said that General Weyand had returned from South Vietnam and that he and Weyand had met with the president and would meet again to discuss the situation in South Vietnam. The president, Kissinger said, had ordered the National Security Council to meet on the following Tuesday or Wednesday to discuss what might be done. Kissinger also used the occasion to answer the criticisms of the way the administration had handled the aid requests and of the way it had reacted to the defeats in Indochina. He emphasized two observations that shifted blame for the defeats in South Vietnam from the executive to the legislative branch. The first was that Congress had reduced aid to Cambodia and South Vietnam and that these reductions had reduced Saigon's military power, undermined the morale of the armed forces, and precipitated the disastrous withdrawal from the Central Highlands.[48] The second was that because the United States had fought for ten years in South Vietnam and had encouraged millions of people to associate themselves with that fight, the United States should not then refuse to give the supplies these people needed and were willing to use to defend themselves.[49]

Kissinger was then asked if the amounts of aid were really at the heart of the matter. Implicitly, the questioner was challenging the soundness of the Paris Accords and of the entire Nixon-Kissinger policy on Vietnam. Kissinger defended the policy by saying, in effect: if Watergate hadn't happened, if there had been enough aid, and if the administration had been free to conduct foreign policy, the United States could have prevented these kinds of defeats for many years. To Dr. Kissinger, one of the lessons of the postwar period was that to gain time was often to gain the chance that things would develop favorably.[50] The United States had no illusions about North Vietnam, Dr. Kissinger said. We knew they would violate the agreement, but we didn't know that "partly through legislative action and partly through our internal divisions," the United States wouldn't be able to conduct a forceful diplomacy and that the North Vietnamese would be in large measure free to violate the accords. If the United States had been able to enforce the Paris Accords aggressively, he insisted, it could have kept North Vietnamese violations under control.[51] "It is not so much a question of what we would have done," Kissinger argued, raising the notion of deterrence. "It is a question of what the other side knew we could not possibly do. . . . We will never know whether [the defeats in South Vietnam] would have happened if enforcement had been carried out more aggressively and aid had been given more substantially."[52]

At the close of the conference Kissinger was again asked what commitments the Nixon administration had given South Vietnam in 1973. Kissinger's standard response was that there were no legally binding commitments, only the moral obligation of a nation to its ally: "something growing out of a ten-year engagement of the United States ended by our withdrawal, not about secret clauses in particular documents."[53] As usual, he added, the American debate in 1973 was over getting American soldiers out of the war, not over giving aid to South

Vietnam. No one questioned the aid in 1973, he said. Then he went farther: "We did not give them any specific figures," he said, "and we did not give them any definite promises, except to indicate that obviously, having signed the Paris Agreement, we would have an interest in its enforcement."

All in all, it was quite a performance. There were appeals for national unity and for ending the finger pointing. There was just a hint that President Nixon, through Watergate, was partly responsible for the weakened morale and unity of the United States. Gone was the simplistic formula that Congress alone has caused the debacle in Southeast Asia. Kissinger even appealed to his listeners to recognize that a great human tragedy was taking place in Vietnam. It was all refreshingly complex. Even so, Kissinger retreated not at all from his belief in the correctness of his and Nixon's handling of Vietnam policy: there were no doubts about the four more years of war, nothing fundamentally wrong with the Paris Accords. Only those unfortunate "internal divisions" and "legislative actions" had sabotaged an otherwise sound approach that would have succeeded for "a number of years." There was not the slightest hint of an admission on Kissinger's part that national disunity and congressional restraint of the executive had resulted largely from the very policy he was defending. Kissinger saved some of his most moving phrases for the moral commitment he saw between the Saigon government and the United States, and dismissed the idea of secret agreements with South Vietnam. Nothing definite had been promised; the United States had merely said it had "an interest" in the enforcement of the Paris Accords. One would have thought the United States had been a bystander all those years rather than a principal combatant and guarantor.

Interestingly, it was Defense Secretary Schlesinger—a man not on good terms with Kissinger—who was the first high official publicly to mute the criticism of Congress. Appearing on the national television news program "Face the Nation" the day after Kissinger spoke to newsmen in Palm Springs, Schlesinger said Congress could not in any way be held responsible for the discipline, leadership, and command of the armed forces of South Vietnam. The reductions of aid had undoubtedly contributed to the defeats, but to ask who was to blame was to put a "simplistic question in a very complex set of events."[54] Schlesinger also repeated several of the standard administration arguments: to fail to give aid, even when South Vietnam seemed lost, would undermine other nations that depended on the United States; and the United States must be seen to be a nation willing to give others the means to survive.

Much more startling was Schlesinger's statement that at the time of the Paris Accords the Nixon administration orally promised to help South Vietnam if the North violated the provision of the agreements permitting one-for-one replacement of equipment. Schlesinger claimed not to know about the oral promises "in detail."[55] As it turned out, the promises were not oral but written, precise, and far-reaching, and one suspects that Schlesinger knew this. Obviously, Schlesinger's statement contradicted Kissinger's of the day before. Attentive observers thus found an unsual situation: the secretary of defense of the United States was contradicting the secretary of state in public on a matter of great importance pertaining to perhaps the most controversial and divisive war in the country's history. Whether or not Schlesinger knew the details of the secret promises is less important than his political intention. He had struck a blow at Kissinger—that much was clear—at a time when Kissinger's diplomacy had run on hard times.

Schlesinger also seemed to be saying that there were secret agreements that wouldn't stay secret for very long if Saigon fell, and he, at least, wouldn't stay silent or try to lie about them, regardless of what Kissinger was trying to do. Nor would he resist turning the knife in the wound. Doesn't this show the risks, a reporter asked, of making secret executive agreements without telling Congress, even though Congress later on will have to provide the funds needed to honor the commitments? Back came the inevitable answer, perhaps a trifle smugly: "[I]n the present climate we must have greater consultation between the executive and legislature on such long-term commitments."[56] Nor was Schlesinger the only official talking about the secret agreements. Senator Henry M. Jackson (D., Wash.), candidate for the presidency and a "hawk" trying to sound like a "dove," also demanded that Secretary Kissinger "make a complete disclosure of commitments that he may have made without notifying the Congress."[57] Kissinger should be brought to Capitol Hill, Jackson suggested, put under oath, and asked, "What commitments?"

The President Addresses Both Houses

As Mr. Ford put his message to Congress in final form, the fighting began to edge perilously close to Saigon itself. On April 8 the North Vietnamese shelled a small town just south of the major base at Bien Hoa. Commandos struck the Thu Duc military academy five miles east of Saigon and cut Highway 14 a dozen miles south of Saigon. Early in the morning the Presidential Palace was bombed. The North Vietnamese promptly claimed the pilot as one of their agents. Other Vietnamese said the attack had been carried out by a befuddled officer who had thought General Ky wanted it done as part of a coup attempt.[58]

General Weyand had recommended that the president ask Congress for at least $500 million in emergency military aid to be used to upgrade the lightly armed regional forces in South Vietnam and to commit them with the remaining regular units to the defense of Saigon.[59] But Mr. Ford had little reason to expect Congress to support any requests for additional aid for Vietnam or Cambodia. During the Easter recess many members of Congress—Republicans and Democrats, senior and junior—had found that their constituents were overwhelmingly against further aid to Indochina, and they said so loudly and publicly when Congress reconvened.[60] Senate Majority Leader Mansfield said there was "a good deal of opposition to military aid to both Cambodia and South Vietnam—that seems to be the consensus."[61] Senate Appropriations Chairman John McClelland doubted his committee would approve even the original $300 million request. In the House, Appropriations Chairman Mahon was unequivocal: "I have said many times the House will not vote any more aid for Vietnam. Nothing has happened to change that estimate."[62]

To make matters worse, the "secret agreements" issue threatened to blow up into a front-page scandal. On the same day that General Weyand's recommendation for additional aid became publicly known, Senator Jackson took the floor in the Senate and charged that the United States had indeed made secret agreements with South Vietnam that called for "fateful American decisions."[63] Senator Jackson added that he would hold hearings, if necessary, in order to compel the administration to reveal the secret promises. When he learned of Jackson's charges, Senator Mansfield told reporters he was surprised to hear the administration might have acted in this way. After each of Kissinger's many negotiations, congressional leaders had always asked him about secret agreements, Mansfield said, and they had never been told any existed.[64]

Elsewhere on Capitol Hill, Assistant Secretary Habib and Major General John Cleland told a closed meeting of the Senate Foreign Relations Committee of the details of the Weyand recommendations and the administration plan to re-equip and reorganize South Vietnam's armed forces. The reaction of the senators could not have encouraged the administration. They doubted the usefulness of the Regional Forces and contradicted the officials' optimism by citing pessimistic government intelligence reports. Senator Humphrey spoke for many: "Everyone goes around with flowers in their ears saying it is going to work out. It isn't going to work out—it is a disaster. . . . I am not ready to give one more dime to people that won't stand up and fight for their existence."[65]

On the eve of the president's address to Congress, a White House spokesman responded to the accusations about secret agreements by asserting that what had been told the South Vietnamese in private was no different from what President Nixon had said at the time in public about U.S. obligations to Saigon. The spokesman quoted various statements by President Nixon that had clearly been intended as threats meant to deter North Vietnamese violations of the Paris Agreements. They were all like the threat he issued on March 15, 1973: "I would only suggest that based on my actions over the past four years, that the North Vietnamese should not lightly disregard such expressions of concern, when they are made with regard to a violation [of the cease-fire and the peace agreement]. That is all I will say about it."[66]

By now, Senator Jackson had concluded that the administration wasn't telling the whole truth, and that far-reaching secret agreements had been concluded with South Vietnam. Jackson renewed his call for Secretary Kissinger to disclose them to the Congress under oath. The *Washington Post* joined in the attack on the administration. In an editorial entitled "Secret Agreements" the *Post* emphatically denied that either Nixon or Kissinger had ever publicly said the United States had promised South Vietnam it would attack North Vietnam, "as a deterrent against violations of the cease-fire by Hanoi." In the editors' opinion such promises were part of the pattern of the American intervention in Vietnam: "At each and every important step along the way, the pledge of the commitment or the involvement was made secretly or without advance consultation, on the assumption that once it was made, Congress would have to honor it."[67]

When President Ford stepped to the podium in the House on the evening of April 10 to deliver his appeal for aid, he knew not only that the presidency had lost substantial powers over foreign policy but that the senators and representatives who sat before him had little inclination to grant the huge sums he was about to ask for Vietnam. Many who sat at the legislators' desks believed the defeats in Indochina had deprived the administration of their policy of military stalemate and negotiation. In its place, they thought, the administration offered not a policy but a posture, a desire to appear before the world as willing to give all necessary aid so long as there remained any South Vietnamese willing to resist North Vietnam. To many senators and representatives this kind of posturing was foolish and inhumane. The war was lost. Voting additional hundreds of millions to continue the fighting would not alter that result or the opinion of other governments about the good judgment and reliability of the United States. They would vote money for the evacuation of the Americans remaining in Vietnam and for the relief of the hardship of the victims of the fighting; they would vote nothing more for the war. In this they apparently had the support of the American people. On the day of the president's address, the results of a survey by the Harris organization were made public. Three-quarters of those asked in March and April opposed giving the $300 million military supplement to South Vietnam, and slightly more than two-thirds (68 percent and 66 percent) opposed the $220 million military supplement for Cambodia. Even if the aid were necessary to avoid a bloodbath in both countries, as the questions was phrased, 57 percent were opposed to additional military assistance and only 29 percent were in favor of it.[68]

Undeterred, Mr. Ford had come to the House to make his case for continued assistance. He spoke of Indochina early in his address on "the state of the world" and devoted almost half his time to the subject. For Cambodia he asked nothing new. He read an appeal for aid from the acting president of Cambodia, recalled the original request for aid he had made three months earlier, and concluded that "as of this evening, it may be soon too late." Two days later he would close the U.S. embassy in Phnom Penh and order American government employees to leave Cambodia.[69] The Khmer Rouge entered Phnom Penh on April 17 and immediately began driving the occupants into the countryside. Only a few would return.

About Vietnam, the president had much to say. First, he repeated the arguments that the peace of 1973 could have endured only if the United States had been able to go to war to "enforce" the agreement and had given South Vietnam the economic and military aid that country needed to sustain itself.[70] Instead, when North Vietnam began systematically to violate the accords, the United States deprived itself "by law of the ability to enforce the agreement, thus giving North Vietnam assurance that it could violate that agreement with impunity."[71] Next, Congress reduced aid to South Vietnam and then appeared unwilling to give any more help at all. Encouraged, North Vietnam intensified its attacks. "Uncertain of further American assistance," South Vietnam tried a strategic withdrawal that failed and turned into a rout.

In response to these tragic developments, the president said, the United States had appealed to Hanoi to cease fire and adhere to the Paris Accords. All the participants in the Paris conference had been asked to help stop the fighting and reinstitute the 1973 terms. The

United States, he said, must choose among four paths: to do nothing more, to go to war to enforce the Paris Accords, to provide the $300 million in military aid that had already been requested, or to increase both military and economic aid to levels that might at best enable South Vietnam to stabilize the military situation and achieve a political settlement of the conflict, and at worst allow an orderly evacuation of Americans and of those South Vietnamese whose lives were endangered by their roles in the fighting.[72]

Mr. Ford chose the last course. Citing General Weyand's report, the president requested $722 million in military supplies. For emergency refugee relief, food, and medicine he asked Congress to provide $250 million. He made two other requests as well. Congress should clarify the restrictions on the use of force to ensure the evacuation of Americans from Vietnam, if that became necessary. Congress also should revise the immigration laws in order to allow the entry of Vietnamese refugees into the United States. Because the situation in Vietnam was critical, the president asked Congress to approve all three requests not later than April 19. With an appeal for Americans to unite and to remain steadfast in their commitments around the world, the president turned to other foreign topics.[73]

Meeting with congressional leaders the day after his foreign policy address, President Ford attempted to close the "secret agreements" controversy by reading to them a statement that had been given to reporters earlier in the day.

> Assurances to the Republic of Vietnam as to both U.S. assistance and U.S. enforcement of the Paris Peace Agreement were stated clearly and publicly by President Nixon.
>
> The publicly stated policy and intention of the United States government to continue to provide adequate economic and military assistance and to react vigorously to major violations of the Paris Agreement reflected confidential exchanges between the Nixon Administration and President Thieu at the time. In substance, the private exchanges do not differ from what was stated publicly.[74]

In this, Mr. Ford was partially successful. His message to Congress and the worsening military situation in Cambodia and Vietnam delayed the conclusion of the "secret agreements" matter, which is discussed in the final chapter. On April 12 the president closed the U.S. embassy in Phnom Penh and evacuated all Americans from Cambodia in an operation called "Eagle Pull." On April 14, as the Congress pondered the assistance package, a new war cabinet was named in South Vietnam.

The president's request for emergency aid for South Vietnam involved eight congressional committees in both Houses. Military aid for South Vietnam went to the House and Senate Armed Services Committees. They had to consider adding $422 million to the unused $300 million they had authorized earlier. The entire $722 million in military aid then would go to both appropriations committees. The requests to clarify evacuation authority and to provide food and refugee relief were referred to the House Foreign Affairs and Senate Foreign Relations Committees, while the entry of Vietnamese refugees lay in the jurisdiction of the House and Senate Judiciary Committees, because of their control over immigration questions.

No Military Aid

During the week that followed Mr. Ford's address, the Senate Armed Services Committee rejected the request for additional military assistance for South Vietnam. A series of identical 8 to 7 votes occurred in that committee, all highly partisan and all narrowly opposed to more aid. Significantly, none of the amounts involved even came close to the requested $722 million. Defeated were proposals to authorize $515 million, $449 million, $401 million, and $370 million. A proposal for $350 million lost 10 to 5 because some of those in favor of more aid thought it too little to make any difference.[75] Voting against more aid were seven Democrats: Stuart Symington (Mo.), Jackson (Wash.), Byrd (Va.), Leahy (Vt.), Culver (Iowa), Hart (Colo.), Nunn (Ga.); and one Republican, Scott (Va.). Voting for the aid were five Republicans: Thurmond (S.C.), Tower (Tex.), Goldwater (Ariz.), Taft (Ohio), Bartlett (Okla.); and two Democrats, Chairman John Stennis (Miss.), and McIntyre (N.H.). After the vote Chairman Stennis said, "The matter of aid is more remote that it was. We disposed of it and that's it insofar as this committee is concerned."[76]

In fact, there was one final effort to supply military aid. On April 21, after hearing testimony from Secretary Kissinger in favor of additional military supplies, the House Appropriations Committee voted 36 to 15 to give $165 million in military aid and $165 million in humanitarian aid. Chairman Mahon had asked for $200 million in military assistance, but the committee reduced the amount and then cleared the bill by voice vote for action by the House. Even though this vote gave the administration an appropriation drawn from existing authorizations, the authorizing House Armed Services Committee again refused to approve the new military funds sought by the president, voting 21 to 17 on April 22 to table Mr. Ford's request.[77]

The requests for humanitarian assistance and permission to use force in evacuating Americans received more favorable treatment. There was general support in Congress for evacuation of the 5,400 Americans and for humanitarian aid, but there was also a widespread concern about the dangers of using American troops in the evacuation. There were two specific worries about the use of force: that using American forces to evacuate loyal South Vietnamese would embroil U.S. combat soldiers everywhere in South Vietnam, resulting in deaths and prisoners all over again; and that a too-broad grant of authority to use force would be misused by the president to try to save what was left of South Vietnam, starting American participation in the war once more.[78] The bills passed by the Senate and House were designed to prevent both of these developments.[79]

In the sections that follow, most attention is given to debate and decision in the House. The actions of the Senate are treated in outline only. This continues the emphasis of the book on the House and is not meant to detract in any way from the roles of the Senate, and especially of the Foreign Relations committee, which, as will be seen, were both imaginative and of great importance in the development of H. R. 6096/S. 1484, the bills that were intended to govern the evacuation of Americans and South Vietnamese from South Vietnam. The general view in the House Foreign Affairs Committee was that H. R. 6096 contained Senate "language" on the constitutional issue of the use of force during the evacuation and House "language" on the funding of the operation.[80]

Vietnam Assistance and Evacuation Authority: H.R. 6096/S. 1484

The Hamilton subcommittee met to discuss the president's emergency proposals concerning Vietnam on Monday afternoon, April 14. They heard first from Assistant Secretary Habib, who acknowledged that "an ominous situation" existed in South Vietnam.[81] According to his brief description, the president asked Congress to do three things: to provide $722 million in military aid to enable the South Vietnamese government to stabilize the military situation; to appropriate $250 million in economic and humanitarian aid for the refugees caused by the current fighting; and to enact legislation allowing the use of American troops "to assist in and carry out humanitarian evacuation from Vietnam, should that become necessary."[82] Habib said he wanted to discuss the economic and humanitarian requests in detail and invited

Arthur Gardiner, assistant administrator for East Asia of the Agency for International Development, to address the subcommittee.

Gardiner, too, spoke briefly and summarized a prepared statement. Even in outline the situation he described in South Vietnam was shocking, while the burdens and responsibilities he projected for the United States were huge. He said that one million people had become refugees because of the latest fighting. The request for $250 million would provide temporary relief for those million people for just six months. To solve the refugee problem would require much larger sums, perhaps $750 million to $1 billion. Only this would allow these million people to resume "tolerable and productive lives," in his words, and would provide work and income for the large numbers of people in urban areas who had become unemployed or destitute after the withdrawal of United States forces.[83]

The opening questions asked by Chairman Hamilton of the executive branch witnesses make the hearing a classic example of a working session in a congressional subcommittee. Proceeding carefully, Hamilton first required Habib to state the political objectives of the administration under the drastically altered circumstances in South Vietnam. It turned out that they were indistinguishable from the old objectives. As the president defined American objectives, Habib said, the United States sought self-determination for the people of South Vietnam. "In terms of an overall international and political objective," he added, "we would hope for, in some way, a return to the basic terms of the Paris Agreement as the framework within which the settlement of the war can be sustained."[84]

Hamilton then quizzed Assistant Aid Administrator Gardiner about the exact amounts of economic aid the administration was seeking ($73 million and the unused authorization) and the waivers of existing ceilings (sections 36 and 38 of the Foreign Assistance Act of 1974) that were necessary.[85] He also established that the $722 million request for military aid belonged in the defense budget and lay outside the jurisdiction of the Foreign Affairs Committee.[86]

Turning to evacuation, Hamilton asked Habib to state which Vietnamese would be evacuated. The assistant secretary answered, in effect, that the president wanted all restrictions removed on the use of American troops during the conduct of any humanitarian evacuation, including one in Indochina, that rescued Vietnam nationals. Since Congress had passed a war powers bill and had repeatedly enacted laws that limited or prevented the use of force in Indochina, the request went far beyond the immediate problems in Vietnam and touched the long-standing constitutional contest between the president and Congress for authority over all of American foreign policy, and especially the use of armed forces. Habib emphasized this point when he stressed that the president had asked for clarification of existing law. It was widely believed, he said, that the president possessed the authority under the Constitution to evacuate Americans whose lives were in danger in a foreign land.

Aware of the traps laid all around this matter, Hamilton promptly asked if the administration sought to alter the War Powers Resolution in any way.[87] Habib said no, that the president wanted the law *revised* to permit the use of force in evacuating Vietnamese. He wanted the Congress *to clarify* the law pertaining to the use of force in the evacuation of Americans in Indochina, even though he was under a constitutional obligation to protect the safety of American citizens.[88] In general terms, he added, the Vietnamese the United States wished to evacuate were those to whom the United States had a "special obligation" and whose lives would be in danger if the Communists took power.

After several representatives had questioned the witnesses, Chairman Hamilton returned to the task of making a clear legislative record: he made certain that the administration had introduced only three bills and put in the record of the hearing the exact texts of the requests for humanitarian and military aid and authority to use force during evacuation; he asked the administration to supply an exact accounting of all aid that had been promised, delivered, or was on the way to Vietnam in the fiscal years 1974 and 1975; he ascertained the best estimate of the number of Vietnamese who were refugees at that time (481,000); he made Gardiner say that the U.S. government was willing to vouch for the ability of South Vietnam to cope with such a huge refugee population; he asked for an estimate of the value of the military equipment lost or abandoned by the South Vietnamese in their retreat ($779.2 million); he asked for an accounting of how the newly requested $722 million in military aid would be spent; and he posed several questions about the nature of the commitments the United States had undertaken toward South Vietnam. Specifically, he asked if the Paris Agreements required the United States to replace equipment lost by South Vietnam one-for-one, and he raised the issue of what had been promised in secret to the South Vietnamese in late 1972 to persuade them to sign the peace agreement.

In reply Habib said that the Paris Agreements allowed one-for-one replacement, but did not require it. Habib answered the second question about secret commitments by reading the White House statement on this matter into the record: what had been said in private had also been said in public. After a final question from Congressman Winn about the activities of the International Red Cross and whether the North Vietnamese would allow the Red Cross to care for the refugees if they conquered South Vietnam—Habib promised to submit a long, written response for record—the subcommittee ended the public session and closed the meeting to discuss the details of the evacuation of Americans and Vietnamese.[89]

While the Hamilton subcommittee listened to Assistant Secretary Habib's testimony and began to acquire the information needed for a decision, the entire Senate Foreign Relations Committee went to the White House for an extraordinary ninety-minute meeting with President Ford and the secretaries of state and defense. On the same day that the senators traveled up Pennsylvania Avenue to the White House, Communist troops fought their way into the outskirts of Phnom Penh.

When they met with the president, the senators could rely on a report by two staff members, Richard Moose and Charles Miessner, who had accompanied General Weyand to Vietnam during the first week in April. Among other things, Moose and Miessner had been told by a CIA officer in Saigon: "The military situation is irreversible. The South Vietnamese will be defeated decisively in the next few weeks unless the United States intervenes."[90] The two passed this information on to the Foreign Relations Committee on their return on April 14, and also warned that Ambassador Martin did not share the view that the military situation in South Vietnam was desperate. Martin did not "perceive or acknowledge" the risks others saw and had declined to hasten planning for an evacuation in order to avoid weakening the resolve of the South Vietnamese government.[91]

According to Moose and Miessner, an appropriate response would be for the Congress to urge a speedy evacuation and waiver of restrictions on immigration. In addition, Congress should postpone debate on the use of force until most Americans had left Saigon in order to avoid provoking the South Vietnamese military. No one, they added, not even the South Vietnamese, believed that additional aid could cause a turnabout in the military situation.[92]

After the meeting with the president, Senators Humphrey and Clark told reporters that final approval would be given to the aid and evacuation request when the committee was certain Ambassador Martin had begun to speed the withdrawal of Americans from South Vietnam. Humphrey and Clark wanted to write the legislation in such a way that the American troops could be used only for evacuation and not for general combat. They also said the bill would authorize the evacuation of some Vietnamese, although far fewer than the 175,000 to 200,000 mentioned by administration officials. Although they mentioned the opposition to the evacuation of several hundred thousand Vietnamese, the senators and many on Capitol Hill had heard and believed rumors that the administration intended to evacuate as many as one million Vietnamese by loading them on boats through Vung Tau under the protection of American troops.[93]

A number of senators, Democrat and Republican, who attended the meeting told reporters afterward that their main purpose was to obtain a promise from Mr. Ford that he would swiftly withdraw the Americans remaining in Vietnam and in this way avoid the risk of embroiling U.S. troops in combat during an evacuation. Once they were certain this was being done, several of the senators said they would be willing to provide the president with the funds needed for humanitarian aid, perhaps in a large contingency fund, as well as authority to use force during an evacuation, provided they were sure the money would be used to bring about a settlement of the conflict. Mr. Ford later said the senators had told him they wanted the immediate evacuation of all Americans but no Vietnamese. He resisted their appeals for several reasons: in his view the United States could not desert the Vietnamese. Moreover, a pull-out of American at this moment could spread panic and chaos in what was left of South Vietnam and jeopardize the lives of the Americans still there. "We need to buy time," he told the senators, "even a few days."[94]

Within forty-eight hours of the meeting at the White House, the Senate Foreign Relations Committee gave tentative approval to emergency legislation providing the president authority to use force if ncessary in evacuating Americans and some Vietnamese, and granting $200 million for him to use as a contingency fund during evacuation. After an all-day closed session, several senators repeated to reporters their belief that the committee would probably give final approval to the bill only when they were certain Ambassador Martin had accelerated the withdrawal of the Americans remaining in South Vietnam, as the president had promised them at the Monday meeting. "Before acting," Senator Church said, for example, "we want to make certain that a plan for the withdrawal of non-essential American citizens from Saigon, including dependents and other civilians, is being effectuated."[95] Senators Humphrey, Church, and Dick Clark (D., Iowa) said the committee would put strict limitations on the use of troops in order to compel their use only in an evacuation and to prevent general combat.

The specific provisions of the Senate committee plan differed substantially from the president's request. The presidential fund of $200 million was not intended for refugee relief but to cover the costs of medicine, transportation, food, and troops involved in a rescue mission. Chairman Sparkman said some of the money could be used to supply arms to the South Vietnamese if they were needed to hold areas whose loss would imperil the lives of Americans. While granting the authority to use force to help with the evacuation, the Senate committee also attempted to limit the Vietnamese evacuees to the wives and children of Americans, to a small number likely to suffer reprisals from the Communists, and to those in the same areas as Americans. These limitations were meant to prevent the extensive military operations that might be needed to reach other Vietnamese in danger of reprisal who might be dispersed throughout the country. All of the changes reflected the fear in the Congress that wide grants of money and authority to use force, and particularly the use of combat forces to evacuate large numbers of Vietnamese would entangle the United States in more warfare in Vietnam.[96] Even so, by moving so quickly and generally in accord with the president's objective, the committee had indicated they accepted the president's assurances that he had no intention of renewing the war.

In the House, the Foreign Affairs Committee was also moving to respond to Mr. Ford's proposals. On April 15 the full committee took testimony on behalf of economic aid for South Vietnam from the head of the Agency for International Development and his deputy for East Asia. The next day, an officer from the Central Intelligence Agency briefed the Hamilton subcommittee on the situation in South Vietnam, and the full committee held a hearing on the legal restrictions governing the use of American troops in the evacuation of Americans and South Vietnamese from Vietnam. Testifying on the legal question were Assistant Secretary Habib; the legal adviser of the Department of State, Monro Leigh; and Congressman Les Aspin.

As this discussion before the committee showed, there was ample reason for the president's request for a clarification and revision of the law concerning the use of American forces in Indochina. A number of laws enacted during the preceding five years appeared to prevent the president from using force anywhere in Indochina, even to evacuate Vietnamese (or Cambodians) from their country, regardless of the moral obligations the United States might owe them. Because of these restrictive laws it was not clear whether or not the president could legally use force to rescue Americans in Indochina.[98]

Over a period of years, Congress had used the power of the purse—the power to authorize and appropriate government funds—to prohibit an increasingly wide variety of military actions in Indochina. First, the limits were applied to American ground combat troops. The Congress forbade their introduction into Laos or Thailand,[99] and then Cambodia.[100] Congress next repealed the Tonkin Gulf Resolution, the legal basis of the original American intervention in Vietnam, although the Nixon administration denied the significance of this move by claiming that the power of the president as commander in chief was sufficient to justify all actions taken to effect the safe withdrawal of American troops from Vietnam.[101] On several occasions, Congress declared it to be the sense of Congress that the United States terminate all military operations in Indochina and withdraw all its forces, subject to the return of all American prisoners of war.[102] In addition, Congress soon held that no more than two hundred members of the Armed Forces of the United States might be present in Cambodia at any one time, and no more than fifteen hundred in Vietnam.[103]

The major limits on military action were imposed in the summer of 1973, after all American troops and prisoners of war had left Vietnam. These were the prohibition of all forms of combat by American forces anywhere in Indochina and the War Powers Resolution. The wording of the prohibition of combat was inclusive and seemed, finally, to close all loopholes: "None of the funds herein appropriated may be obligated or expended to finance directly or indirectly combat activities by United States military forces in or over or from off the shores of North Vietnam, South Vietnam, or Cambodia.[104] Given these restrictions, the administration plainly could not have conducted an armed evacuation of large numbers of South Vietnamese unless Congress changed the law.

The War Powers Resolution appeared to impose even more stringent limits on the use of force in Indochina, not only on the evacuation of Vietnamese from their country, but also on the removal by force of any Americans who might be serving there. The resolution attempted to confine presidential war making to those situations in which Congress had declared war or issued specific statutory authorization for the conduct of hostilities, or when an attack had occurred against the United States, its possessions, or its armed forces.[105] In brief, the law required the president to consult "in every possible instance" with Congress prior to sending U.S. troops into hostilities, and to make a first report within forty-eight hours of such an engagement and thereafter to make periodic reports to Congress. The president was required to terminate the military action unless during the first sixty days of involvement of American forces in hostilities the Congress specifically authorized the continuation of the fighting.[106]

No president has ever admitted that the War Powers Resolution limits his powers, expressly given in the Constitution, as commander in chief. The Nixon administration took the position that the War Powers Resolution, particularly section 2c, "does not constitute a legally binding definition of the President's Constitutional power as Commander-in-Chief."[107]

The view of the Ford administration was that the president's powers as commander in chief were broad indeed and included the constitutional authority to implement security commitments contained in treaties, to carry out the terms of a cease-fire or armistice that terminated hostilities involving the United States, to rescue American citizens abroad, to protect U.S. diplomatic missions abroad, and to suppress civil insurrection.[108] (While promising to follow the letter and spirit of the War Powers Resolution, the Carter administration likewise refused to agree that the law is constitutional and can bind the president when he lawfully acts as commander in chief.)[109]

From these observations, it becomes clear that the president could legally resort to force in Indochina only under the constitutional cover of his power as commander in chief. This could only be construed to cover the forceful evacuation of American citizens, although even this view did not go unchallenged in the Congress. For this reason Mr. Ford asked for both a revision of the law in order to allow the rescue of Vietnamese and a clarification of the law in order to put the use of force on behalf of Americans in Vietnam on the broadest political footing possible. He had sent U.S. combat forces into Cambodia to rescue the Americans there without congressional authorization and in defiance of the standing prohibitions. He was obviously prepared to rely on his powers as commander in chief to bring out the Americans remaining in Vietnam. His request for clarification of the law was an attempt to avoid having to rely solely on his constitutional prerogative in order to act decisively in Vietnam.

While working with the Congress, the Ford administration also attempted to use its dwindling diplomatic assets in South Vietnam and elsewhere. On April 16 Secretary Kissinger told the Senate Appropriations Committee that the president would accept a large contingency fund. The money would not be used primarily for weapons, although it might be necessary for an evacuation to contribute to the formation of a defensive line. Moreover, if some semblance of military stability could be preserved, the North Vietnamese would still have an incentive to negotiate an end to the war rather than to win by all-out assault. The administration then appealed to the USSR for aid in arranging negotiations between the United States and North Vietnam. On April 18, the day after the surrender of Phnom Penh, the president sent a note to Leonid Brezhnev saying that the United States was prepared to discuss a cease-fire and political problems. Above all, the note said, the United States sought to establish "controlled conditions" for the evacuation of Americans and certain Vietnamese. If a cease-fire were arranged, the United States would halt its efforts to provide supplies to South Vietnam. It would expect in return that the North Vietnamese would refrain from attacking Saigon itself and the aircraft engaged in the evacuation.[110]

After delivering the president's note to the Russian ambassador in Washington, Anatoly Dobrynin, Secretary Kissinger told the House Foreign Affairs Committee on April 19 vaguely but emphatically that there were still certain benefits to be gained by North Vietnam from negotiations.[111] The next day a Vietcong spokesman in Saigon appeared to contradict Kissinger's optimism, warning that Saigon would be attacked if negotiations did not begin soon. Then on April 21 South Vietnamese President Nguyen Van Thieu resigned. He left the country four days later. Thieu attacked the United States bitterly and denounced it as "inhuman" for refusing to save his country. He added that President Nixon had agreed with him "on paper" that the United States would give all necessary military and economic support if South Vietnam were again threatened by the Communists.[112] Up to this point only two to four military transports a day had been flying Vietnamese and Americans from Saigon to Clark Air Force Base in the Philippines. Now large numbers of C-141 transports began to arrive, and the evacuation airlift accelerated.[113]

Blaming Congress Again

The desperate situation in South Vietnam, the defeat of any chance for military aid for Vietnam, and the imposition of stringent limits on humanitarian aid and evacuation authority prompted Mr. Ford once again to blame Congress for the defeat of American policy in Vietnam. He did so unequivocally in remarks to the American Society of Newspaper Editors on April 16 and on a national radio and television interview on April 21 with CBS correspondents Walter Cronkite, Eric Sevareid, and Bob Schieffer. To the newspaper editors Mr. Ford said that while China and the Soviet Union had apparently kept their promises to aid North Vietnam, the United States had not maintained its commitment to supply South Vietnam with the military hardware and economic aid it needed to withstand attack by the Communists. "I wish we had," he added. "I think if we had, this present tragic situation in

South Vietnam would not have occurred. If we had done with our ally what we promised, I think this whole tragedy could have been eliminated.[114]

By putting his answer in this way, Mr. Ford raised the question of what had actually been promised to South Vietnam, and the editors promptly asked him what the commitments were and why the correspondence between Presidents Nixon and Thieu on this matter could not be made public. In response, Mr. Ford emphasized the need to keep as privileged communications between heads of state in order to make possible frank exchanges of views. If they knew in advance that their correspondence would be made public, leaders would compromise what they said to one another. About the allegation concerning "secret agreements" the president said he had personally reviewed the Nixon-Thieu correspondence and had concluded that public and private commitments were the same. "The words are virtually identical, with some variation, of course, but the intent, the commitments, are identical with that which was stated as our country's policy and our country's commitment."[115]

It just made him sick, he added toward the end of the session, that "at the last minute of the last quarter" the United States wouldn't make a special, relatively small effort, compared to the $150 billion already spent. If the United States had only been willing to give reasonable sums of military and economic aid to South Vietnam for three more years, South Vietnam would have overcome its economic problems and achieved military security.[116] The reasonable amounts the president had in mind were based on Ambassador Martin's proposal for $2 billion a year for three years, or $6 billion. General Weyand had, of course, said publicly that very substantial military aid would be needed for much longer than three years.

As damning as the accusations were that the president had aimed at Congress, he went much further in a national television and radio interview and heaped all the blame on the legislature. The Congress was to blame for everything from the general failure of U.S. policy to the specific and disastrous South Vietnamese retreat from the Central Highlands. Early in the interview, Eric Sevareid took Mr. Ford back over the questions he had discussed with the newspaper editors. Was President Thieu justified, Sevareid asked, in claiming that the United States had led the South Vietnamese people to their deaths? This time President Ford cast his remarks as a parting shot. These days, he wasn't going out of the way to blame Congress for the tragedy in Vietnam, he said. It was time for a fresh start, a time to pull together, Democrats and Republicans alike. There was enough blame for everybody. The United States had big jobs to do around the world, and treaties to keep. "Now, unless I am pressed, I don't say the Congress did this or did that. I have to be frank if I am asked the categorical question."[117] The three correspondents recognized an invitation when they heard one, of course, and when they pressed Mr. Ford, he let go and blamed everything on the legislature.

It was perfectly natural for President Thieu to react as he did, Mr. Ford said. During 1972 and 1973 the United States promised South Vietnam in public and private that it would enforce the Paris Agreements—by going to war, if necessary—and would keep South Vietnam militarily strong enough to resist any attack by the North. Alas, the Congress in August 1973 "took away from the President the power to move in a military way to enforce the agreements that were signed in Paris."[118] Denied the ability to go to war, or to threaten war, the United States was left with the aid commitment, but Congress refused even to live up to this.

Sevareid pressed Mr. Ford again. Well, he asked, who was more to blame—Congress for giving too little aid, or President Thieu for misusing what was given, and especially for the incredible loss of equipment during the retreat? Without a doubt, Congress is far more to blame, answered Mr. Ford. By failing to give aid in amounts even close to what was asked for this year, Congress "raised doubts" in the minds of South Vietnam's leaders that they would be receiving enough military aid to hold their positions throughout their country. Those doubts surely persuaded President Thieu to order a retreat to narrower lines. "I don't think he would have withdrawn if the support had been there. It wasn't there, so he decided to withdraw."[119] The withdrawal was ill-planned and lapsed into chaos and disaster for the entire country. "But the initial kickoff came for the withdrawal from the failure of our Government to adequately support the military request for help."[120]

How can you say they were short of military supplies, asked correspondent Schieffer, when they left behind such huge amounts of the stuff? That was because the troops were panicky, and of course there's no excuse for poor planning that turns into a rout, answered the president. Patiently, he repeated the elaborate linkages: the troops were panicky because the retreat turned into a rout and a disaster; the South Vietnamese leaders had decided to retreat because Congress had not voted enough military aid. If Congress had just lived up to America's commitments there would have been no decision to retreat; therefore, there would have been no ill-planned withdrawals. If there were no withdrawal there could not have been a rout or a disaster or a failure of American policy. What the president was saying was that there was nothing wrong with South Vietnam or American policy that wasn't caused by Congress or that couldn't have been prevented if Congress had only lived up to the commitments given publicly and privately to South Vietnam during 1972 and 1973.

These remarks by President Ford established the tenor of the public position of the administration during the next two weeks. There was no question who was to blame for the "tragedy" in South Vietnam. Congress had caused it all. Even so, the time had come for Americans to put Vietnam behind them, to look ahead, and to dedicate themselves to solving the problems of the future. These were among the sentiments expressed by Secretary Kissinger in an eloquent address to the same group of newspaper editors the president had spoken to earlier.

Speaking on the day Phnom Penh surrendered, Kissinger chose to call his address "Finding Strength through Adversity." The secretary of state disposed quickly of Indochina. Americans would one day be proud, he suggested, that their president had asked for aid for South Vietnam and had refused to abandon that country, after having encouraged the South Vietnamese to defend their independence and having fought by their side for a decade. Only a very idealistic nation would have persevered in Vietnam for so long at such a heavy material and political price. Then he sought to close the door on the war and all the bitterness and heartache of the past.

> The Vietnam debate has now run its course. The time has come for restraint and compassion. The Administration has made its case. Let us all now abide by the verdict of the Congress—without recrimination or vindictiveness.
>
> Let us therefore look to the future.[121]

Kissinger then set out to explain why there had been setbacks in American foreign policy, why relations were so strained between legislature and executive, what could be done about both the setbacks and the legislative-executive impasse, and what tasks awaited the participation of the United States in their solution. The central concern of the foreign policy of the Nixon administration, Kissinger said, was to adjust the world role of the United States—and the concepts, methods, and commitments defining that role—to the circumstances of a new period in international affairs. Among the most important of those circumstances was the weariness of the American people and Congress with world leadership, a fatigue that had been accelerated by domestic turmoil and the Vietnam War. Other changes that required adjustments in American policy included the decline of bipolarity and the emergence of a prosperous, self-confident Japan and Western Europe; the fragmentation of the Communist world over doctrine and national interest; and the growing strength and willingness of other nations to assume much of the responsibility for their own security and well-being.[122] These developments required the United States to change its role and its policy, to define an effective role, one that while avoiding the extreme of "excessive commitment" did not lurch into "precipitate and dangerous withdrawal" from world commitments and responsibilities.

A great deal had been accomplished toward this end, Kissinger observed, and even more progress was to be expected. There had been setbacks, but these were natural. Much more worrisome was the erosion of mutual confidence between legislature and executive that threatened to end in impasse. Kissinger explained the problems in executive-legislative relations as having both general and specific causes. Part of the explanation lay in the declining ability of all the modern democracies to cope with extremely complex problems that often transcended purely national boundaries. The need to manage bureaucratic bargaining consumed the energy of national leaders. Persuasion, the essence of democracy, often was impossible when the issues were as complex as they had become in the last decade. As a result, the outcome of policy and national effort was ambiguous. Citizens often turned against their governments as incompetent or wasteful or dangerous and at the same time lost the confidence in themselves and their institutions that is the prerequisite for successful action.

These general problems only serve to compound the already difficult relations between legislature and executive. Legislators, frustrated by their inability to influence policy in any important way, reacted by challenging executive authority and blocking or prohibiting actions proposed by national leaders. The technical complexity of contemporary issues defeated legislative oversight even as the issues themselves became ever more important. To these frustrations were added the distrust engendered by the hypothetical and contingent character of diplomacy. Statesmen must act when their assumptions can not be established as valid; they deal in predictions about the future that can be verified only after the developments have occurred while the harm their nations avoid remains unknown and unknowable. The very nature of diplomacy—unless properly understood—conspires to poison executive-legislative relations and sows suspicion and skepticism: "Reasoned arguments are overwhelmed by a series of confrontations on peripheral issues."[123]

No doubt there are elements of Metternich in Kissinger's conceptions, and especially in his personal style, but one finds a striking similarity between Kissinger the statesman and Castlereagh as Kissinger saw him. For example:

> The statesman is therefore like one of the heroes in classical drama who has had a vision of the future but who cannot transmit it directly to his fellow-men and who cannot validate its "truth." Nations learn only by experience; they "know" only when it is too late to act. But statesmen must act *as if* their aspiration were truth. It is for this reason that statesmen often share the fate of prophets, that they are without honor in their own country, that they always have a difficult task legitimizing their programs domestically, and that their greatness is usually apparent only in retrospect when their intuition has become experience. The stateman must therefore be an educator; he must bridge the gap between a people's experience and his vision, between a nation's tradition and its future. In this task, his possibilities are limited. A statesman who too far outruns the experience of his people will fail in achieving a domestic consensus, however wise his policies; witness Castlereagh; a statesman who limits his policy to the experience of his people will doom himself to sterility; witness Metternich.[124]

No one would accuse Kissinger of limiting his policy to the experience of the American people. Rather, his difficulties resembled those of Castlereagh, who failed to achieve a domestic consensus for his conceptions and policies, although Kissinger's end as a world statesman was hardly as gloomy (or fatal) as that of Castlereagh, who committed suicide when his policies were abandoned.

Kissinger then turned to other reasons for the souring of executive-legislative relations and the setbacks to America's policies abroad. A great gap existed, he said, between those whose principal foreign memory was the Vietnam War and those who remembered Munich. Wearied by Vietnam and decades of effort as a world power, many Americans were reverting to earlier attitudes about foreign affairs, attitudes marked by great swings between crusades and isolation, by a failure to grasp the importance of power in international relations, and by a preference for moralism and striking virtuous poses before themselves. Worse, many American opinion leaders had ceased to work to build a national consensus in favor of a leading world role for the United States and had "turned against many of the internationalist premises of the postwar period."[125] The American people would support an active foreign policy, Kissinger said, but only if their leaders would convince them they could be proud of their country's international achievements and that they still had vitally important tasks to accomplish.

Kissinger then attempted to instruct his listeners and, through them, the nation on the proper lessons to be learned from the setbacks and difficulties. The United States, he said, had become more like other nations, less able than it had been in the past to overwhelm problems with resources and energy, more than ever before in need of the virtues of those nations who conduct foreign policy with limited means: alertness, patience, subtlety, flexibility. Because so many other nations depended on or were deeply affected by the actions of the United States, Americans had a special obligation of "steadfastness." Kissinger chose this moment to speak of the "secret agreements" between South Vietnam and the United States. In effect, he confirmed that the promise to go to war had been given and asked that this secret commitment not be made the focus of the national debate in such a trying time. No party had ever sought to implement the agreements, he said, and the resort to war had been prohibited by law for two years. He then added yet another equivocal statement. "It goes without saying that a commitment involving national action must be known to the Congress or it is meaningless."[126] With these words, Kissinger planted a doubt in everyone's mind, as he surely intended to do. The implication was, of course, that the Congress had been told of the promise to go to war and had agreed. Did he mean that? Congressional leaders in both Houses had repeatedly denied any knowledge of the secret promises to go to war again if North Vietnam attacked the South in violation of the Paris Accords. Perhaps he meant only that before the United States honored the promise and attacked the North the administration would have sought the consent of Congress. But the Nixon administration repeatedly ignored Congress when making war plans for Vietnam and Cambodia. Nor would the Ford administration act in a different spirit. By design the administration would ignore the War Powers Act when conducting the evacuations of Americans in Cambodia and Vietnam and the rescue of the Vietnamese whose lives were in danger.

After a slap at the other signatories of the Paris Accords, who had refused even to mention North Vietnam's violation of those agreements, Kissinger again addressed the question of relations between Congress and the executive. As he had throughout his remarks, he both asked for a better future, specified the rather narrow bounds of what the executive branch would do to contribute to improvements, and asked a great deal of everyone else. As he saw it, the executive ought to admit that Congress was now a coequal branch of government. Kissinger was even able to turn a phrase about it: "The decade-long struggle in this country over executive dominance in foreign affairs is over," he intoned. "The recognition that Congress is a co-equal branch of government is the dominant fact of the national politics today."[127]

This was a puzzling statement. One would have thought that the status and powers of Congress depended on the Constitution and nearly two centuries of precedents. Nor was it easy to grasp precisely what concrete actions this new recognition of Congress would lead to. All that Kissinger could suggest was that the executive branch should re-examine policy and explain it to Congress and strive for "mutual respect in the national dialogue."[128] While the changes in executive behavior were to be slight, vague, and, one would have thought, hardly notable or praiseworthy, Kissinger had a catalog of changes he wanted from Congress that were specific, provocative, and, under the guise of mere advice on procedure, were loaded with significance for the goals and methods of American foreign policy. In exchange for better explanations and moderate public statements, for example, Kissinger suggested that Congress ought to stop depriving the executive "of discretion and authority in the conduct of diplomacy while at the same time remaining institutionally incapable of formulating or carrying out a clear national policy of its own." Nor was that all: "The Congress should reconsider the actions which have paralyzed our policies in the eastern Mediterranean, weakened our hand in relations with the USSR, and inhibited our dialogue in this hemisphere."[129] Kissinger then listed the tasks that could not be solved without the leadership of the United States. These ranged from overcoming a world economic and energy crisis to keeping peace in the Middle East and ending the arms race and nuclear proliferation. In his peroration Kissinger pledged that Americans would rediscover faith in themselves, and he ended with a flourish: "We have come of age, and we shall do our duty."[130]

The speech was brilliantly contrived. It glittered and seemed to soar into the clouds. It left the supposedly hard-boiled editors in the audience docile and giggly. Not a tough question was asked the secretary before he left. In retrospect, the speech appears meretricious, a kind of rhetorical fool's gold. There was nothing wrong with American policy, Kissinger suggested. Neither its ends nor its means needed questioning, not in Indochina, or Africa, or anywhere. What had happened was that Americans, wrongly, even perversely, had lost their heads when the going got hard. Worse, Congress was trying to run foreign policy, and that was folly and an institutional absurdity. Let the people get hold of themselves, and let Congress stop its meddling and unite behind the administration. Then the United States could "take up the unprecedented agenda of the modern world." There was nothing in the speech or, quite obviously, in the mind of its author that promised to change the relations between Congress and executive for the remainder of the Ford administration; not the slightest hint that in its objections to the administration's policies on Indochina, or the Soviet Union, or Cyprus, Congress spoke for millions of Americans, much less that in regard to any of these matters Congress might be correct. Kissinger had asked the country to forget the past and had then staunchly defended that same past and promised to act in exactly the same way in the future. The coincidence of the speech with the votes against military aid in the Senate and in favor of humanitarian aid in the House appeared to signal the determination of the Congress to disregard Kissinger's prophecies of doom and his moralizing about a loss of will in Western civilization and to get on with the business of conducting a foreign policy that would be both sensible and widely supported.

5
Last Act

The acid test of a policy . . . is its ability to obtain domestic support.

—Henry Kissinger

As the battle lines in South Vietnam came closer and closer to Saigon, the Ford administration reacted in several ways. Simultaneously it blamed the Congress and appealed to the American people to look beyond the crisis in Vietnam. The administration also chose this moment to establish an interagency task force to handle the evacuation. Ambassador Dean Brown came out of retirement to lead the group. He was told of the negotiations underway through the Russians, but he directed his staff to disregard this hope and lay their plans "as if they were racing the clock and the North Vietnamese army."[1]

Action in the House Foreign Affairs Committee

Ambassador Brown was put in charge of the evacuation on April 17. The same day, Chairman Morgan opened the debate on the administration requests in the full House Foreign Affairs Committee with a proposal that the members consider a single bill written under his direction in place of the two executive bills on Vietnam aid and evacuation (see Appendix 4).[2] Congressman Broomfield, ranking minority member of the committee, supported the proposal. The committee draft, he said, had the approval of senior officials on the White House staff and at the State Department. Moreover, Broomfield said, the bill added "$150 million to the $177 million previously authorized but not appropriated, for a total of $360 million [*sic*] in funds for evacuation and humanitarian aid."[3]

The committee bill, H.R. 6096, combined the purposes of the two administration requests for evacuation authority and humanitarian aid. In simplest terms, the bill accomplished three things: it provided a very large sum for humanitarian assistance in South Vietnam; it gave a substantial amount to pay for the costs of evacuating Americans and

Vietnamese whose lives were in danger; and it allowed the president to use armed force if necessary to assure the success of the evacuation.

Before the committee could accept or reject Chairman Morgan's proposal, Congressman Riegle asked what authority the president needed to stage the evacuation of American nationals from Vietnam. Specifically, he asked if the president needed additional authority to take Americans out with troops. The differing answers from the senior members of the committee highlighted the constitutional and statutory ambiguity in what had become a very complicated political and legal problem. Chairman Morgan answered simply. No, he said, the president needed no additional authority to evacuate Americans, even if this required the use of force. Clement Zablocki, the ranking Democratic member after Morgan (later to be committee chairman) replied that before the president could act Congress had to remove the limits imposed by the various laws prohibiting the expenditure of money for combat anywhere in Indochina. Unless Congress lifted these limits, Zablocki argued, there could be no legal military rescue of anyone, even American nationals. The evacuation of Americans and others from Cambodia was not an apt precedent because there had been no hostilities during that operation. In rebuttal, Lester Wolff asserted his belief that the president had unqualified authority to evacuate Americans from dangerous places or situations abroad. Replying to Wolff and Riegle, Dante Fascell made a subtle case for the committee bill. He conceded that the president had the authority to protect Americans abroad, by force if necessary, but he could not spend any money in Indochina to conduct a military rescue.

Having voiced their different views of the constitutional dimension of the problem, the committee members agreed to consider evacuation and aid in one bill and to take Chairman Morgan's proposal as a working draft. But it was apparent that there was no consensus among them—not even among those willing to grant the president the authority to use force—as to the exact constitutional and legal grounds on which president and Congress would act.[4] This uncertainty recurred throughout the deliberations in committee and on the floor of the House.

As the committee began to consider H.R. 6096, a number of members voiced the two overriding concerns of many in Congress. It was essential, they believed, to prevent the United States from entangling itself once more in the war in Vietnam. It was just as important to protect the prerogatives of Congress in regard to foreign-policy making that they believed had been embodied in the War Powers Resolution. With these concerns in mind, committee members offered four kinds of amendments to Chairman Morgan's proposal: (1) to withhold any authorization for the use of American troops in South Vietnam; (2) to limit the president's authority to conduct an evacuation; (3) to direct all humanitarian assistance through international organizations; and (4) to replace the proposal altogether with a measure whose provisions allowed the president less discretion in spending money and less freedom to try to evacuate South Vietnamese by force.

Opposition to the Use of Force

Congressmen Bingham and Riegle both offered amendments that would have omitted any grant of authority to the president to conduct an evacuation from South Vietnam. The purpose of the proposals was to prevent the use of force in evacuating Vietnamese and to compel the president to rely solely on his constitutional authority to use force to rescue Americans if that became necessary. The amendments also denied the president money to use in buying the cooperation of the remaining units of the South Vietnamese armed forces, or any other group in the country, in order to protect or facilitate the evacuation. With the recent forced departure of President Nixon from office, a barely disguised threat of impeachment accompanied these proposals should the president have strayed far at all from a simple recovery of American citizens (or perhaps even if the rescue were botched).

Bingham's was the first amendment to be considered. The congressman from New York proposed to strike section 2 of the Morgan bill, which authorized $150 million for evacuation and humanitarian aid, waived all legal limits, and left "terms and conditions" up to the president to decide. The Riegle amendment also sought to drop the original section 2, but the young and ambitious congressman wished to replace it. His substitute allowed a larger sum for humanitarian aid only, $200 million instead of $150 million, and directed the president to distribute it through international organizations.[5]

In defense of his amendment Bingham said the Ford administration hadn't asked for any money whatever for evacuation. It had asked for $250 million for vast refugee resettlement projects, which the chairman had no intention of authorizing. The chairman's bill, Bingham continued, would allow the use of $177 million that had been authorized but not appropriated for humanitarian aid (section b). The Department of Defense had funds it could use for a peaceful evacuation, as had been done in Cambodia. Congressman Hamilton supported Bingham's amendment and, in particular, sought to discover a basis for the sums of money. Adding the new money in the bill ($150 million) to the existing authorization ($177 million), and counting the recovery of unexpended aid (perhaps $25 million) gave a huge sum, approximately $350 million. Why was so much money needed? In reply Chairman Morgan confirmed Hamilton's figures. The reason for the large sum was simple: the secretary of state had said that even $200 million in a contingency fund wouldn't be enough. Morgan then hit back at the Bingham amendment. If the money and the authority for air evacuation were deleted, he warned, the members would next attack section 3, concerning the restrictions on spending money for combat in Indochina. If the committee decided to omit the waiver of those restrictions, the president then wouldn't legally be able to use even Defence Department funds for a rescue operation. Then how would he get people out of South Vietnam? Nine Republicans joined ten Democrats to defeat the Bingham amendment 6 to 19.[6] Those voting in favor of the amendment were Bingham, Harrington, Riegle, Collins, Meyner, and Bonker. On most of the votes, these six formed the heart of the opposition to the chairman's bill.

The Riegle substitute allowed only the expenditure of $200 million for humanitarian assistance in South Vietnam and Cambodia, and required the president to disburse the funds through international organizations. In support of his approach, Riegle argued that the president had the authority he needed to accomplish the safe evacuation of Americans from South Vietnam. It would be a mistake to give him a blank check. There was no reason to allow him to use American combat forces again in Vietnam; certainly he shouldn't be authorized to put troops in that country and take out foreign nationals. In essence, the committee bill gave the president the power to put American troops back into Vietnam at whatever level he decided for however long he wished. Then, if something went wrong and major battles erupted with heavy American losses, the president would say that Congress had given exactly this kind of "blank-check" authority in advance.

Congressmen Hays and Buchanan answered Riegle. The UN had the world's biggest bureaucracy, Hays observed tartly, and could be counted on to waste whatever was given them. Very little aid would ever reach South Vietnam. Hays thought that the United States had decided to let Vietnam fall, and there was just no point in quarreling with that now. But the United States ought to get all the Americans out and all the Vietnamese that the Communists would shoot when they took power. Buchanan sought to rebut the idea that H.R. 6096 could in any way become another Gulf of Tonkin Resolution that would plunge the country back into war in Vietnam. The bill specifically prohibited this in section 4, which both confined military action to that necessary to protect the evacuation, and allowed the armed rescue of Vietnamese only if the forces used for that purpose did not exceed the numbers needed to rescue American citizens, their dependents, and those Vietnamese related to Americans. The Riegle amendment lost by voice vote.[7]

Limiting the President's Authority to Use Force

The attempts to set more stringent limits on the evacuation fared better in the committee. Congressman Solarz introduced the first of these measures. Fresh from a meeting with a Vietcong representative in Paris, the young congressman from New York believed the United States should try to negotiate with the revolutionaries before resorting to an armed evacuation. The Solarz amendment to section 2 of the bill allowed the use of American troops for evacuation only after the president certified that it was impossible to reach agreement on an orderly, peaceful evacuation through negotiations with North Vietnam and the Provisional Revolutionary Government (PRG). Solarz told the committee that he had met in Paris a day earlier with a Mr. Ba, an official in the PRG, who had said his organization would make such an agreement. A number of committee members doubted the truthfulness of such a promise and the feasibility of requiring the president to make such a determination. Congressman DuPont tersely gave the two reasons he opposed the change. First, DuPont observed, the Constitution obligated the president to protect American lives, while the Solarz amendment made that obligation dependent on the consent of the Democratic Republic of Vietnam (DRV). Second, DuPont suggested that requiring the president to say it was impossible to negotiate the evacuation of Americans and Vietnamese would have the effect of postponing indefinitely the use of force: the time would perhaps never come when the president would feel justified in saying it was *impossible* to come to an agreement on evacuation with the DRV and PRG. The Solarz amendment lost 7 to 18.[8]

Representative Whalen proposed to qualify the evacuation by making it derive totally from the constitutional authority of the president and his powers as commander in chief of the Armed Forces. To this end, he moved to drop the waiver of all prohibitions on combat in Indochina, contained in section 3, and add a new section saying "nothing in this Act shall be construed to affect any existing authority of the President, in his role as Commander-in-Chief—for evacuating United States citizens from South Vietnam."[9] Whalen justified the deletion of waivers by arguing that in this way no American troops would be introduced to protect non-Americans. The congressional prohibitions of combat in Indochina would remain, and the president would keep his constitutional authority to evacuate Americans from Vietnam, by force if necessary. Adopting this approach would also compel the Ford administration to accelerate the withdrawal of South Vietnamese nationals in order to complete their rescue before hostilities interfered and, by law, their evacuation had to stop. Under his amendment, Whalen insisted, all that became impossible was the introduction of an indeterminate number of troops for an indeterminate period of time to protect the lives of those who are not American citizens.

Clement Zablocki of Wisconsin, the second-ranking Democrat on the committee, took his turn and spoke against Whalen's proposal. In his most telling point, Zablocki said the amendment would not only prevent the evacuation of South Vietnamese whose lives were in danger, but dangerously interfere with the safe evacuation of Americans. Unless the South Vietnamese military were willing to cooperate, it would be extremely difficult and, perhaps, impossible to rescue even the Americans in the country. The only sure way to get the cooperation on the ground needed to make a safe evacuation was to allow the evacuation of the South Vietnamese along with the Americans. Nor was the president given a blank check by the bill. Section 4 restricted force to the minimum necessary and section 5 specifically stated that the War Powers Resolution remained in force. In case of hostilities, the president would have to report to Congress, and Congress would have to give its consent to the actions taken.

Several others spoke after Zablocki: Riegle again stressed the risks of allowing the president to put American soldiers into a war zone; Bingham reluctantly opposed the amendment on the ground that American troops were going into South Vietnam to rescue Americans, whatever the authority for the operation, it made no sense to leave in force laws that appeared to forbid such an operation. The committee obviously found Zablocki's line of argument persuasive and defeated the Whalen amendment 7 to 18.[10]

Like his Republican colleague from Ohio, Congressman Bingham also wished to prevent the use of force in the evacuation of South Vietnamese citizens from their country. The Bingham amendment sought to delete the waiver of the prohibitions of combat in Indochina. In its place Bingham proposed two approaches to the worsening situation in Vietnam: (1) a statement giving the sense of Congress in favor of the early and virtually complete evacuation of all Americans from South Vietnam (even those few essential to the operation of the American embassy in Saigon should prepare to leave and leave if possible) and (2) a grant of authority allowing the president to carry out an armed evacuation if necessary, only of American citizens and those Vietnamese eligible to immigrate to the United States because they are related to American citizens. Bingham's proposal also waived any other legal limits imposed on the use of force in Indochina.[11]

Zablocki immediately objected that this would prevent the evacuation of South Vietnamese. Bingham replied that his approach prevented only their evacuation by force. Wolff moved to strike the waiver of other legal limits, but lost 8 to 18.[12] Those in favor of the Wolff amendment were Wolff, Bingham, Harrington, Riegle, Collins, Solarz, Meyner, and Whalen. Eight members were absent. Solarz then sought unsuccessfully to perfect Bingham's plan by allowing the evacuation of those Vietnamese who could reach American planes and ships; defeated on a show of hands, 11 to 11. Several members then exchanged sharp words. In particular, Don Riegle accused the administration of using the Americans who remained in Vietnam as hostages in order to extort from Congress an open-ended authorization to use force to rescue them. This charge was repeatedly made during debate on the bill on the House floor, and it obviously was widely believed by the opponents of H.R. 6096. Broomfield hotly denied the accusation and registered his disgust at this kind of distrust of the president. On record vote, the Bingham amendment lost 7 to 19.[13]

With the defeat of the Bingham amendment, the opponents of H.R. 6096 lost their final major challenge to the bill. Two additional amendments were offered by Fountain and Solarz, and both passed, although they were of minor importance. Fountain proposed to insert a clause into section 4 that limited the use of the armed forces. His proposal admonished the adminstration to conduct the evacuation without the use of force, if that were possible. It passed by voice vote.[14] Perhaps inadvertently, Solarz took the idea of limits on force to an absurd extreme. His amendment to section 4 allowed the evacuation of Americans and Vietnamese by force, and provided by law that not more than twenty thousand troops could be used and that the troops could conduct an evacuation and nothing else; that the troops could not advance into any areas not controlled by U.S. or South Vietnamese forces; that U.S. naval forces could enter Vietnam's territorial waters only when approaching land controlled by South Vietnamese or American forces; that no fire or attack of any kind could be laid against targets more than fifty miles from areas controlled by U.S. or South Vietnamese units; and that the authority to conduct such an armed evacuation would terminate after thirty days, or an earlier date if set by Congress. In this form the amendment provoked laughter and humorous replies. On the advice of several senior members, Solarz abandoned the impossibly specific limitations. After returning from a quorum call, the committee recognized the concern that had prompted the original wording and passed an addition to section 4 that prohibited "any action or conduct not essential to effectuate and protect the evacuation referred to in this section."[15] Whalen succeeded in freeing some additional funds to pay for the adoption by Americans of South Vietnamese children, and Meyner attempted unsuccessfully to require the distribution of humanitarian aid (section 6) through international or voluntary agencies. DuPont and Biester then offered an amendment limiting the time for an evacuation to fifteen days. The amendment lost 8 to 14. The two then introduced their version of the entire bill—which differed from H.R. 6096 only in splitting the money into two specific amounts for humanitarian aid and evacuation—but their substitute was defeated 7 to 16. In the final vote on the bill, the committee approved H.R. 6096 18 to 7.[16]

Despite the persistent and at times emotional efforts of its opponents, H.R. 6096 passed the committee essentially as it had been written. One admonition had been added about using force only when absolutely necessary, and another warned against going beyond an evacuation in any way. Some additional funds had been found to support the adoption of South Vietnamese children by Americans. That was all. Moreover, the opponents had been beaten by lopsided margins; they never achieved even half the votes of the totally bipartisan coalition in favor of the bill, and repeatedly lost 18 to 7, 17 to 5, and so on. In one sense, Chairman Morgan could be content. The debate in the committee had been vigorous. A variety of points of view and approaches had been aired. And his bill had won handily. It was a good piece of committee work. In another sense, he was worried, for he and the senior staff knew that the committee as a whole stood substantially closer to the administration on this issue than the House did. On the floor of the House H.R. 6096 would again encounter the same kinds of opposition arguments, but there the margin of victory would be much narrower and, conceivably, might not exist. Sentiment in the House as a whole ran strongly against the war and the administration. In addition, the bill was likely to provoke conservatives, who would see it as going too far in limiting the president's powers. If their votes were added to those strongly opposed to the war, who would see the bill as giving the president too much authority and in this way risking war and undercutting the War Powers Resolution, then the bill could run into trouble. At best a close victory lay ahead. Defeat was possible.

For humanitarian assistance the committee authorized a new appropriation of $73 million which, when added to an earlier authorization of $177 million for postwar reconstruction in Indochina, would give the president $250 million for emergency humanitarian aid. This was the full amount Mr. Ford had requested. Both the old and new authorizations would require appropriations. As requested by the executive, the money would be used to move refugees to temporary sites, to care for them, to find work for them, and to settle them in a safe place.[17]

Section 2 of the bill authorized $77 million for the evacuation of Americans and Vietnamese from South Vietnam. Specifically, the money was given to evacuate (a) American citizens, (b) their dependents and the dependents of permanent residents of the United States, (c) Vietnamese related to American citizens, and (d) those foreign nationals whose lives were in "direct and imminent" danger. Still concerned about the risks of falling back into war, the committee limited the size of the armed forces the president could employ to those necessary to rescue only those in categories *a, b,* and *c*.

Because other laws prohibited any use of force in Indochina, the committee explicitly modified five such prohibitions and waived the restraint of all others for this one evacuation.[18] While in this way the committee gave the president the clarification of authority he had requested concerning the use of force to evacuate Vietnamese citizens, they also carefully excluded any possibility that the president might later claim that his authority to use force had been augmented by the bill or by an incident that might occur during the evacuation. The bill itself, for example, defined evacuation as removal to safety "without the use of military force if possible" or only the least use if that became necessary (section 4). Only those armed forces were to be used who were required to evacuate American citizens and their dependents and other relatives; any other actions were specifically forbidden (section 4d).[19] In section 5, the committee said that nothing in the act abrogated any of the provisions of the War Powers Resolution. Finally, section 6 lifted some of the ceilings of the Foreign Assistance Act of 1974 and, by amendment, repealed the ceiling on funds from that act that might be provided for the care of South Vietnamese children adopted by United States citizens.

Plainly, the committee intended to allow the president to conduct a very specific kind of evacuation and, in the meantime, to care for the refugees from the fighting. It had taken care to waive the legal barriers to combat in Indochina; they would not be allowed to impede a quick, limited removal of Americans and South Vietnamese related to Americans or endangered by their association with Americans during the long, bitter war. But no more was to be allowed or attempted. As the committee stated in the section-by-section analysis of the bill: "Section 3 [waiving the legal restrictions on combat] is not a blanket waiver for the use of American forces in Indochina. The use of such forces is carefully limited and circumscribed. . . . The Authority of this section cannot be used to authorize any activities other than those necessary and essential for the evacuation."[20]

Action in the Senate Foreign Relations Committee

The Senate Foreign Relations Committee recommended and the Senate passed a bill, S. 1484, with purposes similar to its House counterpart but containing more stringent limitations on the president's powers to use force. The Senate chose to authorize the president to use force to evacuate Americans as well as South Vietnamese. The executive branch opposed this approach, believing that the president already possessed not merely the legal authority but a constitutional obligation to rescue Americans from danger anywhere in the world. As a result, the executive branch went to conference strongly preferring the House bill.[21]

The bill reported to the Senate by the Foreign Relations Committee on April 18 yielded much less to the discretion of the president than the House version and tied the money far more explicitly to evacuation and relief. Starting with the title—"The Vietnam Contingency Act of 1975"—the Senate established that in their eyes what the president wished to do in South Vietnam was unique, depended entirely on the will of Congress, and would be severely circumscribed by mandatory provisions that limited the use of force and required constant reporting and subordination to Congress. In section 2 the Foreign Relations Committee offered $100 million in new funds for evacuation and relief and waived the key sections of the Foreign Assistance Act of 1974 that would have prevented the granting of new aid.[22] But that money would be spent only by the United Nations and voluntary relief agencies. Obviously the committee sought to remove the United States altogether from Vietnam. The United States was not to be allowed even to direct and control humanitarian relief.[23] In addition to denying the president control of humanitarian relief, the committee required him to report every ninety days to Congress about the use of the $100 million until the money was spent.[24]

While hard on the executive ego, the "strings" on relief were loose compared to the cloying wrapper tied around the use of force during the evacuation. Like the House bill, the Senate began by allowing the use of the armed forces to rescue American citizens (section 3a). Then the differences began: if the president used force to rescue Americans he must comply with section 4a of the War Powers Resolution and report this to the Congress and he must "comply with all the other provisions of that resolution" (section 3b).[25] In addition to the information required by section 4a of the War Powers Resolution the president, in accord with section 4b had to certify to the Congress that American lives were directly and imminently endangered, that every effort had been made to rescue them by peaceful means, and that Americans and their dependents were being evacuated as rapidly as possible (section 3).

In regard to South Vietnamese nationals, the Senate bill narrowed the number of those to be rescued and went further to restrict presidential discretion than the House version had done. The armed forces could be used to evacuate foreign nationals only if, in accord with section 4b of the War Powers Resolution, the president certified in writing to the Congress that every effort had been made by peaceful means to remove the threat to their lives, that their lives were directly and imminently menaced, that no troops additional to those needed to rescue Americans would be required for their rescue, that their rescue would not prolong hostilities, and that their rescue would be attempted only in those areas where American troops were already present to protect the evacuation of Americans.

Returning one final time to the War Powers Resolution, the Senate committee put the use of force under two additional restraints. The bill was meant to provide the specific authorization to use force—in this case to evacuate Americans—required by section 8a(1) of the War Powers Resolution. But it was not to be regarded as either a declaration of war or permission to engage in hostilities. This awkward limitation was made necessary by section 5c of the War Powers Resolution, which allows Congress at any time to direct the president to remove United States forces engaged in hostilities, unless they were fighting with a declaration of war or specific statutory authorization. In other words, the Senate bill allowed the president to use force during the evacuation and preserved for Congress the power, under section 5c, to order the withdrawal of American troops at any time during the operation. As in the House version, the existing limits on the use of force in Southeast Asia were waived (section 6).[26] Plainly, the Foreign Relations Committee wished the Senate to permit the president to use force within very narrow and precise limits to rescue Americans in South Vietnam. In this way, not only would Congress prevent a reengagement of the United States in the Vietnam War, but it would also make future rescue operations dependent on Congress as well as the president. Somewhat unconvincingly, the committee report denied it meant to limit any constitutional powers of the president: "This bill does not attempt to define the nature or scope of any inherent power the President may have under the Constitution to rescue endangered Americans abroad through the use of the Armed Forces."[27] Despite the disclaimer, the committee then proceeded to limit presidential authority. The president may not have a constitutional obligation and authority to rescue Americans abroad, the committee's argument ran, and because the situation in South Vietnam is so grave, the proper course is to enact a statute with specific authorizations to do what is necessary.

There were both practical and political reasons to proceed in this way. The president claimed the constitutional authority to use the armed forces to rescue Americans and any number of foreigners, provided only that the foreign rescue did not significantly enlarge the operation. "That assumed authority might be exercised to unforeseen lengths without the legal and political restraints recommended in this bill," the committee warned. Moreover, the best intentions of policymakers were not proof against the dangers and complications of sending large numbers of American soldiers into a war zone. The report continued:

> Neither the Committee nor the President can foresee all of the pitfalls that could occur in connection with the withdrawal of Americans. Absent the strict guidelines in this bill, the pressures on military forces on the scene and on the President could possibly result in hostile engagement which could lead to some type of reinvolvement in a war which the American people would like to put behind them. . . . [This bill] is not a broad grant of authority but an attempt to spell out the limits to the authority which the President may exercise in the withdrawal of the American community. It is an effort to avoid a situation where events could seize and control American policy options. All too often events have ultimately controlled U.S. policy in Southeast Asia. This bill is designed to prevent that tragedy from happening again.[28]

Despite the disclaimer, the committee majority met serious opposition and saw their bill amended before passage. The committee also recommended that the Senate approve a resolution that gave the sense of the Senate that the president should: request the reopening of peace talks between the Vietnamese combatants, encourage and support those South Vietnamese who favored a political settlement, and tell all Vietnamese that future American aid would depend on the energy and good faith they showed in reaching a cease-fire and political settlement.[29]

Decision in the Senate

Senate deliberations on S. 1484 were marked by the fears of many senators that the rescue operation would by accident or design draw the United States into combat once again in South Vietnam. As a result, the bill had to clear an agonizing delaying action conducted by a number of senators, particularly Dick Clark (D., Iowa) and Joseph Biden (D., Del.).[30] Immediate passage of the bill, Clark argued on April 21, would surrender the ability of Congress to compel the evacuation of Americans from South Vietnam. Moreover, the situation in that country was changing so rapidly that Congress ought to make certain that sending large numbers of troops would not endanger the evacuees and harm chances to arrive at a negotiated settlement of the fighting and an arranged evacuation of South Vietnamese.

In addition to proceeding cautiously, the Senate ought to look closely at the terms of the bill itself, Clark warned. There were disturbing loopholes in it. The $100 million contingency fund for evacuation could be used entirely for military purposes, if the president decided to use it in this way, as Assistant Secretary Habib had confirmed in his testimony before the Foreign Relations Committee. The restrictions on the use of force were also lax. There was no limit on how long American troops might stay in Vietnam and no ceiling on the number of soldiers involved in the rescue operations. The Senate ought to set its conditions and refuse to act until the executive had met them. Above all, the vote should be delayed until all but eight hundred to one thousand Americans had left South Vietnam.[31]

Clark was joined by Alan Cranston (D., Calif.) who suggested that tying the evacuation to the exposure of Americans to danger left a peculiar opening in the bill, one that might be abused by the president. What if Americans were left in South Vietnam indefinitely? Might that not extend U.S. military presence indefinitely? It also appeared to him that a large number of Americans had been left in Vietnam in order to justify the evacuation of large numbers of South Vietnamese.[32] In all, Clark and his allies used their prerogatives cleverly and put off a decision on S. 1484 for three days.

When the Senate finally took up the bill, senators voiced five main concerns. Supporters of S. 1484 sought to protect and implement the prerogatives won in the War Powers Resolution. They shared with the opponents of the bill a desire to prevent the United States from going to war again in South Vietnam and to speed the evacuation of Americans. Opponents of the bill alone wished to evacuate only Americans and to confine U.S. assistance to humanitarian assistance.

Protecting and Implementing the War Powers Act

One of the chief spokesmen for the bill was Jacob Javits. Intervening early in the debate, Senator Javits, an architect of the War Powers Resolution, gave the constitutional and political arguments in favor of the bill. He stressed that S. 1484 marked the first time Congress had exercised the powers it had claimed under the War Powers Act. "For the first time . . ." he observed, "under the War Powers Resolution, it is we who are joining in deciding what is to be done about a war situation."[33] Contrary to what the Ford administration had charged, there was no feeling among America's allies that the United States could not be trusted to keep its commitments because of the failure of U.S. policy in Southeast Asia. He had just returned from a trip to Western Europe, Israel, and Iran, he said. There were no feelings in those countries that the United States was untrustworthy. Rather, these nations now understood that the concurrence of Congress was needed to make valid any commitment given by the executive branch. It was now generally recognized that the War Powers Resolution, and the role of Congress it indicated, had become "a methodology by which the Congress could be joined in the awesome decisions respecting peace or war, rather than to have the President take them unilaterally."[34] Congress had demonstrated its willingness not only to claim the authority but its readiness to take responsibility for the results of its actions. "Congress, knowing the full consequences," he added soberly, "had decided not to give military aid to South Vietnam."[35]

Turning to the specifics of S. 1484, Javits argued that in his opinion the president had some constitutional authority to rescue Americans from a war zone, by force if necessary. But when the rescue required the president to send troops into an area where fighting was under way or was likely, the War Powers Resolution also applied. For that reason S. 1484 specified the conditions in which the president could use force to evacuate Americans from South Vietnam. These were: when their lives were directly threatened; after "every effort" had been made to end the threat to their lives by peaceful means; and when the citizens and their dependents were already being evacuated as rapidly as possible.[36]

The president, Javits continued, lacked any constitutional authority to evacuate foreign nationals through the use of force. He could receive that authority only from S. 1484, and the bill imposed narrow restrictions on the use of armed force to rescue foreigners. These were: that a direct and imminent threat to their lives existed; that every effort had been made to terminate the threat by peaceful means; that only those troops would be used for the evacuation of foreigners that were required for the evacuation of Americans; that the time required not be longer than needed to evacuate all American citizens; and that the American troops would be used only in those areas necessary for the evacuation of citizens.[37]

Javits sought the passage of S. 1484 and of a resolution urging the United States to work for the formation of a coalition government in South Vietnam. "This is the first time in a long number of decades," he concluded, "that the Congress of the United States is beginning to participate in this great issue of peace and war which the President alone for so long has been allowed to decide. . . . we will make mistakes, but what President has not made mistakes? The people have the right to feel that the greatest providence will be exerted by all their representatives, the President, and Congress, in respect of the dread issue of peace and war and the use of the Armed Forces of the United States in any situation which may involve them in hostilities."[38]

Senator Thomas Eagleton (D., Mo.), who voted for the final bill, suggested that a confused legal situation existed in regard to the rescue by force of Americans abroad. Although most constitutional authorities agreed the president could conduct an evacuation by whatever means necessary, an armed rescue was not mentioned in either the assortment of prohibitions of combat in Indochina or the War Powers Resolution. Congress could bring clarity to this confusion by passing S. 1484. At the same time, recalling the Tonkin Gulf Resolution, the Congress should prevent the rescue from turning into war by carefully circumscribing the actions of the commander in chief.[39]

In strong and graceful terms Senator Frank Church (D., Idaho) argued in a similar way in favor of the bill and then went beyond it and forcefully rejected the administration view that the United States in general and the Congress in particular were to blame for the fall of South Vietnam. About the limitations on the use of force, he said:

> Having been burned once by the openended Gulf of Tonkin resolution, Congress must carefully limit any reintroduction of U.S. forces into Vietnam for any purpose other than giving protective cover to the evacuation of American citizens and their dependents. . . . It is a very sorry comment upon this period in our history that such precise

precautions must be written into law. But it is necessary because Congress had learned the hard way not to write blank checks.[40]

In Church's view, S. 1484 restricted the use of force to that needed for a successful evacuation. He supported the bill only because of its limitations on the uses of force, and because he believed the president intended to conduct a limited rescue and nothing more. Nonetheless, the number of South Vietnamese to be evacuated troubled him. The administration had spoken of as many as 175,000. It was a huge number. If their rescue were to be attempted without a negotiated safe passage from Hanoi, the military evacuation would appear to require a huge army, one strong and numerous enough to allow "another Dunkirk."[41] Church was confident the president planned nothing like this, but because Congress had learned the hard way about presidential discretion, it could and should impose narrow limits on the evacuation, like those in S. 1484.

Senator Church then turned to the question of who was responsible for the fall of Vietnam and repudiated the scapegoat tactics of the administration. America's involvement in the Vietnam War had been conducted under a veil of secrecy and lies from beginning to end, he avowed. Even now the administration refused to tell the whole truth to the American people. The executive had asked for $750 million in military aid to "stabilize" South Vietnam. That wasn't possible. The collapse of the Thieu government was not the fault of the American people. Any doubts about this were dispelled by the decision to abandon two-thirds of the country without a fight and surrender huge amounts of equipment. At this moment the North Vietnamese could be firing at their enemies with captured American artillery and ammunition. "The war is finished," Church said.

> The cause is lost. The fault lies not with what we failed to do, but with a policy that was fatally flawed from the beginning. We backed a losing cause in Southeast Asia by embracing leaders who were identified in the eyes of their people more closely with the hated colonialism of the past than with the indigenous struggle for independence. . . . If we fail to learn [the lesson of Vietnam] and, instead, turn upon one another in senseless retribution, then we shall suffer the penalty of Vietnam for years to come and may even live to repeat, in some other Asian land, our awful mistake.[42]

It was thus clear from the opening of the debate on S. 1484 that even the supporters of the bill favored extremely narrow restrictions on the president's freedom to use force in the evacuation of Americans and South Vietnamese from South Vietnam. The debate centered between a bill that imposed these narrow restrictions and either no bill at all or a bill that gave humanitarian aid alone. Opponents sought to show why the limits should be tighter, though after successfully amending the bill many opponents still voted against it. Those in favor of the bill tried to show why the restrictions were adequate and to establish the moral, practical, and political grounds for allowing a circumscribed military rescue.

There were spokesmen for the old policy and the old executive-centered ways of conducting that policy. The colloquy between Senators Hiram Fong (D., Hawaii) and Strom Thurmond (D., S.C.) offers almost the only example of these views.[43] They had long before ceased to persuade, however, and the main concern of the Senate was to prevent the obviously imminent evacuation from turning into another round of the war, and at long last to end American involvement in South Vietnam. Even Senator Barry Goldwater (R., Ariz.) a staunch conservative, chose to criticize not what his fellow senators were doing but their method of doing it. An approach based on the War Powers Resolution was necessarily unconstitutional and unworkable he argued. Before it could properly be used, the War Powers Resolution should be approved by the people as a constitutional amendment.[44]

Preventing a New American Intervention in Vietnam

Supporters of the bill were eager to accept amendments that either helped terminate American involvement or protected against further entanglement in the fighting in South Vietnam, while at the same time allowing Congress to circumscribe a presidential use of force. With these standards in mind, Senators Sparkman, Humphrey, Case, and Javits maneuvered the bill to a successful vote. They readily gave ground and accepted, for example, the amendments by Senator Mark Hatfield (D., Oreg.), requiring food aid for Cambodia to be given through multilateral channels, and the amendment of Edward Brooke (R., Mass.) putting all humanitarian relief in the hands of international or voluntary organizations.[45] Several of Senator Clark's amendments were also accepted for these reasons. They were: first, Clark's proposal to require the president to report daily to the Speaker of the House and the chairman of the Foreign Relations Committee, giving the number of United States citizens and dependents who had left Vietnam, the number remaining, and the number of Vietnamese who had been evacuated by the United States; second, his proposal to increase humanitarian aid from $100 million to $150 million.[46] As a gesture toward the opposition, Senator Humphrey dropped a reference to the

Foreign Aid Act, because a number of senators feared the precedent would broaden the authority of the president to use force or to provide military aid to South Vietnam.[47]

Two amendments submitted by Clark and Cranston were adopted only after they had been altered in important ways, and the alterations illustrate the limits of consensus in the Senate. On April 23, Senator Clark proposed that the Senate require the president within forty-eight hours of passage of the bill to submit to the House and Senate a plan for the withdrawal of Americans and Vietnamese from South Vietnam. The managers of the bill, Case and Sparkman, both attempted to persuade Clark to withdraw the amendment. Case argued that it was unnecessary. The bill already required the president to make daily reports on the progress of the evacuation, and because unforeseen events could arise, it would be better if the exact nature of the plans were not made public. Enough was enough, Case argued, even though he understood fully the "lingering suspicions" of those who had been misled in the past by executive secrecy. Sparkman added his concern that the Senate not take action that invaded the presidential powers inherent in the Constitution. Senator Javits reinforced the opposition to Clark's amendment by adding that in his view this kind of amendment threatened the entire new cooperative relationship in foreign-policy making that had been established following passage of the War Powers Resolution. The Senate had already "locked in" the evacuation by limiting it to that size, duration, and violence needed to remove Americans from South Vietnam. If the amendment were passed, he asked "Will the price paid for the partnership be a breach of the ability to really function?"[48]

Senator Clark answered his critics by saying that the bill gave the president the authority to use force in unlimited numbers and to spend $100 million. The administration obviously intended to evacuate a very large number of South Vietnamese—at least 130,000, for that many had received parole—but there apparently existed no plan for their evacuation. The amendment imposed no limits on the president but simply asked that Congress be advised of the general plans for the evacuation of foreign nationals. The plans could, of course, be communicated in confidence and need not be made public. Senator Humphrey attempted to bridge the gap by saying he saw nothing to oppose in the Clark amendment. Were there in fact any plans for the evacuation of such a large number of Vietnamese? Perhaps the problem was the very short time limit of forty-eight hours. In response, Clark first altered his proposal and dropped the requirement that the president inform Congress "fully and completely" of his evacuation plans. When that did not satisfy the sponsors of the bill, Senator Humphrey proposed that Clark withdraw the proposal and bring it back after it had been altered to meet the good arguments against it, without sacrificing its own merits. Clark agreed, with the understanding that he would introduce the amendment again later in the debate.

When he brought his proposal before the Senate a second time, Senator Clark had dropped not only the requirement for a full and complete report on evacuation planning but asked instead for notice of a "general plan" for evacuation. This change made the amendment acceptable to the managers, and the proposal was accepted. Immediately after the adoption of the Clark amendment, Senator Case made a change in the wording of the bill that allowed the expenditure of the money in the contingency fund not only to help the evacuation from Vietnam but also afterward should people need additional assistance following their departure.[49]

Speeding Evacuation

Senator Cranston proposed that the bill require the evacuation of all Americans until not more than five hundred were left and that the evacuation be carried out in a single operation in case it became necessary to use force. The purpose of the amendment, Cranston said, was quite simple. It was to reduce to a "bare minimum" the number of Americans in South Vietnam to make it as simple as possible to get them out should it be necessary to use force. The State Department and others in the executive branch had said that no more than five hundred Americans were needed in South Vietnam, and yet the administration appeared to have fixed on the number of fifteen-hundred, and was dragging its feet. Javits answered by saying pointedly: "We cannot be armchair generals." It had been left up to the president to decide precisely how many Americans should remain in the country at any given time. Moreover, there were sharp limits on the permissible uses of force, and the prerogatives established for the Congress in the War Powers Resolution had been reserved. At any moment Congress could direct the president to withdraw any armed forces from combat. Cranston then responded that he had no intention of compelling the withdrawal of all Americans, and repeated that he wanted the Senate to reduce the number of Americans in order that they could be rescued easily, if it became necessary to use force.

The answer given by Javits can be taken as a valid interpretation of the attitude prevailing in the Senate at the time as to the proper limits in congressional participation in foreign-policy making, particularly in regard to war and the use of force abroad:

> I am one of the most ardent advocates of congressional power over war and over the use of armed forces. I certainly have shown that in many ways, including the War Powers Resolution. But at the same time I think it would be a disservice to the whole idea if we allowed the pendulum to swing so far that we are going to take over the management of tactical operations. It just cannot be done. Though I know the intent is of good will and faith . . . if we get to that position where we will prescribe the number, not in excess of 500, that is where I argue against him. We did not decide that anyone would be left or 1,500 would be left. All we did was prescribe the policy—and we have done that very well, I think—within which the President must operate.[50]

After describing the rationale for the bill, Senator Javits then proposed that the Cranston amendment could be made to fit with this view of congressional participation in foreign-policy making if the precise number of five hundred were dropped. Cranston promptly accepted the change, and his amendment was adopted. In final form, it required the evacuation to be carried out in a single operation, if feasible, and stipulated that only the minimum number of personnel essential to the work of the embassy should be allowed to stay in Vietnam; all others should be removed as rapidly as possible after the bill became law.[51]

The Evacuation of South Vietnamese

The amendments rejected by the Senate also reveal much about the prevailing view in the Senate in regard to both a forceful evacuation of Americans and South Vietnamese and the proper role of the Congress in ending the Vietnam War and participating in foreign-policy making. Senator Floyd Haskell (D., Colo.), a former Republican who had long opposed the Vietnam War, introduced an amendment to drop all provisions of the bill save those allowing humanitarian assistance.[52] Haskell argued that the president already had the authority he needed to use the armed forces to rescue American citizens in Vietnam. He also wished to strike the authorization allowing the use of force to rescue foreign nationals. "If we want to launch a bloodbath in South Vietnam," he said, "the best way to do so would be to send in United States troops to get out South Vietnamese nationals."[53] Moreover, by limiting the American role at this moment to humanitarian aid, Congress would cause the administration to speed the removal of Americans from Vietnam.

Senator William Scott (R., Va.) then joined the debate to make clear he, too, wished to prevent the use of force to rescue Vietnamese. Scott wished, however, to have Congress authorize any use of forces by the president to rescue even American citizens, and he proposed that Haskell accept an amendment to this effect as a substitute for his own. Because the two amendments are so similar, and the same arguments were used to defeat both, they are examined here together even though they were offered on the floor at different times.

Haskell refused to allow the substitution of Scott's proposal, saying that no new authority was needed to rescue Americans and that the $100 million contingency fund allowed the president to give Saigon military aid, and he particularly opposed this. Senator Biden of Delaware supported the Haskell amendment, although he was the only one to do so. Biden said the president has used force to evacuate Americans from Cambodia, and no one in the administration or the Foreign Relations Committee doubted he possessed this authority under the Constitution. Moreover, the provision connecting the evacuation of Vietnamese to the evacuation of Americans meant that so long as Americans stayed in South Vietnam the administration could continue to use force to evacuate South Vietnamese. Biden then returned to what might be called the "Tonkin Gulf theme." There were still some twenty-five hundred Americans and their dependents in South Vietnam. The United States had also assembled a large military force off the shores of Vietnam. What if the North Vietnamese sent their small boats to attack that naval force? Would the president then hand the Senate another Tonkin Gulf resolution? The initiative in the situation was entirely in the hands of the North Vietnamese. "It seems to me," Biden added,

> [that] all we are doing is increasing the risk that . . . we would be presented with a situation which I would find intolerable, which is that there are Americans being killed, and what do we do? Well, obviously, as ardent an opponent as I have been of our involvement in Southeast Asia, I would be the first to stand up on the floor of the U.S. Senate and say that we must send military force to protect those people, and we would all be in that position, and we would be ramrodded into a situation that nobody intended, not the President, not we Senators, nobody intended, but, nevertheless, we would end up in such a perilous situation.[54]

Far from protecting the lives of American citizens in Vietnam, Biden said, the bill actually endangered their lives. Pass the humanitarian aid, he argued. Let it be given through multilateral channels. Get American citizens out of Vietnam, and let the administration negotiate for the safety of the Vietnamese everyone was worried about.

In his rebuttal, Senator Humphrey stressed the limits imposed on the president by the bill. He reminded the Senate that the numbers of American troops the president could use in the evacuation of Vietnamese and the time they could be employed were both tied by the bill to the numbers and time needed to evacuate American citizens. It was the Haskell amendment that promised to expand the president's powers by declining to impose specific restraints on his use of force in the evacuation. The Department of State had already claimed for the president the authority to evacuate Vietnamese if that could be done as part of the American rescue effort. "This bill," Senator Humphrey insisted, "would restrict the authority they say the President has now."[55] Haskell's amendment drew only ten votes, and was defeated.[56]

Senator William Scott's proposal to strike the provision allowing the use of American forces to evacuate foreign nationals won about as many votes as Haskell's and was defeated 12 to 80.[57] Scott based his amendment on the "Tonkin Gulf lesson." That resolution had been passed, he said, without any realization of what it might lead to. Regardless of the sponsors' disclaimers, the bill before the Senate would return American troops to South Vietnam without a time limit and under an excessively broad grant of authority. His sympathies were with the Vietnamese, he said, but he wished the Senate to put Americans first. The amendment didn't stop the evaucation of anyone, Vietnamese or Americans, but only prevented the use of American troops for any purpose other than the protection of American citizens. "I just do not want to see a reintroduction of American troops into South Vietnam," Scott said.[58] In reply, Senator Javits answered that for the United States to fail to take out the Vietnamese in danger of reprisal would be morally shocking and racist. Moreover, Javits added, if Congress wanted any South Vietnamese evacuated, it had to give the president that authority. Otherwise it could not be done.[59]

Humanitarian Aid Alone

A proposal by Senator Clark to limit the discretion allowed the president in spending money from a contingency fund was also defeated, although the amendment won the support of a third of the Senate. As written, the bill left open the possibility that the $100 million contingency fund could be used for military aid, and Assistant Secretary Habib had confirmed that the administration believed they could use the contingency fund in this way. With his amendment, Clark attempted to prevent the use of any money for any form of military assistance to South Vietnam.[60]

Senator Herman Talmadge, (D., Ga.), a cosponsor of the amendment, spoke eloquently in support of the change. "We cannot continue to deny the obvious," he began. "We cannot continue our attempt to delay the inevitable. Cambodia has fallen. South Vietnam is in a shambles economically, politically, and militarily. . . . Now . . . after ten eventful and traumatic years, the end is near." It was not a time for recrimination, he said: "Vietnam and Cambodia were never ours to lose." Moreover, in aiding South Vietnam, the United States had given lives and money unstintingly and had ended with its own economy in chaos. America had clearly lived up to its obligations. Now, with the end in sight, the United States must not reenter the conflict. Yet this bill allowed exactly this to happen by creating a contingency fund for the president to use for military assistance. What was the situation in South Vietnam, Talmadge asked:

> The President of the country has resigned, presumably to flee. The armies of South Vietnam have collapsed, and in recent weeks the North Vietnamese and their allies have taken billions of dollars worth of military equipment that the United States had furnished South Vietnam. Much of this equipment is still workable. Our planes were abandoned, filled with gasoline, ready to fight. The South Vietnamese did not use them to fight. Instead, they abandoned them. Tanks were ready to fight, but the South Vietnamese did not use them to fight either. They abandoned them. . . .
>
> In my view there is no chance whatever for South Vietnam to win a military victory. If more equipment is sent to South Vietnam, it will almost surely fall into the hands of the Vietcong and the North Vietnamese. For what purpose? To turn and use against us?[61]

It would be futile to spend any money trying to salvage the shattered armies of South Vietnam, Senator Talmadge added, and to disguise military aid as humanitarian assistance would be tragic. There was a pressing need for humanitarian aid, and it should be given openly. Senator Talmadge opposed both using the funds to give military aid to South Vietnam and making payments of any kind to the new government in Saigon, which might well be Communist. In his view, most Americans didn't want "one more cent" to go to the armed forces of South Vietnam. They certainly didn't want to fatten the Swiss bank accounts of South Vietnamese politicians. "Most Americans want—and have the right to expect—an open and straightforward end to our involvement in that part of the world. The time has come," he concluded, "to call a halt."[62]

The effect of the Clark-Talmadge amendment was to force the advocates of the bill to state their exact reasons for creating a contingency fund and allowing the president to use it as he thought would help the evacuation, and including military assistance for what was left of the South Vietnamese armed forces. Two points had already been made in the course of the debate, and Senator Humphrey, taking the lead on behalf of the bill, reemphasized them. The point of the bill, he said, was to leave the president the proper degree of flexibility to plan and execute a military rescue of American citizens, and, at the same time, to impose strict and severe limits on the use of force. Congress should set the direction but not foolishly obstruct the president and make ridiculous their congressional role in foreign-policy making. It was a matter of high policy, common sense, and the unwritten rules essential to the success of a government based on separation of powers. In a revealing exchange with Senator Talmadge, Humphrey stressed all these elements:

> I want to tell you that the President, as Commander in Chief, has got to have some flexibility here when the purpose . . . is not to continue the fighting. We have already made up our mind to get out of South Vietnam. We already have a law that says you cannot have American forces in South Vietnam.[63]

Calmly, Talmadge interrupted to say that S. 1484 allowed the reintroduction of American troops and gave the president $100 million to spend as he pleased. Humphrey granted that the bill opened the door "a crack." But he returned to the common sense and to unwritten comity that must exist between the branches in the American system. "I think we have got to trust somebody. . . . We cannot run the evacuation program from this Congress, let us face it. We are not in charge of running evacuation programs."[64]

Earlier in their exchange Senator Talmadge had forced from his colleague the other reason for giving the president a large discretionary fund. Are you against military aid, Talmadge had asked. Humphrey admitted he was. That's all the amendment does, Talmadge said. It just prohibits military aid. Why are you against it? "Let us just lay it on the line," Humphrey answered. It might happen that in order to rescue some Americans the United States would have to give military aid for a time to one or other South Vietnamese contingents. As an example, he said, consider one hundred Americans surrounded by the Vietcong and out of the reach of the American rescue force. If the U.S. military commanders on the scene could get arms to a South Vietnamese force and the South Vietnamese were able to rescue them, it would be worth it. No one could predict the circumstances.

It was at this time that the critics pointed to the reference in the bill to the Foreign Assistance Act, which allows military aid, as further evidence of the administration's intention to give military assistance and, perhaps, to prolong the fighting in South Vietnam. In response, Senator Humphrey, speaking as manager of the bill, offered to delete the reference. The presiding officer ruled that such a change could be made only with the unanimous consent of those present, and Humphrey's attempt failed when Senator Clark objected out of fear that the actual effect would be to broaden the president's discretionary power. After the defeat of the Clark amendment, Senator Humphrey made good his offer to delete the reference to the Foreign Aid Act by winning approval of an amendment to that effect. Although the effort to block all military aid lost by a two to one margin, it drew thirty-two votes—a third of the Senate—including several conservative and moderate senators in addition to Talmadge.[65] The large number of votes against even the very indirect and self-interested form of military aid allowed by the bill helped establish even more clearly, if any clarification were needed, that the Senate was extremely wary of all measures that in the slightest degree would bring the United States into what were obviously the last days of fighting for control of South Vietnam.

With the passage and defeat of the last amendments, S. 1484 came before the Senate and passed by a vote of 75 to 17.[66] The final arguments for and against the bill rehearsed the arguments already given and repeated during the debate.[67]

After their victory, the sponsors of S. 1484 correctly felt that the Senate had accepted their two main points: Congress would seize the chance to use its new foreign-policy-making powers; and the United States would not rejoin the war in Vietnam. Skirting the constitutional question, Senators Humphrey and Case had argued that the use of force to rescue foreigners required legislative consent. Because the rescue itself might lead to hostilities, Congress was obligated by the War Powers Resolution to set the terms even for the rescue of Americans, despite the admitted obligation of the president under the Constitution to safeguard the lives of American citizens. Boldly—and successfully—the senators had staked the claims of Congress to a major role in the formulation and conduct of foreign policy, and some of the boundaries ran over prize presidential turf. At the same time, the Senate had rejected amendments that would have fastened so much congressional metal on the rescue as to make it cumbersome, ineffective and ridiculous. Of particular importance in this regard was the defeat of Senator Clark's amendment calling for the president to inform Congress of his plan for the withdrawal of all Americans from South Vietnam. The preservation of a contingency fund falls in this category and in the following category as well. If the claim were to be staked, the

Senate had to allow the evacuation by force of South Vietnamese whose lives would be in danger when Saigon fell. The critics had wanted to strike the provisions allowing and setting guidelines for the rescue of South Vietnamese and confine all aid to humanitarian assistance. If this had been done, the entire rescue could have been conducted by the president on the basis of his authority under the Constitution to protect American citizens. There would have been no role in policymaking of any kind for the Congress, no first act under the War Powers Resolution, no check on the president, nothing but Congress passing another foreign aid act. There were important changes made in S. 1484 before it passed the Senate: all humanitarian aid was to go through multilateral or voluntary channels, the funds for humanitarian assistance were increased, and the administration was required to share its information and plans with Congress. Even so, none of the changes altered the claim to a major foreign policy role that had been boldly asserted and tenaciously, cleverly, and successfully defended.

Decision in the House

The critical debate on H.R. 6096 began in the House at noon on April 23 and lasted into the early morning of the next day. In comparison to the bitter and at times even wild encounter in the House, the Senate deliberations on evacuation and aid seem pale, terse, and for all their thoroughness, unimaginative. Acting as a Committee of the Whole, with the regular very strict time limits and procedures suspended, the House members engaged in elaborate parliamentary maneuvers. They stalled, snapped at each other, spoke passionately and sometimes eloquently.

The Edgar Substitute

Hardly had debate begun than an amendment in the form of a complete substitute was introduced by Robert W. Edgar (D., Pa.). Thus began a round of intricate parliamentary maneuvers that would end with Edgar declaring his own substitute to be out of order as a way of defeating a major amendment to it. The original Edgar substitute posed one of the two sides of the debate on H.R. 6096. It authorized no armed evacuation of anyone, American or Vietnamese. It required the evacuation of all Americans and their Vietnamese relations within ten days after the act became law. It also set aside $150 million in humanitarian assistance, stipulated that the money be given only through international and voluntary relief agencies, and directed the president to report every ninety days on the recipients and methods of assistance.[68] Here was dramatic evidence of the desire of many in the House to keep the United States out of another round of war in Vietnam. Simultaneously, the Edgar proposal skirted the constitutional issue, neither circumscribing nor expanding presidential or congressional powers in foreign-policy making.

The Edgar proposal was amended six times. Two amendments were particularly important. The first, offered by Moffett of Connecticut, allowed the use of humanitarian aid money for the peaceful evacuation of South Vietnamese in danger of reprisals because of their past association with the United States. The measure passed narrowly on a division of 43 to 37.[69] Ashbrook of Ohio proposed a second amendment that passed by a huge margin and testified to the continued political vitality of anti-Communist sentiment in the country and the Congress. Ashbrook's proposal forbade passing any of the aid money in any way to North Vietnam or the Vietcong. The assistance would neither aid nor be administered by either of them.[70] A record vote was demanded and the measure passed 340 to 70.[71]

The Eckhardt Substitute

In order to forestall a vote on the Edgar proposal, Bob Eckhardt of Texas introduced a substitute for it that was virtually identical to H.R. 6096.[72] Eckhardt offered his substitute just as the time for debate on the Edgar amendment expired, thus effectively avoiding debate on any amendments to his substitute.*

Members offered numerous amendments to the Eckhardt proposal as well, but all those that threatened to move back toward the Edgar substitute were rejected by large margins or not allowed by the chairman. In this category were the amendments unsuccessfully proposed by Solarz to set a thirty-day time limit on combat; by Abzug to deny any use of the armed forces; by Harkin to prevent the armed rescue of South Vietnamese facing reprisals; and by Ottinger to remove the sweeping nature of permission to use force "notwithstanding any other provision of law."[73] Ashbrook won approval of his measure to deny all

*Technically the Edgar proposal was known as "an amendment in the nature of a substitute." The Eckhardt measure was thus a "substitute amendment for the amendment in the nature of a substitute." Someone wishing to change the Eckhardt proposal had to offer "an amendment to the substitute amendment for the amendment in the nature of a substitute." A clear head and a quick tongue didn't hurt, either. Under the rules of the House, because time on the Edgar substitute had expired, amendments to the Eckhardt substitute for it could be proposed but not debated.

funds to North Vietnam and the Vietcong, and Montgomery gained the acceptance of his colleagues for a proposal asking the president to use diplomacy to obtain an updated list of Americans missing in action and the return of the remains of those known to be dead. After several attempts by conservative House members, John Rousselot (R., Calif.) won approval (345 to 68) for his version of language condemning North Vietnam and the Vietcong for violating the Paris Agreements. The earlier similar amendments by Bauman and Buchanan, which were not allowed by the chairman, had also condemned the USSR and the People's Republic of China for their support of the aggression of Vietnamese Communists.[74] The chairman also refused to allow an inflammatory measure by John Burton of California that sought to make the operation of the act dependent on the findings of an investigation into the attempted export to Switzerland of sixteen tons of gold that apparently belonged to the governments of Cambodia and Vietnam. William Clay of Missouri attempted to introduce a measure to prohibit the administration from sending refugees into any congressional district where the unemployment rate exceeded the national rate, but the chairman ruled against the proposal as unrelated to the purpose of the bill.

After the chairman ruled against the Clay measure, he asked for additional amendments. Hearing none, he ordered a vote, and the Eckhardt substitute—essentially H.R. 6096—passed 272 to 146.[75] Defeated in their hopes of blocking an armed evacuation from South Vietnam, Edgar and the other opponents of the Foreign Affairs Committee's approach resorted to parliamentary niceties to beat H.R. 6096. Edgar raised a point of order against the Eckhardt amendment on the ground—made precise by Abzug—that part of the money to be used in the Edgar proposal came from a previous appropriation and an authorizing committee could not properly dispose of appropriated funds. The chairman agreed and ruled the Edgar proposal out of order, which necessarily voided all amendments, including Eckhardt's.[76]

After six hours of debate a decisive majority had passed what amounted to H.R. 6096, only to have it snatched from them on a parliamentary technicality. Their anger and feelings of frustration were aptly expressed by Foreign Affairs Committee Chairman Morgan as he argued against calling an end to the debate. "The passage of the Eckhardt substitute by a vote of 242 to 146 definitely illustrates this House is ready to vote now. . . . It was not the committee that started the tactics of delay," he said. "It was not the committee that started the abuse of parliamentary procedures on this floor over a period of five or six hours in order to prevent the majority from working its will. . . . Let us go on with this bill, work all night tonight if we have to in order to mark it up. The Senate passed its bill this afternoon. We want to go to conference tomorrow. . . . If we are going to do something to the crisis in South Vietnam we had better do it now."[77] Rejecting a motion that the Committee of the Whole rise and report against the bill, the House finally turned to H.R. 6096.

Return to H.R. 6096

The debate in the House would not end until well past midnight: Chairman Morgan's prediction of an all-night effort almost came true. As the hours passed, the same conservatives won approval of their condemnation of aggression by the Vietnamese Communists, and of the request for an updated list of the missing and the return of the dead, as well as a prohibition of aid of any kind to the North Vietnamese and Vietcong.[78] The prohibition of all aid passed 343 to 71.

Only five other amendments passed.[79] Bingham of New York obtained approval of a provision that specifically stated that H.R. 6096 did not authorize the use of force for war within the meaning of the War Powers Resolution. Collins of Illinois further limited the evacuation of South Vietnamese by obtaining approval for a change in the wording of section 4d to describe exhaustively the kinds of military action U.S. Armed Forces could not employ on their behalf.[80] Holtzman offered a change in wording, and McHugh a classification.[81] That was all. The remainder of the long, exhausting evening passed in a series of defeats for the opponents of H.R. 6096. One after another, the major criticisms of the bill were offered as amendments and were rejected. Whalen tried and failed to remove the waiver of the laws prohibiting combat in Indochina. Riegle tried for a ten-day time limit and lost. Seiberling proposed to limit the evacuation of Vietnamese to those who could be removed by peaceful means, and failed. O'Neill offered without success a full substitute that was, in essence, the same as the Edgar proposal: it didn't provide for the evacuation of Vietnamese, compelled the president to extend aid through international agencies of his choosing, and required reports every ninety days. Eckhardt tried and failed to pass his substitute, with a new section denying that war powers were being granted. Anderson of California and Casey of Texas attempted to control the introduction of Vietnamese into the United States. Anderson wished to require the federal government to pay all costs for five years; Casey, to prevent their arrival in any state without the consent of Congress. The chairman refused to allow either amendment to come to a vote.[82] At last, with the fund of amendments exhausted, the Committee of the Whole rose and the Speaker then resumed the chair. Pike had served as chairman of the Committee of the Whole, and he formally reported H.R. 6096 to the House as amended. The House agreed to the amendments by voice vote and then, on a record vote, passed the bill 230 to 187.[83] The way was now clear for compromise with the Senate in conference, approval of the conference report, and signature by the president. It was early in the morning of April 24.

For a decade nothing had been straightforward about the war, and few who had followed H.R. 6096 through subcommittee and committee hearings and through the tortuous debate that evening expected it would move easily through the last stages of enactment. They were right. There were more surprises ahead. When the final vote occurred, it was clear that all the main points had been made for and against the bill, and that further discussion would change no one's mind. The debate thus served a double function. First, and most obviously, it openly and systematically revealed the support of a majority of the entire House (230 votes of 435) for the approach developed and approved by the Foreign Affairs Committee. Legitimacy was conferred on the bill and regular and visible procedures were followed. Second, and perhaps less obvious but no less important, the debate allowed the strength and conviction of the opposition to be seen. Counting 187 votes, more than 40 percent of the entire House, the opponents of a new use of force in South Vietnam made a showing that neither the highest officials in the administration nor anyone in Vietnam, North or South, could ignore. There was support in the House for a limited evacuation and some humanitarian aid as a last American effort in Vietnam; anything more than that would fail to win the consent of the legislature.

Conference

The view in the House Foreign Affairs Committee after the conference on H.R. 6096 was that the House had its way over funding and that the Senate won agreement for its approach to policy governing the evacuation and the use of force.[84] The conferees would have agreed. After accepting the House name for the bill, they incorporated all the House funding provisions into their final report. As in the House bill, restrictions were lifted on the use of past authorizations ($177 million) for humanitarian aid and evacuation, and an additional $150 million was allowed for both purposes.[85] The conferees, nonetheless, adopted a requirement from the Senate bill that obligated the president to describe in detail every ninety days the amount and manner by which the humanitarian assistance had been distributed.[86]

The provisions authorizing the use of force in an evacuation closely resembled those in the Senate bill. The conferees rejected the House approach, which neither allowed nor denied but merely limited the use of force to that needed to evacuate American nationals. Instead, the conferees accepted the Senate version, which was much more complicated and imposed the strictest kind of limits on the president's freedom to conduct an armed evacuation. In final form, the agreed bill allowed the president to use force to evacuate American citizens only if (1) he submitted a report to Congress in compliance with section 4a of the War Powers Resolution; and (2) certified, in compliance with section 4b of the War Powers Resolution, that a direct threat existed to the lives of Americans in Vietnam, that every effort had been made to terminate the threat by peaceful means, and that all but the most essential officials were being evacuated as rapidly as possible.[87] The evacuation of South Vietnamese and other foreign nationals whose lives were in danger was allowed only if the president certified in writing to Congress in accordance with section 4b of the War Powers Resolution that (1) every effort had been made to terminate the threat by peaceful means; (2) no more American soldiers would be used than were necessary for the evacuation of Americans and their dependents; (3) the rescue of Vietnamese and others would not prolong the evacuation; and (4) the evacuation would occur only in those areas where U.S. forces were already present to protect and evacuate Americans.[88]

The two matters of funding and the use of force were the heart of this piece of legislation. In addition to settling them as already described, the conferees also waived all existing prohibitions of combat in Indochina in order to allow an armed evacuation. Their agreed bill stated that the act granted authority to use force within the meaning of section 8a of the War Powers Resolution but not sections 5b and 5c. This meant that Congress wished to allow the use of force (8a), and at the same time to oblige the president to terminate the operation within sixty days unless Congress authorized longer engagement (5b); and to remove U.S. troops whenever Congress required it by concurrent resolution (5c). The bill also obliged the president to give daily to Congress an exact accounting of the number of Americans who remained in Vietnam, the number of Americans who had been evacuated, and the number of Vietnamese who had been evacuated the previous day with American assistance; and required the president within four days to submit to Congress his general plan for the evacuation of Americans and Vietnamese. The House provision denying aid to North Vietnam and the Vietcong was also accepted, as was the measure giving the sense of Congress in favor of an updated account of Americans missing in action in Southeast Asia and the return of those known dead.[89] The final bill was reported to both houses on April 28, and the Senate passed the conference report without delay. The bill went on the calendar of the House for immediate action on April 29. Final approval and submission to the president seemed assured.

The President Calls Time

As he watched the House and Senate come to agreement on an evacuation plan, President Ford was still deeply concerned that congressional action would spread panic in Saigon before the United States could complete the evacuation of all U.S. personnel and as many South Vietnamese as possible. Determined to prevent this, he called House Speaker Carl Albert to the White House on April 29 and told him that approval of the conference report on that day would shorten the time for evacuation and jeopardize American and South Vietnamese lives. Time is of the essence, the president argued. Postpone consideration of the conference report, he pleaded, and give me more precious hours for the evacuation of Americans and of the South Vietnamese who have been loyal to us.[90] This is the strongest kind of appeal a president can make and it convinced the Speaker, who promptly telephoned from the White House and removed the conference report from the agenda.[91] Meanwhile, President Ford sent nine hundred Marines into Saigon by helicopter to complete the evacuation, which he ordered to end not later than 3:45 A.M., April 30. Saigon fell the same day. When the House met again two days later, the conference report was resoundingly defeated, 162 to 246, by a coalition of liberals who disliked the troop authority and conservatives who feared the aid would fall to the Communists.[92]

Carl Albert was not the first American to conclude that he must honor this kind of appeal from the president, and he will not be the last. But his action deeply upset Chairman Morgan and the others in the House and Senate who formed the majorities in favor of protecting the War Powers Act while providing for an armed evacuation and substantial humanitarian assistance for the evacuees. At the same time it is clear that President Ford's appeal may have had a double motive.

While obstensibly intended to win time for evacuation, the postponement also allowed him to escape having to act on the bill until after the surrender of South Vietnam. It would not have required much political imagination to perceive that sentiment in Congress could turn against the bill once the immediate crisis was past. If that happened, as it did, not only would he have won time for a safe evacuation but Mr. Ford would have spared future presidents, and that included himself, the burden of the precedent of H.R. 6096 which, had it passed, would have fastened congressional shackles even on the president's authority to evacuate Americans whose lives were in danger abroad.[93]

When he pulled the conference report off the agenda in response to Mr. Ford's plea, the Speaker knew his action would allow Mr. Ford and the presidency to escape an additional limitation on his authority and would keenly disappoint Chairman Morgan and the other leaders of the effort to pass H.R. 6096.[94] Speaker Albert's action was consistent with the original House version of H.R. 6096, which contained no specific authorization for an evacuation, unlike the Senate version. The postponement and then defeat of H.R. 6096 had the effect of forcing the president to rely on his constitutional prerogatives to conduct the evacuation. The action against abuse of those prerogatives was and remains impeachment. A ridiculous situation might have arisen if, after the fall of Saigon, the House had passed the conference report and then tried but failed to override a certain veto. H.R. 6096 was the way chosen by the Congress to deal with the crisis caused by the overthrow of the governments of Cambodia and Vietnam. With the cooperation of the Speaker using his legitimate powers to control the agenda of the House, President Ford evacuated the last few hundreds of Americans and Vietnamese from Saigon on his own authority as president. At the same time, it was undeniable that the development of H.R. 6096/S. 1484 by the Congress had decisively reduced the freedom of the president to intervene in the climactic final days of American involvement in the wars of Vietnam and Cambodia. Working through legislation—the only available means of expressing their will—majorities in the House and Senate had tried to stop the president from returning the United States to war. Events dictated that Congress also lost the chance to extend by statute the reach of the War Powers Resolution. The result was to put off a decisive test of the war powers of the executive and legislative branches.

On May 5, President Ford asked Congress for $507 million in aid to assist in the transport and resettlement of the Vietnamese and Cambodian refugees. The matter was referred to the Judiciary Committee in the House. Final action on the request occurred on May 21 when the House and Senate approved the conference report on H.R. 6755, authorizing the aid.[95] With the approval of the aid for the refugees the United States reached the end of its long, bitter involvement in the Vietnam War.

6
The Lessons of Failure

Government and cooperation are in all things the laws of life.

—John Ruskin

Legislative Stalemate

The Ford administration had been of two minds about H.R. 6096/S. 1484 from the start. On the one hand, both houses had granted the money and authority necessary for the president to conduct an armed evacuation of Americans and Vietnamese from South Vietnam. The president had asked for the money and authority to stage a rescue and, presumably, he was glad to have it, even in the highly qualified form in which it emerged from conference. But the administration had also asked for additional military assistance on the assumption that the United States should attempt to sustain the government of South Vietnam in its hour of peril, and that such an effort could be successful. Congress denied this second request early in its deliberation, saying, in effect, that the fate of the South Vietnamese regime depended on the will of its citizens, and not on additional military aid from the United States.

Congress also made clear that *as the two requests were presented* they bore an ominous resemblance to the Gulf of Tonkin Resolution: here again was the president proposing to deal with a crisis in Indochina by asking for huge amounts of money and open-ended authority to use force. President Ford claimed he wanted the authority to use force just in case it became necessary to rescue Americans and those South Vietnamese loyal to the United States who might lose their lives to Communist reprisal. Congress would grant the authority for a rescue operation, but it would allow the use of force only for a last-minute rescue. There would be no broad grant of authority and no large sums for aid. In short, Congress meant to deny the president any plausible negotiating position out of the dual conviction that the war was lost and that a sweeping grant of authority to use force was an invitation to disaster and war.

If this is an accurate view of the intentions of the administration and the congressional majority, it is clear that there are two aspects of the failure of H.R. 6096/S. 1484 that deserve attention. These occur chronologically. In the first phase, the disagreement between legislature and executive is fundamental and unavoidable. According to the statements of the administration, from the opening of the North Vietnamese offensive in the winter of 1974–75 until sometime between the calamitous retreat from the Central Highlands and a few days after the return of the Weyand mission, the administration hoped to sustain an ally—the government of South Vietnam—as it fought desperately for its survival. Shortly after General Weyand returned, President Ford, Secretary Kissinger, and General Scowcroft concluded that barring a miracle the effort to sustain South Vietnam had turned into a rescue operation.[1] As President Ford's national security advisor, General Brent Scowcroft, described it, there was "some lag before the Administration realized that a psychological collapse had occurred [in the South Vietnamese government and armed forces]. . . . At the last stages the point was to rescue as many South Vietnamese as possible."[2]

Once the administration adjusted its view, gave up trying to sustain the Thieu regime, and began to concentrate on a rescue, the aims of the legislative and executive branches in South Vietnam became identical. This occurred nearly three weeks before the fall of Saigon. One can't help asking why, if the two branches were after the same goals, it should have proved so difficult to reach agreement and actually pass a bill well in advance of the collapse in South Vietnam—a bill, moreover, that the administration would have liked far better than it liked either the House or Senate versions of H.R. 6096.

To find out why this was impossible, the author asked both General Scowcroft and Peter Rodman, a close associate of Secretary Kissinger, the following question: "After General Weyand returned from South Vietnam and everyone realized the war was lost, did the administration tell the Congress publicly or privately that they were preparing a rescue and not a Gulf of Tonkin resolution?" Both men answered that Congress was not told. If the matter had been addressed publicly, General Scowcroft said, the administration would have lost the confidence of the South Vietnamese. If the relevant committees or significant numbers of senators and representatives had been told in private, there would have been leaks to the press, and the rescue would have been compromised just as surely as if the announcement had been made in public. "We couldn't say it was a rescue for fear of leaks," Peter Rodman said. "That's the problem you have whenever you talk to Congress. That's the dilemma."[3] There is a self-serving aspect to this kind of answer: the executive constantly "leaks" information and truly opposes only those leaks it does not originate; or, as members of the executive branch would put it, congressional leaks harm the interests of the United States. Leaving this aside, the point is one that must be taken seriously, for there surely would have been leaks if such a message had been passed to Congress, and the leaks could well have hastened the collapse of all organized resistance in South Vietnam; this in turn would have cut the number of Vietnamese who ultimately escaped and might perhaps have trapped many Americans as well, or at least have made their rescue much more costly and difficult.

A first cause of the failure of H.R. 6096 would thus appear to be the logic of the relationship within the American government and between the Ford administration and both sides in Vietnam. As the interviews with General Scowcroft and Peter Rodman established, by the time President Ford asked for the $700 million in additional military assistance for South Vietnam and Secretary Kissinger testified on Capitol Hill in favor of the aid, the administration had already concluded that all was lost. The charade was necessary, according to the administration, in order to foster an environment in South Vietnam in which a rescue operation could succeed.[4]

A second cause for the failure of H.R. 6096 would appear to be the bill itself and the restrictions the Congress felt compelled to impose on the president's authority to use force to rescue the Americans and Vietnamese in South Vietnam. The reasons behind the administration's opposition to H.R. 6096 were clearly presented in the executive branch position paper on the conference. On every important issue the administration favored the House position.[5]

The administration's opposition to H.R. 6096/S. 1484 began with the full title of that bill, which included the words: "to authorize the President to use the Armed Forces of the United States to protect citizens of the United States." The Senate title raised a constitutional red herring, the administration insisted, because the president already possessed the authority to use force to rescue Americans. The title of the House bill clearly avoided the constitutional issue—"A bill to authorize funds for humanitarian assistance and evacuation"—and was preferred.[6] In regard to funding authorizations, the administration preferred the larger amounts given in the House bill and disliked the restrictions in the Senate version concerning how humanitarian assistance could be distributed.

While the House prevailed on both these questions, to the satisfaction of the executive, the Senate had its way in regard to the use of the armed forces and the relevance of the War Powers Resolution. Here, the administration's dislike of the bill was fundamental. The Senate version gave permission for the president to use the armed forces to rescue Americans under certain conditions and required this to be accomplished in a single operation, if possible. Strong, if unavailing, objection came from the executive. It was bad enough, the position paper argued, that the Senate bill called into question the president's authority to use the armed forces in situations where there were no hostilities. What was much worse, the bill "raises questions as to whether it is intended to interfere with the president's constitutional authority and duty to protect American citizens."[7] Moreover, the Senate bill added to the requirements of section 4 of the War Powers Resolution. Before the president could use force to rescue the Americans in South Vietnam he would have to certify that their lives were in danger, and that he had tried and failed to safeguard them by peaceful means, and that they were already being evacuated as rapidly as possible. The executive branch opposed this kind of reporting for two reasons. First, it implied without good reason that the president might send in the armed forces when it wasn't really necessary, and would not try for a peaceful evacuation. In addition, the administration opposed the inclusion of reporting requirements beyond those already in the War Powers Resolution.

The House approach to the evacuation of South Vietnamese also won the support of the executive branch. The Senate version, which prevailed, limited very narrowly the manner in which the rescue of foreign nationals could be accomplished. As with the rescue of Americans, the president was required to certify that the foreign lives were threatened, and that he had tried and failed to remove the threat by peaceful means. Force could then be used, but with no more soldiers for no longer a period in no larger an area than was already required for the rescue of Americans. Tartly, the position paper stated in rebuttal: "If the precise time necessary to evacuate Americans only could not be exceeded at all there could be no significant evacuation of Vietnamese nationals. The Americans would all be evacuated first and the evacuation effort would have to be ended."[8] What was more, by making the evacuation of South Vietnamese virtually impossible, the Senate bill ignored the moral obligation of the United States to those Vietnamese loyal to the United States, an obligation which existed whether one believed the original involvement in the war was right or wrong.

As the position paper made clear, the administration had little reason to cherish H.R. 6096 as it emerged from conference. In the last hours before Saigon fell, the president, acting on Constitutional authority alone, rescued the Americans with what amounted to a show of force, certainly without having to engage in combat. Meanwhile, tens of thousands of South Vietnamese escaped by sea to the Seventh Fleet. Then Saigon changed hands, and it was over.

A combination of distrust and a bill unacceptable to the executive caused the defeat of H.R. 6096. The administration, taken at its best, feared to take Congress into its confidence, even after it had concluded the war was lost, because publicity would have destroyed its hopes first to preserve the South Vietnamese government and then to conduct a safe, effective evacuation. Never invited to share the confidence of the administration, Congress suspected the worst, denied military aid, and circumscribed even the rescue of American citizens. The two branches of the government never joined in productive accomplishment. Fearing and distrusting one another to the end, they made one last show of the disunity in American society and government that grew out of the Vietnam War.

Of the two it is easier to understand the reaction of Congress than to comprehend the strident criticisms of the legislature by President Ford and Secretary Kissinger. Again and again, the highest officials in the administration poisoned the well of legislative-executive relations. Scolding and condemning Congress as cowardly, immoral, even decadent, they then marched back up the Hill to ask for more money, more authority to use force, more cooperation.

It seems clear in retrospect that the stridency of the criticisms surpassed the immediate cause—the denial of emergency military aid when the administration already knew the war was lost. Instead, Secretary Kissinger was giving voice to the frustrations born of the collapse of his entire Vietnam policy. He had been nurturing them since at least the summer of 1973 when Congress prohibited combat in Indochina. Now, at last, his frustrations could come out, and he dressed them in cataclysm and the decline of the West. Why President Ford should have been so willing to echo the charges is less clear. Perhaps he saw some advantage in his struggle to defeat S. 1484 and to preserve the constitutional authority of the presidency as he saw it. It was, after all, a Democratic Congress, and he could rally his supporters by running against a legislative branch in the hands of the other party.

In a sense, Secretary Kissinger was correct. The reductions in aid had hurt the South Vietnamese government militarily and psychologically. But to suggest that this was the sole, or even the primary, cause of the failure of the Nixon-Kissinger Vietnam policy was to ignore the faults of the South Vietnamese regime, something even their own officials refused to do, and to ignore the fragility of the structure Nixon and Kissinger had created to maintain the peace in Vietnam. That structure depended on deterrence. Both Vietnams had been made to believe that the North would suffer overwhelming and unacceptable punishment if they started the war again. Ironically, Nixon and Kissinger could achieve more with the Communists of Vietnam, China, and the USSR than they would with their own countrymen.

The fragility and eventual collapse of deterrence in Vietnam stem from the inability of Nixon and Kissinger to persuade the Congress and the American people to support it. Ultimately, peace in Vietnam depended on the ability of the United States to go to war there once more. When they concluded the Paris Agreements, Nixon and Kissinger knew the Congress and people of the United States would not return to war in Vietnam. Otherwise they would have asked the Senate to give its consent to a treaty of alliance with South Vietnam. Instead, they made the commitment to go to war in a series of secret letters kept hidden from the Congress and the people. In the failure of that policy one sees the limits of the politics of acquiescence. It will not serve to protest, as Secretary Kissinger protested, that had Congress only granted adequate aid and not deprived the president of the power to "enforce" the treaty, he could have preserved South Vietnam. The point is that the promises to President Thieu, and in them the entire Vietnam policy of the Nixon administration, were based on a fiction: the appearance but not the reality of national power. The essence of the politics of acquiescence is for the executive to be limited only by what the Congress and people will reject forcefully and effectively. Neither Congress nor the people can reject what they don't know about. Secrecy can thus give an astonishing, almost magical, extension to the limits of policy. But it is alchemy: the base metal is always there after the fireworks subside. Long before taking office, Kissinger wrote: "The acid test of a policy . . . is its ability to obtain domestic support."[9] That thought serves as the epitaph for the Vietnam policy of the Nixon administration, a policy that ended in ruins on April 29, 1975.

The enduring lesson for democratic societies, however, is more profound. To confuse acquiescence with consent is to court failure, and perhaps much worse. There is no substitute for the painstaking education of a government and a people so that their newfound knowledge and understanding will enable them to discern what is irrelevant in their past and what must be done in the future. When this task of education is well performed, democratic leaders who base policy on what the people will support find they have all the authority and freedom of action they require. Then acquiescence becomes consent, and the hands of democratic leaders are strengthened by the unity of their nations.

The "Secret Agreements" Controversy

On April 30, the day after the surrender of Saigon, the former South Vietnamese minister of planning, Nguyen Jien Hung, gave to the newspapers two letters and portions of two others from President Nixon to South Vietnamese President Nguyen Van Thieu. The letters were published on May 1, 1975[10] A spokesman for the Ford administration said the documents appeared to be authentic, but the president wrote Senator Sparkman and said he would not release the originals on the ground that public and private statements were consistent: "There was no secret from the Congress or the American people," Mr. Ford told the chairman of the Senate Foreign Relations Committee.[11] The White House also sought to prove this by releasing copies of statements by various administration officials, for example, Secretary Kissinger (the U.S. "had the right" to use force); former Secretary of Defense Elliot Richardson (the use of force couldn't be ruled out); and State Department official William Sullivan (there are "no inhibitions" on the United States if the cease-fire is breached).[12] The letters from Nixon to Thieu, however, show that no American official had ever said in public anything even close to what had actually been promised President Thieu in writing at least twice by President Nixon.

Both letters were written to persuade Presidient Thieu to accept the Paris Agreements. In particular, President Nixon promised help in relieving Thieu's fears, principally over the continued presence of North Vietnamese forces in South Vietnam. This was to be done by improving the terms of the negotiated documents and, above all, by the joint action of the United States and South Vietnam. Specifically, in the letter dated November 14, 1972, President Nixon made this far-reaching promise: "You have my absolute assurance," he wrote, "that if Hanoi fails to abide by the terms of the agreement it is my intention to take swift and severe retaliatory action." The bitter with the sweet: if South Vietnam refused to sign the accords, the United States would continue along the path it had begun at Paris. Quickly, Nixon added another soothing word: "I repeat my personal assurances to you that the United States will react very strongly and rapidly to any violation of the agreement."

A sample of what this reaction might be came in December, when for twelve days the administration sent B-52s to bomb selected targets in the Hanoi-Haiphong area. The administration was punishing Hanoi for refusing to allow progress in the peace negotiation in Paris. Nixon, Kissinger, and Haig argued that Hanoi had made a strategic decision "to prolong the war, abort all negotiations, and at the last moment seek unconditional victory."[13] According to Kissinger, North Vietnamese stalling forced the United States to choose between two options: to take a "massive, shocking step" designed to end the war, or to see the fighting continue, the negotiations languish, and the divisions in the United States intensify without end.[14] The bombs falling in Hanoi were noticed in Saigon, as the administration intended them to be.[15] On December 22 the United States proposed to reconvene talks between Kissinger and Le Duc Tho and to conclude the negotiations in three days. On December 26, eager to stop the bombing, Hanoi accepted the American terms for the renewal of negotiations. It remained to bring the South Vietnamese to agree. A letter from Nixon to Thieu dated January 5, 1973, replayed the earlier letter and, as is obvious from references in it, at least one other letter that had unsuccessfully urged Thieu to accept the peace agreement. Nixon was blunter about going ahead. Without further concern for the Demilitarized Zone and "supervisory machinery," Nixon said, " we will proceed to conclude the agreement." He urged Thieu to sign. To split with the United States was to invite disaster. He then repeated the assurance about American retaliation: "You have my assurance of continued assistance in the post-settlement period and that we will respond with full force should the settlement be violated by North Vietnam."[16] President Thieu neither accepted nor rejected the agreements and the American promises of assistance until Nixon, having agreed with North Vietnam, threatened to conclude peace with the Communists over the head of the Saigon government. An ultimatum went to Thieu from Nixon on January 16 announcing his intention to sign the peace agreements on January 27—alone, if necessary.[17] Thieu quibbled. Nixon demanded a reply by January 20, and on that day Thieu at last relented. He gave final consent the next day.[18]

When the copies of the letters were published two years later, Senator Jackson took up the issue he had already raised. Because these commitments had been kept secret, Senator Jackson said, the Nixon administration had misled both the Congress and South Vietnam. There was, Jackson added, a "fateful difference" between saying in public that the United States retained the option to use force and committing the government in secret to attack North Vietnam if it violated the peace. Admiral Elmo Zumwalt, former chief of naval operations and a member of the Joint Chiefs of Staff from 1970 to 1974, confirmed that the promises had been made to the South Vietnamese. It was Thieu's price, he added, for accepting a "very unfavorable truce"—one that left the enemy in place in South Vietnam.[19]

Elsewhere on Capitol Hill, the Senate Foreign Relations Committee was reported to be considering an inquiry into the promises, and Senator Sparkman repeatedly asked Mr. Ford for the text of all private commitments to South Vietnam. The fall of South Vietnam made confidentiality a poor justification, the senator argued.[20] Eventually, hearings were held by Senator James Abourezk (D., S.Dak.) before his Subcommittee on Separation of Powers of the Senate Committee on the Judiciary. On May 2, Senator Abourezk wrote to President Ford and requested the letters sent by President Nixon to President Thieu. President Ford replied on May 27, refusing to release the Nixon-Thieu correspondence. In his reply, the president said flatly: "Neither this administration nor its predecessor has ever regarded or cited these documents as constituting a contractual agreement binding upon the U.S. Government."[21]

Mr. Ford was, of course, playing with semantics. Whether or not the letters created a binding "contractual agreement," President Nixon and Secretary Kissinger obviously meant to abide by them. They had invaded Cambodia and Laos, mined and blockaded the ports of North Vietnam, and sent American troops deep inside North Vietnam itself in a futile attempt to rescue American prisoners of war. Everything about the international behavior of the Nixon administration supports the contention that they would have used force—perhaps a reinstitution of the blockade of the North—to preserve the regime in the South in the event of an escalation of the fighting. Moreover, unless the Nixon administration had intended to use force against North Vietnam, there is no merit to one of secretary Kissinger's principal reasons for blaming Congress for the fall of Vietnam. Repeatedly, Secretary Kissinger said that Congress had contributed to the downfall of Saigon by prohibiting combat in Indochina and denying the administration the ability to enforce the Paris Peace Agreements. This criticism makes no sense unless the Nixon administration intended to honor the promises to President Thieu and use force to compel the North Vietnamese to leave the South alone.

Additional support for this view came in Admiral Elmo Zumwalt's testimony to Senator Abourezk's subcommittee. In 1973, Zumwalt was chief of naval operations. He had not been aware of a written agreement, Zumwalt testifield under oath, until he read the letters in the press. However, it was clear, he said, that verbal commitments had been given to President Thieu promising "a vigorous response with force in the event of major truce violations by the North."[22] He had been told of the verbal commitments on at least two occasions: at a meeting in the president's Oval Office in the White House on November 30, 1972, attended by President Nixon, the secretary of state, the secretary of defense, all of the Joint Chiefs of Staff, and the president's assistant, General Haig; and at a routine briefing by the chairman of the Joint Chiefs for the chiefs or their deputies at the Pentagon in December 1972.[23] In Zumwalt's view, the August 1973 act of Congress that prohibited the entry of American troops into combat in Indochina had caused the fall of South Vietnam. Accordingly, he had been mystified when the administration had decided to obey the prohibition, "because it did seem to me it would be quite contrary to the commitments [to Thieu] that I thought had been made."[24]

Although a number of officials in the Nixon administration often threatened to punish North Vietnam if it violated the Paris Agreements, there is little question that they kept secret the commitments to use force that were given to President Thieu. In fact, they went out of their way to deny that any kind of secret commitments existed that obliged the United States to come to the aid of South Vietnam. For example, Kissinger, then national security adviser, noted on January 24, 1973, "There are no secret understandings. . . . The formal obligations of the parties have all been revealed, and there are no secret formal obligations."[25] A few days later, Secretary of State William Rogers flatly denied that any commitment of any kind had been given to President Thieu. The denial occurred during an exchange between Congressman Benjamin Rosenthal (D., N.Y.) and Secretary Rogers:

> MR. ROSENTHAL: Mr. Secretary, have we any commitments at the present time to the Governments of Laos, Cambodia, or South Vietnam which have not been made fully public? Any agreements of any kind? . . . I worry about what has been the growing trend in the executive branch, not only of this administration but of earlier administrations, of entering into executive agreements rather than treaties.
>
> SECRETARY ROGERS: I see; the answer to your question is "No."
>
> MR. ROSENTHAL: There is nothing pending that you would want to tell us?

SECRETARY ROGERS: No, nothing that I want to tell you. There is no executive agreement, or anything of that kind.[26]

On May 5, 1975, Senator Case accused President Nixon of violating the Case-Zablocki Act, which required the executive to report any agreement with a foreign nation within sixty days of its conclusion. If the promise to South Vietnam did not constitute an agreement, Case said, then Nixon had grossly deceived an ally. In the senator's view, additional grounds for an inquiry lay in the failure of the Nixon administration to report on the effect of the promises to Thieu of the Case-Church Act of 1973, which banned combat anywhere in Indochina.[27]

As it turned out, this was the last round fired in the controversy over the "secret agreements." Within a week, Cambodia seized the U.S. freighter *Mayaguez,* and all attention shifted to the dramatic attempt to rescue the ship and crew. When Senator Jackson's presidential campaign fizzled, the last bit of fire under the pot died out, and the issue was forgotten. Before returning to the fate of the president's final appeal to Congress, it is interesting to examine the way the administration dealt with the revelation of the promise to attack North Vietnam. In essence, the administration denied there was anything new in either Senator Jackson's accusation or the two letters.

It is clear that Kissinger contrived the response of the Ford administration and that the president agreed to it and issued it in his own name. Mr. Ford's press spokesman, Ron Nessen, explained the half-truths and the refusal to publish the Nixon-Thieu correspondence in the lofty terms of executive privilege and the national interest:

> By 1975, with the war nearly lost and Congressional limitations blocking American military involvement, the question of carrying out these secret Nixon promises to Thieu was moot. Why, then, did the Ford White House fudge on the truth and play word games to avoid revealing the now-irrelevant contents of Nixon's letters?
>
> Mostly, to protect the principle of confidentiality, the necessary ability of a president to communicate privately with foreign leaders. But also because the letters could be used as ammunition in any postwar recriminations over who was responsible for losing the war.[28]

But the response was more complicated than this, and the logic behind it was used to justify the president's refusal to disclose any of the official records concerning the negotiation of the Paris Accords. Essentially, Ford and Kissinger argued that whatever the commitments were that had been given Thieu to persuade him to sign at Paris—and they never denied making commitments—one could not regard them as "secret agreements" because their substance had repeatedly been stated in public. This was an odd position for the president and secretary of state to assume, even if it had been correct, which it was not. The secret promises to South Vietnam were far more definite and sweeping than anything Nixon, Kissinger, and Ford had said in public about them. If it meant anything at all, the argument of Ford and Kissinger was that it was perfectly all right for the president and his advisers secretly to promise the most drastic and dangerous actions without frankly conveying these promises to the Congress or the people—let alone seeking their approval—so long as what was said in Aesopian language in public did not contradict the secret undertakings. Because President Nixon had publicly stated he might use force against North Vietnam, he or any of his successors could resume the American combat role in Vietnam whenever they judged it necessary to "enforce" the peace and cease-fire agreements. A commitment to use force had been given secretly to South Vietnam. Congress, North Vietnam, and the American people could learn of it indirectly through the vague threats issuing periodically from the White House. They would learn directly only when the bombs again began falling from the B-52s over Vietnam. In other words, until Congress prohibited combat in Indochina and passed the War Powers Resolution, the executive-legislative struggle over the American role in the Vietnam War had not been concluded. Unless the promise to attack North Vietnam was mere bluff—and no one in the Ford administration was ever to suggest he had been bluffing—President Nixon fully intended to make war again on his own prerogative, without reference to the Congress or, one might add, the Constitution of the United States. Secretary Kissinger might speak of the effectiveness of deterrence as often as he liked; he and the president had obligated the United States to go to war when deterrence failed, as fail it must, considering the post-1945 history of Vietnam and the determination of the Communist leaders and movement to unify the country under their rule.

There is something else. Accepting as given that the North Vietnamese would resume the war casts doubt on the sincerity of Nixon's and Kissinger's promises to South Vietnam. Did they give the promises just to extricate the United States, the reasoning would run, without any intention of honoring them? In short, hadn't the United States already "sold out" South Vietnam in 1973? The evidence remains circumstantial, but the promises appear to have been genuine; Nixon and Kissinger were ready to resume the war, although they surely hoped and had reason to believe it would never be necessary. Three points can be made in favor of this conclusion. First, when the promises were made in late 1972 and early 1973 the president had just ordered exactly the kind of massive aerial punishment of North Vietnam that he promised to repeat if they violated the Paris Accords. There had been very little effective opposition in the United States to the "Christmas bombing," and there was no reason to expect that opposition to grow or to tie the president's hands in any way.

Second, the heavy bombing of Hanoi, the blockade, and even the unsuccessful attempt to free the American prisoners at Tay Ninh must have made Nixon a very credible adversary. Deterrence is a compound of will and means, and Nixon had amply demonstrated both. No North Vietnamese political or military leader would have dared ignore Nixon's threats to attack them. That it was, therefore, unlikely that North Vietnam would soon attack the South makes it even more probable that the promises were genuine, for the Nixon administration could reasonably expect never to have to honor them.

Finally, the domestic American political scene suggests the pledge was a genuine one. When the promises were given to the South Vietnamese, Congress was six months away from prohibiting combat in Indochina and passing the War Powers Act. It is at least an open question whether or not Congress could have overridden Nixon's veto of the War Powers Act if the president had not already been tainted by the Watergate scandal. In January 1973, Nixon's control over foreign policy was undimished, and he had just won reelection by a huge majority over Senator McGovern. Kissinger discussed the rationale behind the peace agreement in his memoirs, and it is clear that he and the president pinned their hopes on deterrence both to prevent a resumption of the war by North Vietnam and to allow the United States to escape being forced to return to the war. They believed Saigon could survive guerrilla and low-level conventional attacks. "The implicit threat of our retaliation," Kissinger argued later, "would be likely to deter massive violations."[29]

By April 1975 all this belonged to another time, almost another era, or so it seemed, for the term "pre-Watergate" has been coined to describe it.[30]

In retrospect it is clear that Nixon and Kissinger had never told the American people and Congress that the United States had promised to go back to war if North Vietnam attacked the South in "massive violation" of the Paris peace accords. In the end, therefore, the administration had the worst of both worlds: a collapsed policy rolled up by the armies of North Vietnam, and no support from Congress in the time of trial from August 1973, when Congress prohibited combat in Indochina, until April 30, 1975, when Saigon had fallen. This failure of conception and execution cannot be made to go away by saying that Congress was to blame, for Congress had never been publicly asked to support the policy.

Had the secrecy imposed by the politics of acquiescence led to the collapse? In one sense it clearly had, since Congress could not be held responsible for something it knew nothing about. In another sense, the verdict must be more ambiguous, for it is quite possible there could have been no peace without the secrecy. Congress and the public would almost certainly have balked at a commitment to return to the war. Was the nation and the world better off to have this secret peace, even though it might fail, than to have no peace at all? Whatever one's answer to this question, it is obvious that in concluding the peace by the politics of acquiescence, the administration reached far beyond the bounds of popular support. While subtlety is a part of successful diplomacy, the manner in which the Paris Accords were concluded and failed renders Kissinger and Nixon merely devious and throws doubt over their other accomplishments—for example, in the Middle East, where Kissinger appeared to be all things to Arab and Jew, as well as in Soviet-American relations. The case thus becomes a classic example of the dangers of the politics of acquiescence, and suggests a cautionary rule: the more important the undertaking, the more essential it is to handle it through the politics of support and not the politics of acquiescence.

Inevitably, one's judgment of the appropriateness and wisdom of Congress's refusal to permit combat in Indochina after August 15, 1973, or to supply extra military assistance in early 1975 depends on one's attitudes about the war and about the Nixon-Kissinger policies in Vietnam and Cambodia. There is a temptation to see this as a judgment to be made in the simplest terms. If one hated the war, one ought to like anything to do with ending it. Or, if one liked the war or responded to arguments about the importance of maintaining the credibility of the United States as a guarantor of its allies around the world, one must lament the collapse of the Vietnam policy. But there is a need to go beyond uncomplicated judgments of this kind and to ask what Congress's action suggests about what kind of foreign policy role Congress will and should have in the future.

Consensus and Foreign Policy

The part of Congress in the fall of Cambodia and Vietnam was to undo the politics of acquiescence. In this sense it is a calling to account of the government by itself, which is the essence of limited, constitutional government. In enacting strictures on the president, Congress was implicitly, and often explicitly, blaming itself for foolishly having surrendered initiative to the president. The politics of acquiescence were not practiced only by the Nixon and Ford administrations. They merely brought it to its highest level. All the post–World War II presidents resorted to acquiescence because they could. So strong was the national consensus on foreign policy—its anti-Fascist and then anti-Communist fevor—that presidents could take congressional consent for granted and take liberties with the spirit of legislation without fear of reprisal.

The early presidents who depended on the politics of acquiescence did so secure in the knowledge that the nation and Congress would have supported virtually any and all measures, including war, that they proposed to take. At the outset the politics of acquiescence was preferred not because acts regarded as necessary or vital could not have been taken in any other way, but because it was simpler to operate in this manner, and because it avoided embarrassing one's enemies—always dangerous in a nuclear age. Less admirable, perhaps, was the wish to conceal one's diplomatic, intelligence, and military mistakes. The last presidents in line—Johnson, and especially Nixon and Ford—were forced to depend on the politics of acquiescence because they could not act or might not obtain popular and congressional support to act as they thought they must. With the loss of consensus, what had once seemed appropriate became suspect, what had seemed to be a logical and sensible way to conduct foreign and military operations appeared instead to be conspiratorial, dangerous, immoral, and even unconstitutional.

Acquiescence is crucial to a coherent and successful foreign policy for a number of reasons. It is too awkward and time-consuming to get support for every imaginable executive initiative. Mandatory legislative prohibitions as a means of confining executive prerogative kill good and bad alike. There is no room left for flexibility or creativity in response to political, bureaucratic, congressional, and international realities. An executive deprived of reasonable latitude and flexibility in action is compelled to resort to demagoguery as he struggles to build the power to do what he judges he must.

At present there still lingers a confusion between the substance and the conduct of policy. This is inevitable because process is never neutral and always shapes substance. It is understandable, therefore, that those who found the Vietnam War to be unwise should have turned against the methods used to conduct and legitimate it. But process is not the same thing as substance. Taken to an extreme, the determination to deprive the executive of flexibility and prerogative in the conduct of foreign affairs can be self-defeating and even dangerous to the Constitution itself. Secrecy, flexibility, and force are necessary to diplomacy, as necessary to a president as the forward pass and the run are to the coach of a football team. To learn from the debacle in Indochina that the president cannot be allowed these essential tools would be to argue that a coach whose team had lost three of the last four games because of interceptions and fumbles may not use the forward pass or the run in any future games.

If acquiescence is crucial to successful diplomacy, it must depend on consensus. The greatest success of the Nixon-Kissinger-Ford years was to extricate the United States from Vietnam without detonating a prolonged internal witch hunt and without dismantling the existing international order. The greatest failure of the administrations from 1969 to 1977 was their inability to build a new consensus about foreign affairs. There wasn't time or energy; one shouldn't ask too much of them. There was little interest in it in any case, despite the state of the world messages, and the whole government was upset by Watergate.

The critique of the fall of Vietnam and Cambodia and of the part of Congress in the tragedy thus inevitably moves outside the halls of the Capitol or the White House or Pentagon and into the minds of the people of the nation and the minds of its foreign-policy leadership. The people as a whole and those who assume directly the responsibility for foreign affairs must move beyond the denial of acquiescence to the fashioning of a new consensus on United States foreign policy. There are two elements to such an effort. They have always marked every such effort in the past, and most notably the two greatest accomplishments in contemporary American foreign policy, the Marshall Plan and the North Atlantic Treaty. First, Congress and executive must reach a common understanding of international and domestic reality. Congress cannot and must not be allowed to lag behind the executive in this. There was no such lag in understanding the economic and political situation in Europe and the United States in 1947. Second, workable plans must be devised to cope with these realities. But these two elements will be possible only if there is a common understanding of what is the international purpose for which the United States is to commit its great power abroad. In the late 1940s not only was this purpose clear—the well-being and security of the United States—but the means were traditional and obvious: through alliance and economic assistance to build the military strength and prosperity of those nations outside the Soviet Union, eastern Europe, and China. Today, not only the means but the ends of U.S. foreign policy have become complex and ambiguous. Nations outside the Soviet sphere are no longer interested in alliance and economic assistance simply in order to add to the strength of those opposed to the power of the USSR, while the selfish national interest of any single nation, even one as powerful as the United States, seems to them an inadequate standard by which to guide their behavior.

The search for a new understanding of international and domestic reality and for an appropriate consensus on the goals and means of American foreign policy has begun, of course. It is, therefore, necessary to examine the case for a new understanding of both international reality and national consensus. With this in mind, one may then specify what part Congress could play in both understanding and adapting to the new requirements for a wise and effective foreign policy.

The Content of the New Consensus

For two decades and more, Stanley Hoffmann has offered subtle, elegant, and provocative commentaries on major international subjects, combining in a felicitous way a continental European perspective and an affectionate familiarity with the United States.[31] He was one of the most perceptive analysts of the foreign policies of Nixon, Kissinger, and Ford, a practice he continued in his latest book, where he again faults Kissinger's preference for a balance of power system and secretive foreign-policy making, a combination Hoffmann regards as internationally obsolete and domestically self-defeating.[32]

The latest book, however, is much more than a pointed analysis of the foreign policy of the United States from 1969 to 1977. Although he claims to have written an essay for fellow citizens, his book is ambitious and thorough. It is at once a diagnosis of the nature of contemporary international politics and a prescription for an effective foreign policy for the United States in the 1980s and beyond. In addition to offering his own original interpretations of these issues, Hoffman brings together, analyzes, and amends the perspectives and research on international affairs of many different authors and scholars. In regard to substance, the greatest virtue of the book is to test the recent explorations of international interdependence of Keohane, Nye, Morse, Brown, and others against theory, rigorous argument, and practical experience.[33] Out of this testing come diagnosis and prescription and a set of proposals for institutions and procedures of U.S. foreign-policy making, including much on the reform of executive-legislative relations, which is discussed later. It is the transformation of international politics that makes reform imperative, and before examining the ideas for institutional and procedural improvement, it is necessary to summarize Hoffman's observations of this larger change.

The world has become one for the first time in history, Hoffman begins, and one must grant the theorists of interdependence their principal argument. In this single international system, there are many kinds of relationships of interest, dependence, and influence in which the use of force is unlikely. The economic and social issues of domestic politics intrude into and sometimes usurp the international sphere, once reserved for war and diplomacy. In the process states lose their ability to control their own affairs; their monetary, credit, and taxation policies, for example, become subject to the wishes and needs of others caught in the same web of "complex interdependence," as Keohane and Nye call it.

But neither theory nor logic nor experience allows one to stop here. In addition to the many kinds and degrees of functional interdependence, Hoffman cautions, there remains the problem of relationships in the strategic-diplomatic arena, those contacts that are "dominated by the possibility of violent conflict and characterized by the threat or use of force."[34] Because these kinds of relationships endure, one must assume that advanced states will resort to force to prevent drastic economic loss, for example, and that the poorer nations are equally capable of violence, with the attendant risk of escalation as the great powers maneuver to block gains or support clients.[35]

For these reasons, the contemporary international system is fragmented into novel and traditional spheres: in what is novel there is new complexity and restraint; in what is traditional the dangers are both "huge and familiar."[36] Security remains the overriding concern of states, for they must make their way in a "coercive universe."[37]

For these reasons there is no going back to more familiar approaches to world order, such as the balance of power or the hopes for peace through the spread of prosperity and free trade, for they are inapplicable to a world dominated militarily by two nuclear superpowers who seek fundamentally different ends in a world remarkable for its heterogeneity of values, history, levels of industrialization, and social and political progress.[38] A new concept of world order is needed to cope with an international system fragmented by nuclear weapons and interdependence. In the strategic-diplomatic arena general war must be avoided, for it would destroy all, and violence must be moderated in order to escape the evils of escalation.[39] Beyond the strategic-diplomatic arena, it is essential not only to use resources safely and wisely, but to seek to reduce, if only gradually, the inequalities of wealth and power that exist among nations at present.

The rules that states would have to accept if such a world order were to be established run against all experience and logic of traditional international behavior. In Hoffmann's version these rules are:

> 1. The actors must prefer what is collectively beneficial over what serves individual national interests.
> 2. The actors must commit tangible resources in advance—food, money, raw materials, peace keeping forces—to the maintenance of a moderate world order, rather than for the benefit of specific national interests.
> 3. Each actor must reduce internal vulnerability to loss of control over energy or other crucial internal needs, in order to reduce the costs of breakdown of order or manipulation of dependency.
> 4. The actors must be willing to allow the growth of effective international institutions to tend the collective problems; such institutions can be more than "fields of hostile maneuvers."[40]

Hoffmann's list is representative of the views of many analysts, scholars, and politicians about the kind of outlook and foreign policy required both to escape nuclear disaster and to bring order out of heterogeneity. It is obvious that such rules and the outlook and policy they imply could not be adopted without substantial change in the views of Congress and the public and in the procedures and institutions involved in U.S. foreign-policy making. Although the argument of Hoffmann and the others is persuasive, one need not endorse their viewpoint in order to favor procedural and institutional reform, for in the end, reform attempts to answer the two important questions about U.S. foreign policy: (1) assuming one knows what must be done, how can a new consensus on foreign policy be established in the United States? and (2) what procedures and institutional arrangements are conducive to the development of a wise, effective foreign policy for the United States? Both questions may be given a more precise turn to bring them within the scope of this study: (1) what part should Congress play in the establishment of a new American consensus on foreign policy? and (2) what procedures and institutional arrangements for executive-legislative relations will aid the development of a wise and effective foreign policy?

The need to reestablish a consensus behind American foreign policy has been widely discussed in the decade since the protests against the Vietnam war first revealed the absence of consensus. When the substance of policy is ignored, the discussions have become excessively mechanical, as if the results achieved by adopting new organizational charts or following the recommendations of efficiency studies, or launching media campaigns would be unaffected by the content of the policies on whose behalf consensus was sought. A policy whose ends and means were widely understood and supported would be easily put into practice without any special efforts. A policy distasteful to many Americans, on the other hand, would complicate and perhaps even defeat efforts to build consensus for it, regardless of its merit. A good example of the effect of content on the process of consensus would be John Connally's controversial peace plan for the Middle East, which he announced in the fall of 1979 as part of his campaign for the presidency. The plan called for a number of major short-term concessions by Israel—withdrawal from the West Bank and Gaza, and demilitarized sovereignty for the Palestinians in those territories—in return for a military guarantee of Israel's security by the United States and an agreement with Saudi Arabia assuring the stability of the supply of oil to the West.[41] The ideas are controversial and any attempt to act on them would provoke widespread and bitter opposition regardless of the procedures followed by president and Congress.

If the president and Congress nonetheless believed the policy was essential to the security of the United States and its allies and wished to establish widespread agreement about it, they could do so only by recognizing the need to allow more time, effort, imagination and resources in order to reach their goal than they would allow for a less controversial proposal.

Second, it is a mistake to expect generalized educational efforts to have much politically relevant effect on public and congressional opinion. The lead time is too long, and politicians and events won't wait. Consensus can best be established in reference to a specific series of projects and goals which proceed from a definite understanding of risks, costs, and benefits that can be demonstrably linked to the well-being of the nation and of individuals. The outstanding examples here are the Marshall Plan, the North Atlantic Treaty, and the long-running negotiations on multilateral trade that were launched by the General Agreements on Tariffs and Trade.

The primary responsibility both for advancing the projects and winning widespread consent to them belongs to the president, and his resources are not meager. In the order of things Congress plays a subordinate but important role, a role made all the more agonizingly difficult by the dispersion of authority within both houses of the legislature. But it is not clear that this dispersion causes greater problems today than at other important moments in the nation's history. One need only recall the difficulties in establishing a coherent foreign economic policy for the United States in the years immediately after 1945 to realize this. "More than half of the nineteen standing committees of the House of Representatives, and several special, joint, and select committees, held pieces of the puzzle, themselves components of the overall foreign economic policy objectives of the United States." Committees worked on different aspects of the same problem without telling each other what they were doing, and they liked to vote in favor of their constituents' interests without much regard for the foreign-policy implications of their actions.[42] It is true that the number of standing committees in the House has increased (to 22) and especially the number and power of subcommittees has grown (from 108 to 146 in the last decade.) But two thoughts, both heretical and practical, suggest themselves. Isn't the problem facing the president and the congressional leadership essentially the same kind of problem both have faced for decades when creative and novel foreign policy programs were started and widely supported in Congress and public opinion? And second, assuming that the recent greater dispersion of authority has worsened the problem in the House (the Senate cut its committees from 31 to 21 in the Ninety-fifth and Ninety-sixth Congresses), consensus has to be rebuilt within the existing political and institutional realities.[43] The dispersion of authority may be mitigated in the short term, but it cannot be made to vanish. "We must," as Bayless Manning observed, "as a practical matter, take the fundamentals of the existing structure as a given."[44] The existing structure is the starting point, one might add, for proposals for institutional and procedural reform as well as for ideas about the role of Congress in rebuilding a national consensus on foreign policy.

Congress, Consensus, and Reform

There are two methods of building consensus in Congress and among the public that are immediately available to the legislature and that ought to be used. The first is the appointment of select committees to consider executive proposals. Either House by resolution may establish a select committee to investigate a particular problem or issue for a limited time. Recalling an earlier observation, one would caution mildly against the use of the select committee for general educative purposes. A great deal of valuable time and effort may be expended without any sure returns. Instead, the inquiry should be directly related to a major executive proposal and conducted in such a way that its findings may be reported at a timely point in the deliberative process leading to the passage of legislation. The House Select Committee on Foreign Aid established in July 1947 and led by Christian Herter is an example of a select committee used in this manner.

In his account of the work of the Herter committee, Holbert Carroll stressed the delicate timing of its establishment and reports, the care with which its members and staff were appointed, the vast scope of its inquiry, and the positive effect of the committee's activities on the passage of foreign aid and Marshall Plan legislation in 1947 and 1948. The procedure was not without its costs, chiefly in the rivalries and hostilities of other chairmen and representatives who felt their jurisdictions had been invaded or slighted, but these appear to have been more than overcome by the benefits of the inquiry.

In regard to timing, the establishment of the Herter committee was delayed until July 1947, after the June speech of Secretary Marshall announcing the willingness of the United States to help in the economic recovery of Europe.[45] House Speaker Joseph Martin (R., Mass.) drew members from twelve different committees, each of which had a piece of the foreign-aid problem. Most were conservatives who, initially at least, disliked the idea of large-scale assistance for Europe. A staff of more than forty consultants was built inside and outside the Congress. The chief of staff of the Foreign Affairs Committee became director of the Herter committee staff, and care was taken to maintain close relations with the staff of the Senate Foreign Relations Committee. Chairman Charles Eaton (R., N.J.) was named head of the Select Committee, but the most active role was given to Christian Herter, then a member of the Rules Committee.[46]

In addition to foreign aid, the committee also studied the resources available to the United States for assistance, and the possible ways to organize the executive in order to carry out the foreign-aid program. Subcommittees were sent to Europe for firsthand observation and study, and the staff added studies of problems concerning areas outside Europe.

The greatest accomplishment of the Herter committee was to change the minds of the opponents of large-scale foreign assistance and to persuade them either to support the program for European recovery or, perhaps equally important, not to oppose it. In addition to altering the opinions of influential representatives who took part in the inquiry, the committee's work also won over Republican party leaders in the House who were opponents of foreign aid.[47] Carroll observed that select commmittees are not popular among members of Congress because they tend to encroach on the work of other committees and subcommittees. This obvious source of opposition to the substance of the recommendations that might issue from a select committee must be balanced against the potential gains in consensus building. In the case of the Herter committee, the gains were real and crucial for the success of the Marshall Plan and other major programs of foreign assistance that followed it. In offering advice as to when the appointment of a select committee would be appropriate, Carroll emphasized the usefulness of the method for building consensus:

> The select committee device ought to be employed when the situation requires the development of a fresh consensus in the lower chamber regarding a major policy area. Such occasions arise every few years. The Colmer (Postwar Economic Policy and Planning) and Herter Committees were formed at critical junctures of major shifts in policy and helped the House to rise to a higher plane of agreement. A wholesale change in party control such as occurred after the election of 1952 provides another great occasion when a slow and deliberate select committee inventory seems desirable. The election year 1956 opened up festering differences about security policy generally, and the campaign naturally contributed to the confusion over military and foreign economic and foreign aid policy which developed in 1955 and in 1956 with the shifts of Soviet tactics. Under these circumstances, select committees might heal wounds and induce a fresh consensus.[48]

It is obvious that the device could be abused.[49] It could be wielded as an instrument to undermine the president's position because of different assessments of the problems facing the country or out of partisan or personal conflicts. The best way to reduce the risk of abuse would appear to be to use the device sparingly at critical moments when confusion must be overcome or areas of agreement widened. In addition, it must not be used abstractly but only as part of an effort by the executive and the leadership in Congress to win agreement to specific international programs and proposals.

A second method of building consensus derives from the power of legislators to call national attention to problems and to new methods of dealing with them, to bring proportion to American diplomacy, and to ground policy and statecraft in a well-informed general opinion. For members of Congress to perform in this role they must change an increasingly widespread attitude toward power and public service and alter the direction of their legislative work. Of these, the first is probably the most difficult. The difficulty no doubt arises, as former Senator J. William Fulbright suggested, from a preoccupation with getting and keeping office rather than using power constructively for the common good. This selfishness is emphasized by the modern techniques of political salesmanship. "It appears," Senator Fulbright observed:

> that in this age of poll-taking and image-making, of mass media and political salesmanship, the attributes required for winning public office have become quite distinct from the qualities needed to govern responsibly. . . . The qualities needed to govern well—wisdom, intellect, competence and character—are of little use in modern election campaigns and may, if not suppressed, be significant handicaps.[50]

A change of the kind advocated by Senator Fulbright is fundamental. It is also difficult to accomplish within a short term, for the integrity of legislatures, their ability to be guided by "the general reason of the whole," in Burke's phrase, derives from the mores of a society and in significant measure from the nature of the education afforded the young, as Senator Fulbright acknowledged.[51]

That is not the case with the direction of daily legislative work. Here the concern should be not to abandon the oversight of executive action, for if the Congress ceases such examinations there is no one else to conduct them, but to temper the supervision with an appropriate attention to both the examination of the assumptions of U.S. foreign policy and communication of those assumptions to Congress and the public. "Most major decisions," as Douglas Bennett argued, "take place in an atmosphere of long-standing prior assumptions about how the world works, about the direction in which Americans want to move, and about the political alignments bearing on a given issue."[52] By influencing the assumptions underlying policy, the Congress would join the executive in shaping the policies that are drawn from those basic assumptions. Through hearings, and the individual and collective efforts of committee members, a consensus about assumptions could be widened within Congress and the nation.

One approaches the topic of institutional and procedural reform with a sinking heart. Most of the proposals made over the years about this are obvious and politically irrelevant. One notes sadly, for example, that Holbert Carroll two decades ago advanced the idea for standing select committees on national security and foreign economic policy. The rest of the proposals are most often ineffective. No doubt it is true that Congress must allow the president a sensible latitude in action, or see everything botched by too many cooks. Given the constitutional separation of powers, there will have to be informal rather than formal arrangements to bring this about. The essence of the American political order, to recall Louis Fisher, lies in "a respect for procedure, a sense of comity and trust between the branches, an appreciation of limits and boundaries . . . the delicate system of nonstatutory controls, informal understandings, and discretionary authority."[53] As Stanley Hoffmann put it, "There will have to be an understanding, a kind of gentleman's agreement, on the boundary between the domain of legitimate congressional intervention and the area of necessary executive autonomy."[54]

Such informal agreements and the tolerance of discretionary authority have existed in the past and will surely exist again in the future. The question is how Congress and president should act to arrive at a new understanding that will lead to wise and effective policies that will be spontaneously and generally supported. Again, the obvious intrudes itself, and one flirts with banality. The executive can expect Congress to surrender the degree of control it has won over the detail and daily conduct of action and negotiation only if the president allows both houses a significant part in setting the original direction of policy. Cannot one take the analysis further? Specific institutional changes have been proposed, and they will be examined here. But it is appropriate to insist on the need for mutual trust and an appropriate autonomy for each. An observation that is needed and is generally overlooked is that informal understandings of this kind are never worked out in the abstract. It is no doubt important to develop the rationales for executive discretion and congressional participation, for some minds will be changed and some dangers avoided by clarity and the study of implication. But the stuff of comity and trust, nonstatutory control, and discretionary authority is to be found in the repeated direct encounters of the representatives of the two branches as they seek to accomplish specific international goals and to devise and win approval for specific international programs. Few minds in Congress will be changed by appeals to the principle of executive autonomy, but ample cooperation and the surrender of necessary authority is to be found in joint initiatives that serve and protect the common good.

While the correct mix of discretion and supervision that defines legislative-executive relations is elusive and changes constantly, it is appropriate to ask what concrete institutional and procedural reforms might be made to improve U.S. foreign policy. Recalling the rule that all procedures and institutions affect the substance of policy and were intended to affect it, one is not surprised to find that those most insistent about the need for reform of the congressional foreign-policy process have strong substantive views they wish to advance. At the present time it is the advocates of the idea of interdependence, whose point of view was summarized earlier, that seek important changes in the ways in which Congress conducts its foreign-policy business. In general terms, their concern is to ensure that Congress recognizes and accommodates the international as well as the domestic effects of legislation. This requires, in Joseph Nye's words, "an early and close relationship between the executive and Congress and a reorganization of congressional procedures and committees."[55]

To this end, Bayless Manning has proposed the creation of a Joint Committee on International and Domestic Affairs. This committee would receive all proposals from the president that have a mixed international and domestic character. It would not replace the work of the existing committees on such legislation, but ideally it would report on the bills reported by the other committees.[56] The intention is twofold: to focus attention on interdependence in the executive and Congress, and to test all relevant legislation for attention to the international as well as domestic aspects. The larger concern that moves Manning and Nye, and others such as Graham Allison, Seyom Brown. I. M. Destler, Hoffmann, Morse, and Peter Szanton, is not, of course, the addition of a particular congressional committee.[57] Their concern is, instead, that the diverse elements of foreign and domestic affairs be made to mesh in sensible and constructive ways that contribute to world order. This is the problem of coordination and, as such, has always been particularly troublesome in the American system. The need for coordination between and within both branches of the American government is now not only difficult but crucial in a world that is fragmented and partially interdependent, where one encounters constantly what Hoffmann termed "the risk that the very diversity of ideological, political, and economic systems will make the definition of common rules and international regimes impossible, or their survival unlikely."[58] The point, therefore, is not whether Bayless Manning's proposal for a Joint Committee on International and Domestic Affairs is adopted or spurned, but that the need for coordination is perceived and acted upon at both ends of Pennsylvania Avenue.

For this reason it is appropriate to consider other methods of coordinating foreign policy in the U. S. Congress and ways of relating foreign and domestic concerns *before* action has been taken. One must keep in mind that no institutional solution will "fix" a problem as difficult or as intimately connected to policy as is the problem of coordination. Instead, one must think of an endlessly evolving series of institutional and procedural accommodations that cope with immediate needs and then must be repaired or replaced as domestic and international conditions change and policy is altered to meet new developments. Logically, Congress would be most involved in efforts to coordinate foreign-policymaking in regard to three areas: within the House and Senate; between the House and Senate; and between Congress and president.

Foreign-Policy Coordination in House and Senate

The Select Committee as a device to foster consensus has already been discussed. Select Committees may also serve as coordinators of policy, particularly if their members and staffs are carefully chosen, and the moment is appropriate. Carroll observed that Select Committees proved especially useful when major shifts in policy were required. An equally useful moment may arise when the partisan control of the government changes hands, as in 1952 and again in 1968, 1976, and 1980. In seeking the appointment of Select Committees, however, the president must remember that they will be most useful if their activities are directly related to specific legislative proposals. "The typical legislator places a low priority on deliberation detached from specific action."[59] Permanent Select Committees might be established to coordinate all the elements of military and foreign policy. Select Committees on International Security Policy in both houses logically ought to take under their wings the existing committees on intelligence in both Houses. It is not that the intelligence committees are inappropriate; the close involvement of Congress in this area was long overdue. But the committees should not exist in isolation and ought to form part of a larger effort at coordination.

A second method by which both Houses could improve their coordination of foreign policy is by strengthening the powers of the leadership of the political parties in House and Senate. At present, the party leadership plays only a marginal role in the critical committee work on foreign affairs.[60] A party leadership group might be created, for example, to oversee foreign-policy concerns at all levels of activity in the Congress. Through the deliberations and interventions of such a group, pressure might be brought to bear on committee chairmen and subcommittee chairman and on individual committee members to pay attention to ideas and problems that would otherwise be overlooked, and to relate their work to the activity of other committees and to the executive.

Easiest to accomplish, and potentially most important, would be the establishment of formal and informal cooperative efforts between committees and subcommittees. This practice would be particularly important in the House if members from the authorizing committees could serve on the relevant appropriations subcommittees when foreign money bills are considered. It is a practice often used in the Senate, and would seem to be a desirable way to further policy coordination, despite greater obstacles to its use in the House deriving from the differences in prestige and size between the committees involved.[61] Cross membership—committee assignments that match areas of policy overlap—would also seem a reasonable way of increasing the likelihood that important issues will not drop through the cracks of decentralized inquiry and recommendation. Nor should one forget the need for cooperation between committee staffs, a matter that has increased in importance as staffs have grown in size and degree of specialization.

Foreign-Policy Coordination between House and Senate

Whenever important foreign questions must be dealt with there is a real possibility that the president and the most important Senators, aware of the greater prestige of the Senate in foreign affairs, and preferring to deal with a smaller group, will rely excessively on the Senate and poison the well of House-Senate cooperation (let alone coordination). This has happened repeatedly since 1945, from the secret negotiations between Marshall, Vandenberg, and Dulles at Blair House in regard to the United Nations in April 1948 to the formulation of measures to implement the Panama Canal Treaty in the fall of 1979. If the House feels left out of these kinds of deliberations, the inevitable result is a loss of coherence and even of majorities in favor of administration proposals.

Conference committees present an outstanding opportunity for policy coordination, and the conferees often make good on the chance. In addition, there is close consultation with the executive during conference. For these reasons the conference is treated (and should continue to be treated) as a device of coordination. This should be reflected in the appointment of conferees, including those from committees with related interests, for example. The drawback, of course, is that conference occurs nearly at the end of the legislative cycle and not at the beginning. Errors or oversights can be and often are corrected in conference, but earlier intervention is necessary, for the farther along a piece of legislation has moved, the larger the number of hostages that have been given and taken and the greater the resistance to change, however necessary or important.

Joint Select Committees are one method of making House-Senate cooperaton systematic. There are obvious difficulties. Jealousy, lack of clear legislative jurisdiction, the drain on time and energy—all weigh against this device. Even so, the Joint Select Committee has been effective in a number of areas for both short and long terms: the Joint Economic Committee, the Joint Committee on Atomic Energy, the Watergate Committee, and a number of others. Because of their joint nature, these committees function best when they gather information, promote understanding between executive and legislature, and aim at changing attitudes. As Holbert Carroll observed: "Over a Congress or even a decade, while not subject to exact measurement, these changes in the attitudes of individual men serve to elevate the deliberations of particular committees to a higher plane and infuse Congress with a more acute sense of the inter-relatedness of policies."[62] To match the picture drawn within each House, one should add the need for cooperation between committee staffs from House and Senate and between the party leaders in House and Senate. Considering the powers of the party leaders again, there would appear to be every reason to establish a formal foreign-policy group composed of senators and representatives who lead their parties. The responsibility of the group would be to oversee the general nature of foreign-policy deliberations in House and Senate and to superintend executive-congressional relations in this area. Normally this kind of coordination is left to the president, but there seems to be little reason for this not to be performed by party leaders themselves. Acting in this way they would enhance the degree of coordination of policy substance and would increase their ability to make executive proposals conform to the dictates of political feasibility.

Foreign-Policy Coordination between Legislature and Executive

In broad terms, the problem in this area is to prevent president and legislature from flying off in different directions and bringing each other crashing to earth periodically in mutual confrontation and paralysis. In the terms of analysis on which this book is based, the problem is how to achieve support and acquiescence. Acquiescence that is not induced by emergency can only follow the winning of support. Support is unquestionably won by proposals whose excellence alone sways opinion in Congress and the public. But excellence in conception and design is seldom enough. The gap between the vision of the statesman and the experience of his nation is not so easily closed. In the present American system, consultation is surely the means by which executive and legislature, at least, may close that gap. There is, of course, no guarantee that consultation of the kind proposed here *will* lead legislators to grant support, let alone that degree of acquiescence without which no executive may function effectively. The argument is of necessity rather than sufficiency. Consultation with the Congress by the executive will never be sufficient to win the consent of the American people to major foreign programs; it will always be necessary. The goal must be the creation of networks of continuing relations that will carry the weight of creative advances in American policy.[63]

An extremely helpful outline of what such networks of continuing relations would include has been provided by Congressman Lee Hamilton and Foreign Affairs Committee Staff Consultant Michael Van Dusen, both already much involved in this book. "From the viewpoint of the Congress," they write, "the crux of the problem between the executive branch and the Congress, which prevents the formulation and execution of a more coherent foreign policy, is the inadequate system of consultation between the two branches." It ought to be possible for the two branches to agree informally on what constitutes adequate consultation, who in Congress is to be consulted, and at what stage in the policymaking process consultation should occur. In the absence of such consultation two things happen in Congress, neither of which is necessarily helpful to the development of wise and effective policy. In the event of failure or scandal, the absence of early and adequate consultation rebounds against the executive and contributes to a confrontation between the branches. Moreover, in its desire to obtain consultation Congress resorts to mandatory legislation that compels consultation, as in the case of the War Powers Resolution and the restrictions on military sales. These methods are clumsy and may produce informaton after the fact rather than prior consultation. They invite executive evasion without providing a sure congressional remedy because of the separation of powers. It is, in short, in the interest of both branches to avoid this kind of mandatory legislation if possible.

With these ends in mind, Hamilton and Van Dusen proposed an interesting variety of means to improve consultation in regard to foreign policy between legislature and executive:

1. The formation of ad hoc consultation groups in Congress in times of crisis or when unusual foreign policy problems are encountered; these groups would be easily identifiable by the executive, legitimate in the eyes of Congress, and would enormously simplify the sheer mechanics of consultation.
2. The improvement of the system by which the executive briefs the Congress on foreign concerns. An improved briefing method ought to offer regularly scheduled information meetings, special sessions in times of crisis, and frequent informal briefings at the request of individuals or committees or executive officials.

> 3. The initiation of frequent question periods during which the president, secretary of state and other high officials would answer questions on foreign policy for members of Congress.
> 4. The establishment by Congress of a statutory basis for the security classification of information.
> 5. The continued use of the legislative veto—by which Congress reserves the ability to disallow specific executive actions taken under general statutory authority—as a means of compelling prior consultation between the branches.[64]

The goal of Hamilton and Van Dusen in proposing these procedures is to identify the channels through which executive and Congress together may achieve the changes of opinion and attitude that alone make possible a wise and effective foreign policy for the nation. They discount the kinds of institutional changes mentioned in the earlier discussions of policy coordination because they believe those changes to be politically unrealizable at present and because they doubt the fundamental importance of institutional settings.

> The nature of executive-legislative interaction will be more instrumental in shaping a coherent foreign policy than the forum in which the executive and the legislature meet. History supports the proposition that structural changes in both the legislative and executive branches only tend to slice the bureaucracy differently: they do not change attitudes or modify behavior.[65]

While granting the notion that attitudes are fundamental and content is more important than form, and while strongly supporting the proposals Hamilton and Van Dusen have made in regard to consultation, I must add two points. Structure does alter content—nothing demonstrates this better than the separation of powers itself. For this reason, the effort to bring greater coherence and wisdom to American foreign policy must tap the structural resources available to the Congress.

Partners in Collapse

The nature of the American political order, which shares responsibility as well as power, made Congress and the president partners in the failure of American policy in Vietnam. One of the objectives of this book has been to untangle the final developments in that doomed policy and to discover what lessons may be learned that would help the two branches avoid the mistakes of the past, both in the day-to-day workings of the policy process and when the next major controversy develops over a costly, difficult, and painful foreign intervention. The natural inclination of policymakers is to project the familiar into the future. Moreover, they do this badly, as a rule, seizing on the first analogy that occurs to them—without careful study and without even making the effort to ask whether the analogy is apt or misleading.[66] "Seeing a trend running toward the present," as Ernest May observed, "they tend to assume that it will continue into the future, not stopping to consider what produced it or why a linear projection might prove to be mistaken."[67]

Applied to legislative-executive relations during the fall of Vietnam and Cambodia, this way of using the past could produce a grim and gloomy prediction about the future of cooperation between president and Congress in their handling of important foreign-policy questions. In extreme form, the analogy policymakers could draw would read as follows: "The behavior of Congress in the last phases of the Vietnam War shows that Congress cannot be trusted to support the national security of the United States when American lives are at stake and large sums of money are involved." This was the conclusion President Ford and Secretary Kissinger stressed when they publicly and repeatedly blamed Congress for the fall of Vietnam. In effect, they told the American people and the world that Congress had overthrown Vietnam. To the president and secretary of state, Congress provided both the proximate and the long-term cause of the downfall of South Vietnam and of American policy in Southeast Asia by cutting aid and depriving the administration of power to punish North Vietnam by bombing or naval blockade or some other resort to force. The lessons to be learned from this analogy would then be of two kinds: either the president must at all costs avoid military action anywhere in the world until Congress comes to its senses, or the executive must not shrink from conducting the necessary interventions covertly, keeping all knowledge of them from the public and the Congress.

The covert American intervention in Angola suggests that the Ford administration learned the second lesson, until public disclosure of the operation and a desperate need for money forced the policy into the open and Congress stopped it. Afterward, the Ford and Carter administrations appear to have learned the first lesson and to have studiously avoided military collisions with the Soviet Union or Cuba in Africa and the Middle East, for at least four years, until the invasion of North Yemen by its southern neighbor in the spring of 1979.

The dangers of either of these lessons are obvious. To abide by the first would be to deny the United States the means of protecting its own security and well-being and that of its allies until so many precious advantages had been surrendered that resistance had become futile. The second course is just as dangerous, although in different ways. If a covert intervention is begun and runs into difficulty, it will become publicly known. At that point, if the executive fails to win congressional support, the president faces the unattractive choice of abandoning the operation in the face of domestic opposition or continuing in defiance of Congress and precipitating a constitutional crisis. The first course endangers national security, the second undermines the republic itself.

Both "lessons" would appear to be inappropriate and based on a mistaken reading of the past. Instead of accepting the analogy and the gloomy lessons painted by Ford and Kissinger and incorporated into accepted wisdom about American foreign policy, it is necessary to look for other analogies and parallels and, as Ernest May advised, to ask whether or not the moral seen in the one case of Vietnam is a principle suitable for projecting into the future. The forces that produced the actions of Congress in regard to Vietnam must be examined, and it must be asked whether or not they will persist and operate in the same ways in the future.[68]

The attempt to understand the forces that produced the actions of Congress in regard to Vietnam must begin with the uniqueness of the Vietnam war in American domestic life. More people opposed the Vietnam war with more energy, and even bitterness, than have opposed any other foreign policy in this century, perhaps in the life of the republic. The "peace movement" became a national convulsion that forced the withdrawal from politics of an incumbent president, disrupted national life (particularly in the universities) and ate away at the morale and efficiency of the Armed Forces of the United States. The uniqueness and vehemence of opposition to the war should warn against easy generalization about congressional and popular support for American foreign policy. Surely, no other event will soon strike the American people with the force and repugnance of "the War."

In addition, errors in executive policymaking account for the defeat in Vietnam at least as much as or more than the collapse of congressional support. Two of the multitude of errors are mentioned here. First, the United States forced on the South Vietnamese a military organization and style of fighting that was American, one that depended on mechanical mobility and high rates of fire. Neither of these could survive the gradual removal of the American military presence from the country or the reductions in aid imposed by the Congress.[69] Saddled with an extremely expensive manner of waging war, the South

Vietnamese were undeniably hurt by the increases in American prices of petroleum products and brass that occurred in 1974 just as the Congress began to impose reductions in aid.

A second executive blunder also contributed to the defeat of South Vietnam. The Nixon administration made peace dependent on the recourse of renewing the war against North Vietnam, but never made this commitment public or sought its approval by Congress. It was therefore absurd for President Ford and Secretary Kissinger to accuse Congress of denying the executive branch the power it needed to enforce the peace agreements. Congress could not deny what it did not know existed. What pained Secretary Kissinger was the magnitude of his miscalculation. He and President Nixon had hoped to keep the peace by deterrence. They believed they had cowed the North Vietnamese sufficiently to prevent them from attacking the South. In the breathing space thus provided South Vietnam could strengthen itself and, above all, the United States could withdraw honorably. All depended, nonetheless, on the ability to use force if the North attacked. By prohibiting combat by American forces in Indochina, Congress was, in effect, saying clearly what it would support. It was not and could not have been balking at or understanding the peace agreements, because it had not known the United States had promised to return to the war. Of course, many in the Congress feared that such a promise existed, or at least that President Nixon might order United States forces back to war. That fear was behind their votes in favor of the combat ban. It can be said that Congress defeated the Paris Agreements, but at the heart of the failure of the accords lay executive inability to fashion a policy capable of commanding public support. That the promise to return to war was without public support is revealed clearly by its secrecy. Had the policy stood a chance of winning popular approval there would have been no need to keep it secret.

A third aspect of executive-legislative relations in the last months before the fall of Vietnam merits attention. As the House and Senate deliberated on the administration requests for additional military and economic aid and approval of a forceful evacuation, both followed established procedures. There were no procedural innovations working. The requests were treated essentially as more or less normal program decisions and not as crisis actions that justified departure from regular committee procedures. Lengthy hearings were held, bills were carefully debated and repeatedly amended in committee. Ostensibly, the committes were deciding whether the military aid program for Vietnam and Cambodia should be supplemented and whether there should be a substantial increase in economic assistance for the care of the tens of thousands of new refugees. Back came the judgments from the committees that the programs were adequately funded and that, while additional monies might be spent for evacuation, none would be allowed in the current fiscal year for military or economic aid. Meanwhile, the tide of battle turned against South Vietnam and Cambodia and these countries as they had been constituted for years entered their last days. That might have provoked a crisis atmosphere and have driven the requests out of normal channels, but it did not.

There appear to have been several reasons for the "business as usual" approach that marked deliberations in both House and Senate. The first surely comes from the indifferent handling of the requests by the Ford administration. The original request for an increase had been postponed until after the November elections, and the administration never quite managed to convey a sense of urgency to the Congress until after the disastrous defeat in the Central Highlands. That defeat, of course, tended to work against the approval of additional aid by making clear how poorly the South Vietnamese government had performed and giving the opponents of aid the easy argument that more arms would hardly make a difference for a government that had just surrendered tens of millions of dollars' worth of weapons without a fight.

For the most part, the management of the aid requests was left to low-level officials in the administration. President Ford did not clearly engage his office in the requests until quite late in the crisis, and Secretary Kissinger was not even in the country throughout much of the period. At the very least, the administration sent confusing signals to the Congress, and this made it all the more likely that the requests would not be lifted out of the normal channels of congressional procedure.

If this is an accurate account of the forces that produced the behavior of the Congress and that defined legislative-executive relations during the fall of Vietnam and Cambodia, then the lessons to be learned would appear to be quite different from those suggested by President Ford and Secretary Kissinger in their petulant and angry attacks on the Congress for overthrowing allies of the United States. In its opposition to adminstration policy Congress was not signaling its isolationist sentiment or its wish to run out on American allies. Rather, it was giving what it gives best, an estimate of political feasibility. In denying the aid requests in early 1975, just as in prohibiting combat in Indochina in August 1973, Congress gave notice that it was not feasible for the administration to base its policy on the assumption that it might wage war in Indochina or provide substantially greater amounts of aid to Vietnam than had been appropriated for 1975. Congress was setting limits to American policy based on its judgments of the wishes of its constituents and the merits of the alternatives it foresaw.

The irony of the fall of Vietnam and Cambodia is that the executive concluded it could not devise a workable policy within these limits. It chose instead to work by secrecy and reliance on the prerogatives of the president as commander in chief of the armed forces. The lesson would therefore appear to be that unless the executive bases its actions on policies capable of winning widespread popular support the Congress will not hesitate to refuse the funds and authority needed to carry out its plans. The novelty in this, of course, is the willingness of the legislature to contest with the executive about the substantive adequacy of policy. The executive has brought this on itself through a series of blunders and scandals. Time and the natural advantages of information and initiative the president possesses will remedy this. But neither will detract from the need to depend on support as well as acquiescence in the making of American foreign policy.

Appendix 1: H.R. 2704

H.R. 2704, a bill to provide additional military assistance authorizations for Cambodia for the fiscal year 1975, and for other purposes.

Be it enacted by the Senate and House of Representatives of the United States of America in Congress assembled,

That section 504(a) of the Foreign Assistance Act of 1961 is amended by adding at the end thereof the following sentence: "In addition, there is authorized to be appropriated to the President not to exceed $222,000,000 for additional military assistance for Cambodia for the fiscal year."

Sec. 2. Section 655 of the Foreign Assistance Act of 1961 is amended by repealing subsection (a) and subsection (b) thereof.

Sec. 3. The value of orders of defense articles and services ordered under Section 506 of the Foreign Assistance Act of 1961 for military assistance for Cambodia shall not exceed $75,000,000 in the fiscal year 1975.

APPENDIX 2: Subcommittee Draft and DuPont Substitute

SUBCOMMITTEE DRAFT PROVISION

Section 655 of the Foreign Assistance Act of 1961 is amended by adding the following new subsection:

"(h) An amount equal to 10% of any ceiling provided for in this section may be provided which shall be in addition to the amount authorized under such ceiling in each successive thirty day period beginning on the date of enactment of this subsection, subsequent to a report by the President to the Congress during such thirty day period which states—

(i) That United States is seeking an immediate end to the conflict without requiring the participation of the present government in any subsequent government of the Khmer Republic;

(ii) That the Government of the Khmer Republic is pursuing a similar objective; and

(iii) That initiatives have been taken toward the other side in the conflict to achieve a peaceful conclusion under which Cambodians who wish to do so may be permitted a reasonable time to leave the country.

And which provides specific details of such activities; *unless* the Congress, within 10 calendar days after receiving any report under this subsection adopts a concurrent resolution stating in substance that it does not favor the provisions of the report."

REPRESENTATIVE DUPONT DRAFT PROVISION

Section 655 of the Foreign Assistance Act of 1961 is amended by adding the following new subsection:

"(h) Any ceiling provided for in this section may be exceeded by 10 percent of such amount in each successive thirty day period beginning on the date of enactment of this subsection, subsequent to a report by the President to the Congress during such thirty day period which states—

(1) that it is recognized that the only objective of any further aid is to relieve human suffering by ceasing military action.

(2) that the Government of the Khmer Republic is pursuing a similar objective; and

(3) that to this end, military supplies are being provided only until such time that our government is assured by the Government of the Khmer Rouge that non-combatants and prisoners will be treated in accord with the provisions of the (Geneva) Convention.

(4) that initiatives have been taken toward the other side in the conflict looking to a controlled solution, and which provides specific details of such initiatives; *unless* Congress, within 10 calendar days after receiving any report under this subsection adopts a concurrent resolution stating in substance that it does not favor the provisions of the report."

Appendix 3: Hamilton-DuPont Compromise

Strike all after the enacting clause and insert in lieu thereof the following:

That section 655 of the Foreign Assistance Act of 1961 (21 U.S.C. 2415) is amended by adding at the end thereof the following new subsection:

"(h) The Congress directs that United States policy shall be to achieve an end to the conflict in Cambodia no later than June 30, 1975, and to end all U.S. military assistance by such date. To achieve the policy stated in the first sentence, notwithstanding any other provision of law, in addition to any amounts included in subsection (a)—

"(1) of the amounts authorized to carry out chapter 2 of part II of this Act, not more than $20,000,000 may be provided for military assistance for Cambodia;

"(2) of the defense articles and services which may be ordered under section 506 of this Act for fiscal year 1975, not more than $7,500,000 may be ordered for Cambodia; and

"(3) of the amounts authorized under the Agricultural Trade Development and Assistance Act of 1954, not more than $17,700,000 may be provided for economic assistance for Cambodia.

for each of three successive thirty-day periods beginning on the date of enactment of this subsection, but only (A) after the President reports in detail during such thirty-day period to Congress that at the time of such report—

"(i) the United States is undertaking specific steps to achieve an end to the conflict in Cambodia not later than June 30, 1975, in order to relieve human suffering and to end all United States military assistance to Cambodia by such date;

"(ii) the Khmer Republic is actively pursuing specific measure to reach a political and military accommodation with the other side in the conflict;

"(iii) initiatives have been taken toward the other side to achieve a peaceful and orderly conclusion to the conflict, including safe passage out of Cambodia for those persons who desire to leave the country, appropriate care and help for the refugees and victims of the conflict, and assurances that combatants and prisoners will be treated in accordance with the provisions of the Geneva Convention on Prisoners of War; and

"(iv) the United States, pursuant to United Nations General Assembly resolution 3238, is requesting the Secretary-General, after due consultation, to lend assistance to achieve a peaceful and orderly conclusion to the conflict, including, if appropriate, the use of peacekeeping forces; and

"(B) if the Congress, within 10 calendar days after receiving such report, does not adopt a concurrent resolution stating in substance that it does not favor the provisions of such report."

APPENDIX 4: H.R. 6096

Union Calendar No. 68

94th CONGRESS
1st Session

[Report No. 94-155]

IN THE HOUSE OF REPRESENTATIVES

April 17, 1975

Mr. Morgan introduced the following bill; which was referred to the Committee on International Relations

April 18, 1975

Reported with amendments, committed to the Committee of the Whole House on the State of the Union, and ordered to be printed

[Insert the part printed in italic]

A BILL

To authorize funds for humanitarian assistance and evacuation programs in Vietnam and to clarify restrictions on the availability of funds for the use of United States Armed Forces in Indochina, and for other purposes.

1 *Be it enacted by the Senate and House of Representa-*
2 *tives of the United States of America in Congress assembled,*
3 That this Act may be cited as the "Vietnam Humanitarian
4 Assistance and Evacuation Act of 1975".
5 SEC. 2 There is authorized to be appropriated to the
6 President for the fiscal year 1975 not to exceed $150,000,-
7 000 to be used, notwithstanding any other provision of law,
8 on such terms and conditions as the President may deem

2

1 appropriate for humanitarian assistance to and evacuation
2 programs from South Vietnam.
3 SEC. 3. Nothing contained in section 839 of Public Law
4 93-437, section 30 of Public Law 93-189, section 806 of
5 Public Law 93-155, section 13 of Public Law 93-126,
6 section 108 of Public Law 93-52, or any other comparable
7 provision of law shall be construed as limiting the availa-
8 bility of funds for the use of the Armed Forces of the United
9 States for the purposes of section 2 of this Act.
10 SEC. 4. For the purposes of section 2, evacuation shall
11 be defined as the removal to places of safety as expeditiously
12 as possible, *without the use of military force, if possible, but*
13 *should it become necessary and essential,* with the minimum
14 use of necessary force, the following categories of persons:
15 (a) American citizens;
16 (b) dependents of American citizens and of per-
17 manent residents of the United States.
18 (c) Vietnamese nationals eligible for immigration to
19 the United States by reason of their relationships to
20 American citizens; and
21 (d) such other foreign nationals to whose lives a
22 direct and imminent threat exists: *Provided,* That
23 United States Armed Forces necessary to carry out their
24 evacuation do not exceed those necessary to carry out
25 the evacuation of (a), (b), and (c) above.

3

1 *The authority granted by this section shall not permit or*
2 *extend to any action or conduct not essential to effectuate*
3 *and protect the evacuation referred to in this section.*
4 SEC. 5. Nothing in this Act shall be construed to abro-
5 gate any of the provisions of the War Powers Resolution,
6 Public Law 93-148.
7 SEC. 6. Funds heretofore or hereafter made available
8 under section 36 of the Foreign Assistance Act of 1974 may
9 be used for humanitarian assistance purposes without regard
10 to limitations contained in subsections 36(a) (1), 36(a)
11 (6), and 38(a) (1) *and in the third sentence of subsection*
12 *37(b)* of that Act.
13 SEC. 7. Any of the provisions of this Act may be re-
14 scinded by concurrent resolution of the Congress.

Notes

1 Introduction

1. See, for example, Merlo J. Pusey, *The Way We Go to War* (Boston: Houghton Mifflin, 1969); Arthur Schlesinger, Jr., *The Imperial Presidency* (Boston: Houghton Mifflin, 1973).

2. See, for example, Alton Frye, *Toward a Responsible Congress*. (New York: McGraw-Hill, 1975).

3. Scholars on the radical left would prefer quite a different analysis than the one favored by liberals, an explanation at once more systematic and "scientific," one that casts the president and executive branch as a tool of one or another ruling group or class. See Gabriel Kolko, *The Roots of American Foreign Policy* (Boston: Beacon Press, 1969); Joyce and Gabriel Kolko, *The Limits of Power: The World and the United States Foreign Policy 1945–1954* (New York: Harper and Row, 1972).

4. One need not be a doctrinaire of left or right to be dissatisfied and alarmed over the explanation of Vietnam and other errors as the result of "executive aggrandizement." It is intellectually dissatisfying because it ends inquiry precisely where it should begin. Why was executive power allowed to grow so great—to what end and in service to what kinds of causes? It is alarming because given the separation of powers the apparent remedy is an increase in congressional influence over foreign-policy decisions. This is hardly reassuring to anyone with a slight knowledge of the history of American diplomacy; one need go back no farther than the 1930s to find decisive—and calamitous—evidence that a great role for Congress, even dominance over the executive, offers no guarantee of wisdom.

5. The last is a reference to David Halberstam, *The Best and the Brightest* (New York: Random House, 1969). See his portrait of MacGeorge Bundy, pp. 39–60, and his summary of the principals, pp. 656–58.

6. One thinks of the works of Richard Neustadt, *Presidential Power: The Politics of Leadership from FDR to Carter* (New York: Wiley, 1979) and Arthur M. Schlesinger, Jr., *The Age of Roosevelt: The Crisis of the Old Order* (Boston: Houghton Mifflin, 1957) and *The Age of Roosevelt: The Coming of the New Deal* (Boston: Houghton Mifflin, 1959), perhaps because the authors are such well-known public figures. James M. Burns, *Presidential Government: The Crucible of Leadership* (New York: Houghton Mifflin, 1965) is another example. Deeply impressed by Franklin Roosevelt and the New Deal, these men tended to measure other presidents and policies against the Roosevelt standard and to find them wanting, both in style and substance and in their willingness to use presidential power. See also Aaron Wildavsky, ed., *Perspectives on the Presidency* (Boston: Little, Brown, 1975).

7. J. M. Burns, *Uncommon Sense,* (New York: Harper and Row, 1972) pp. 172–73, italics added.

8. Ibid., p. 170.
9. Ibid., pp. 180–81.
10. Emmet John Hughes, *The Living Presidency: The Resources and Dilemmas of the American Presidential Office* (New York: Coward, McCann & Geoghegan, 1972) p. 248.
11. Dean Acheson, "The Responsibility for Decision," in *This Vast External Realm* (New York: Norton, 1973), pp. 196–97. See also the testimony of Nicholas de B. Katzenbach, while under secretary of state, giving the rationale of presidential supremacy in foreign policy, excerpted in Robert A. Goldwin and Harry M. Clor, eds., *Readings in American Foreign Policy,* 2nd ed., (New York: Oxford University Press, 1971) pp. 36–45.
12. Acheson, *This Vast External Realm,* p. 197.
13. Ibid., p. 201; for a discussion of the decentralized structure of influence and decision making in the House, see Richard F. Fenno, Jr., "The Internal Distribution of Influence: The House," in Raymond Wolfinger, *Readings on Congress* (Englewood Cliffs, N.J.: Prentice-Hall, 1971), pp. 208–11. Even the parties, the strongest centralizers in the House, Fenno observed, contain "disparate factional blocs and conflicting policy viewpoints" and remain "loose coalitions of social interest and local party organization."
14. Acheson, "Legislative-Executive Relations," in *This Vast External Realm,* p. 211.
15. Ibid., p. 212.
16. Ibid.
17. Ibid., p. 220.
18. Ibid.
19. Ibid., p. 221.
20. George F. Kennan, *Memoirs, 1925–1950* (Boston: Little, Brown, 1967), pp. 413–14.
21. For an account of the American intervention in Angola, see John Stockwell, *In Search of Enemies: A CIA Story,* (New York: Norton, 1978). See also Nathaniel Davis, "The Angola Decision of 1975: A Personal Memoir," *Foreign Affairs* 57, no. 1 (Fall 1978): 109–24.
22. Garry Wills suggested in his study of Kissinger that the secretary's virtuosity as a negotiator was, in fact, the pursuit of complexity for its own sake, that Kissinger was "ultimately a master of the supererogatory maneuver, of the paradoxical act as lovingly shaped as the quaint antitheses of his prose—that he traveled around the world to arrive next door, thus making the obvious look like a miracle, threading with admitted dexterity labyrinths of his own making. . . . One advantage of the approach was that it always suceeded because it always vanquished hypothetical enemies. Henry had only to imagine some disaster that did not, in fact, come about—and then claim credit for preventing the catastrophe he had been the first to imagine" (*Playboy,* December 1974, pp. 296, 300).
23. Sydney Hook, *The Hero in History: A Study in Limitation and Possibility* (New York: John Day, 1943), pp. 114, 147–48, 153.

2 Nixon, Kissinger, and the Politics of Acquiescence

1. The secret U.S. bombing and much more about the part played by the United States in Cambodia are discussed in William Shawcross, *Sideshow: Kissinger, Nixon, and the Destruction of Cambodia* (New York: Simon and Schuster, 1979). See especially pp. 19–32.
2. Quoted in ibid., p. 217.
3. Ibid., pp. 205–8.
4. Ibid., pp. 198–99.

5. This discussion of the legal basis of the Nixon administration's Cambodia policy owes much to Lehman, *The Executive, Congress, and Foreign Policy: Studies of the Nixon Administration* (New York: Praeger, 1976). The text of the Byrd amendment is given on p. 59.

6. Ibid., p. 72.

7. Ibid., p. 178.

8. See Shawcross, *Sideshow;* and Gareth Porter, *A Peace Denied: The United States, Vietnam, and the Paris Agreement* (Bloomington, Ind.: Univ. of Indiana Press, 1975), pp. 83, 200, 205.

9. See Lehman, *The Executive, Congress, and Foreign Policy,* pp. 186 ff.

10. Ibid., pp. 186, 191–93.

11. Ibid., p. 209.

12. A third of the Senate voted in favor of an amendment proposed by Senator Mike Gravel (D., Alaska) to strike the supplemental aid for Cambodia. See ibid., pp. 198–201.

13. Correspondence with John H. Sullivan, senior staff member of the House Foreign Affairs Committee.

14. For examples and an elegant discussion of the politics of support see Dean Acheson, "Legislative-Executive Relations," in *This Vast External Realm.* Joseph Marion Jones, *Fifteen Weeks* (New York: Harcourt, Brace, Jovanovich, 1955); and Acheson's *Present at the Creation* (New York: Norton, 1969) also show how pervasive the concern was in the Truman administration to obtain the widest possible measure of public and congressional support for their policies.

15. Among the works I have read with this theme are Henry Brandon, *The Retreat of American Power* (Garden City, New York: Doubleday, 1973); Stephen R. Graubard, *Kissinger: Portrait of a Mind* (New York: Norton, 1973); Marvin Kalb and Bernard Kalb, *Kissinger* (Boston: Little, Brown, 1974); David Landau, *Kissinger: The Uses of Power* (Boston: Houghton Mifflin, 1972).

16. John Campbell, *The Foreign Affairs Fudge Factory,* (New York: Basic Books, 1971), p. 229.

17. Ibid. Campbell mentioned the Hoover Task Force of 1949, the Jackson Subcommittee hearings of the early 1960s, the reforms proposed by William Macomber, and the Fitzhugh and Peterson reports on bureaucratic reorganization as examples of the frequency with which the institutional problems have been studied and the consistency of their diagnosis.

18. Henry Kissinger, "Domestic Structure and Foreign Policy," *Daedalus* 95 (Spring 1966): 503–29; and "Central Issues of American Foreign Policy," in Kermit Gordon, ed., *Agenda for the Nation* (Washington, D.C.: Brookings Institution, 1968). What is fascinating about these articles is, of course, the total absence of Congress. They are representative of Kissinger's other works. In Graubard's intellectual biography only the Congress of Vienna is mentioned in the index. Kissinger's concerns were and are substantive and centered on the executive branch, a preoccupation he shares with the "bureaucratic politics" school of political analysis in which Congress, if it appears at all, is lumped into the same scheme as the executive agencies, despite the substantial differences in responsibilities, constituency, capability, structure, and process.

19. Anthony Hartley, "American Foreign Policy in the Nixon Era," *Adelphi Papers,* no. 110 (Winter 1974–75), published by the International Institute for Strategic Studies, London, p. 2.

20. To have tried instead to heal and unite the country would have required a combination of unselfish purposefulness and foresight that is not easy to discover in the factional backbiting and private discussions, so starkly revealed in the "tapes," of the Nixon

administration. It may be that Nixon's strategy was not so much Republican as personal, not for the party but for himself, a course marked, as it was, by "vindictiveness and self-righteousness." See Theodore H. White, *Breach of Faith: The Fall of Richard Nixon* (New York: Atheneum, 1975), pp. 424–27. See also Ripon Society and Clifford W. Brown, Jr., *Jaws of Victory: The Game-Plan Politics of 1972, the Crisis of the Republican Party, and the Future of the Constitution* (Boston: Little, Brown, 1973), chap. 1, "Strategic Politics," and chap. 5, "Watergate."

21. By far the most penetrating analysis of the relevance of the balance of power to contemporary international politics is Stanley Hoffmann's "Weighing the Balance of Power," *Foreign Affairs* 50 (July 1972), especially p. 627.

22. Stanley Hoffmann, "Will the Balance Balance at Home?" *Foreign Policy,* no. 7 (Summer 1972), p. 73. Hoffman argued that consensus must be restored in order to avoid "a paralyzing, destructive continuation of indifference and distrust."

23. Louis Fisher, *Presidential Spending Power,* (Princeton, N.J.: Princeton Univ. Press, 1975), p. 201.

24. Hartley, "American Foreign Policy in the Nixon Era": "The principal innovations introduced into the methods of American foreign policy by the Nixon-Kissinger conjuncture can be defined as centralization and secrecy" (pp. 1, 9, 12). See also Marvin and Bernard Kalb, *Kissinger,* especially chapter 5 on the organization of National Security Council by Nixon and Kissinger: "Henry's Wonderful Machine," pp. 97–119 in the Dell edition.

25. Lehman, *The Executive, Congress, and Foreign Policy,* p. 215.

26. See Hughes, *The Living Presidency: The Resources and Dilemmas of the American Presidential Office,* pp. 248–68. Hughes attributed the crisis of confidence in the presidency to Vietnam. He believed that the war had overturned "the familiar political and ideological premises that had shaped and directed, year after year, all partisan debate over the rightful role of America in the world" (p. 248). The cost to the presidency was heavy indeed, no less than "the disenchantment of those political forces for so long most eloquent in its defense and most eager for its leadership. Almost certainly, no other war in the Republic's history forced so sharp a change in national attitude, or so great a surge of popular doubt about the range of Presidential power and the reliability of Presidential decision." Moreover, Hughes concluded, "such a penalty to the office would not be considered historically unjust. For so much as any conflict could be, this was a Presidential war" (p. 251).

3 The Fall of Cambodia

1. One of the most interesting of these is the substantial reform of United States foreign aid policy in the Foreign Assistance Act of 1973 (P.L. 93-189). See U.S., Congress, Committee on Foreign Affairs: Mutual Development and Cooperation Act of 1973. House Report #93-388, July 20, 1973: and Implementation of New Directions in Development Assistance Comm. Print (Washington, D.C.: U.S. Government Printing Office, July 22, 1975). For a fascinating interpretation of the presidency based on the idea of government by prerogative, see Richard M. Pious, *The American Presidency* (New York: Basic Books, 1979).

2. Congress had previously forbidden the introduction of American ground combat forces into Laos or Thailand (P.L. 91-171, 29 December 1969, sec. 643) or of advisers in Cambodia (P.L. 91-652, 5 January 1971, sec. 7); and stipulated that aid to Cambodia

should not be construed as a commitment to the defense of Cambodia (P.L. 91-652, sec. 7b); had required the president to notify Congress thirty days before granting special assistance to Cambodia (P.L. 91-652); had repeated the refusal to pay for American ground troops in Laos or Thailand (P.L. 91-668, 11 January 1971, sec. 843; 92-204, 18 December 1971, sec. 742; 92-570, 26 October 1972, sec. 741); had repealed the Gulf of Tonkin Resolution (P.L. 91-672, 12 January 1971, sec. 12); had declared it the sense of Congress and "the policy of the United States" to terminate all military operations by U.S. forces and to withdraw all American military forces by a certain date, subject to the release of prisoners of war and an accounting of the missing (P.L. 92-129, 28 September 1971; sec. 401; P.L. 92-156, 17 November 1971, sec. 601); and had limited the number of foreigners who were not Cambodians and yet were to be paid by the United States in Cambodia to eighty-five (P.L. 92-226, 7 February 1972, sec. 656). The Senate in 1972 passed a restrictive war powers bill, S. 2996, but the House passed a far milder version, and the bill died in conference. For a summary of key votes on Vietnam see *Congressional Quarterly, Weekly Report,* April 26, 1975, pp. 846 ff. See also Marjorie Niehaus, Robert Shuey, *Legislation Restricting Involvement of U. S. Military Forces in Indochina,* Congressional Research Service Issue Brief IB75022 (Library of Congress, January 21, 1975).

3. Senator Henry Jackson first released word of the correspondence. The letters then surfaced. See *Washington Post,* April 9, 10, May 1, 1975.

4. The original prohibition applied only to funds supplied under a single supplemental appropriation act (P.L. 93-50). This language was repeated in other important pieces of legislation including the Department of Defense Appropriation Acts for fiscal years 1974 and 1975, the Foreign Assistance Act of 1973, and two additional supplemental appropriation acts (P.L. 93-305 and 93-324): "None of the funds herein made available shall be obligated or expended to finance directly or indirectly combat activities by United States military forces in or over or from off the shores of North Vietnam, South Vietnam, Laos or Cambodia." The ban was also made to apply to funds already appropriated (P.L. 93-52) and to any money appropriated in the future (P.L. 93-126, 93-155). Ironically, it was the signing of the Paris Accords, the cessation of American bombing, and the return of American prisoners that persuaded supporters of the war to join opponents and force a halt in the bombing of Cambodia and a ban of all combat activities in Indochina. See the discussion of the prohibition of bombing in Daniel Rapoport, *Inside the House* (Chicago: Follett, 1975).

5. P.L. 93-148, War Powers Resolution, 7 November 1973.

6. Many students of American government have taken a skeptical view of the War Powers Resolution. A good summary of their doubts that it will prevent the president from taking the nation to war in whatever manner he judges appropriate may be found in Pious, *The American Presidency,* pp. 414–415.

7. Alarmed American officials began to warn that Congressional cuts in military assistance impaired the military effectiveness of the South Vietnamese armed forces. Their warnings came on August 8 from the highest ranking military officer in South Vietnam, Major General John E. Murray; on August 26 and September 5 from "military sources" in Saigon; and on September 12 from President Ford himself. For these dates and the others mentioned in this section see the excellent *Chronologies of Major Developments in Selected Aread of International Relations,* cumulative edition, January–December 1974, House Foreign Affairs Committee Print (Washington, D.C.: Government Printing Office, n.d.) pp. 21 ff. See also Frank Snepp, *Decent Interval: An Insider's Account of Saigon's End Told by the CIA's Chief Strategy Analyst in Vietnam* (New York: Random House, 1978).

8. Public Law 93-437. See U. S., Congress, House, Committee on International Relations, *Congress and Foreign Policy: 1974,* 94th Cong., 1st sess. (Washington, D.C.: Government Printing Office, 1975), p. 27.

9. Senate Report 93-1134, quoted in *Congressional Quarterly, Weekly Report* [hereafter, *CQ*], September 14, 1974, p. 2508.

10. Public Law 93-559.

11. H.J. Res. 1178. This was the fourth consecutive year in which Congress failed to pass a foreign aid appropriations bill before the end of December. See *Congress and Foreign Policy: 1974,* p. 7.

12. See *CQ,* December 21, 1974, pp. 3361–63.

13. Public Law 93-475 passed Congress on October 11, 1974.

14. Public Law 93-563, the Agricultural-Environmental and Consumer Protection Appropriation Act.

15. U. S., Congress, House International Relations Committee, *Chronologies of Major Developments in Selected Areas of International Relations,* January–June 1975, House Foreign Affairs Committee Print (Washington, D.C.: Government Printing Office, n.d.), p. 9.

16. Shawcross, *Sideshow,* p. 347.

17. Snepp, *Decent Interval,* p. 142.

18. *New York Times,* January 12, 1975.

19. *Washington Post,* January 13, 1975. In the *New York Times* article on the topic on January 13 a "Pentagon official" was reported to have confirmed that the reconnaissance flights also covered North Vietnam.

20. January 11, 1975, *Chronology, January–June 1975,* p. 9

21. *Weekly Compilation of Presidential Documents* [hereafter, *WCPD*], February 3, 1975, pp. 109–11.

22. *WCPD,* October 14, 1974, p. 1250.

23. Ibid., January 6, 1975, p. 3.

24. Ibid., February 3, 1975, p. 110.

25. Ibid.

26. Ibid.

27. See the Agency for International Development table and discussion of U.S. Economic and Military Aid to Indochina, 1962–1974, reproduced in *CQ,* February 1, 1975, p. 229.

28. See "Democrats Oust Hebert, Poage, Adopt Reforms," *CQ,* January 18, 1975, pp. 11–19; and "House Democratic Revolt Claims Three Chairmen," *CQ,* January 25, 1975, pp. 210–15. See also Norman J. Ornstein and David Rhode, "Congressional Reform and Political Parties in the U.S. House of Representatives," in *Parties and Elections in an Anti-Party Age: American Politics and the Crisis of Confidence,* ed. by Jeff Fishel and David Braden (Bloomington, Ind.: Univ. of Indiana Press, 1978); H. Davidson and Walter J. Oleszek, "Adaptation and Consolidation in the U.S. House of Representatives," *Legislative Studies Quarterly* 1 (1976: 37–65; and Larry Dodd, "Emergence of Party Government in the House of Representatives," *DEA News Supplement* (Division of Educational Affairs of the American Political Science Association), Summer 1976, pp. S-1–S-5.

29. See "The House: More Than Two-Thirds Democratic," and "Labor, Liberal Groups Score Election Wins," *CQ,* November 9, 1974, pp. 3064–67, 3077–84.

30. A summary of the Bolling plan, H.Res. 988, is in "Showdown Near on House Committee Reorganization," *CQ,* April 27, 1974, pp. 1026–28.

31. A useful summary of the origins and initial accomplishments of the Hansen com-

mittee is in Dodd, "Emergence of Party Government in the House of Representatives," *DEA News Supplement,* Summer 1976. For the text of the Hansen substitute as passed by the House see U.S., Congress, House, *Committee Reform Amendments of 1974: Explanation of H. Res. 988 as Adopted by the House of Representatives, October 8, 1974,* Staff Report of the Select Committee on Committees, 93rd Cong., 2nd sess. Committee Print (Washington, D.C.; Government Printing Offices, 1974).

32. Except the Budget Committee. This change was aimed at Wilbur Mills, chairman of the Ways and Means Committee. Despite his committee's very heavy work load, Mills had refused for years to establish subcommittees. See "Hansen Reorganization Plan Adopted," *CQ,* October 12, 1974, pp. 2896–98.

33. Dodd, "Emergence of Party Government," p. S-2.

34. "New Congress Organizes; No Role for Mills," *CQ,* December 7, 1974, p. 3247.

35. The members of Ways and Means had held this power since 1911. Membership of the Steering and Policy Committee was: three members elected by the caucus as a whole; the Speaker (then Carl Albert); the majority leader (then Thomas O'Neill); the caucus chairman (then Phillip Burton); twelve regional members, elected by members of Congress from their regions (West, Midwest, South, Northeast); and nine members appointed by the Speaker to represent several different constitutencies: the party whips, second- and third-term members, the black caucus, women members, and first-term members. This committee also selects committee chairmen, subject to the approval of the caucus.

36. "Congressional Government: Can It Happen? *CQ,* June 28, 1975, p. 1335.

37. In early May 1975, a few days after the fall of Vietnam, officials in the executive branch bitterly criticized the reforms in almost exactly these terms:

> "What they've got up there [on Capitol Hill] right now is an attitude of anarchy," protested one Kissinger associate, expressing a widespread complaint among foreign policy strategists.
>
> "They've overturned the seniority system in the House in committee control," said another frustrated official. "Nobody is in control in the House or the Senate. The old power centers are gone. You cannot count on anybody to deliver votes. We have to search out centers of influence. Do we have to bargain with every individual House member, every senator? Who speaks for the United States?" *(Washington Post,* May 7, 1975)

38. Murrey Marder quoted two congressional responses to these charges: "'Their problem,' a congressional veteran wryly replied with a laugh, 'is the plague of democracy.' They're not used to it; they're going to have to cope with it.'"

"'It may look like anarchy,' conceded a Senate specialist, 'for it will be a groping process. It will not be merely a process of ratification. They [the executive branch] are going to have to trim the kind of arrogance we have had for years. I think it will be healthy—very healthy.'" Ibid.

39. The House approved the name change, H. Res. 163, on March 19, 1975. Committee on Foreign Affairs, *Survey of Activities,* March 25, 1975, p. 1.

40. Ibid. The other new subcommittees were: International Operations (Wayne Hays), International Resources, Food, and Energy (Charles Diggs), International Economic Policy (Robert Nix), International Organizations (Donald Fraser), Special Subcommittee on Future Foreign Policy, Research and Development (Lestor Wolff), and International Trade and Commerce (Jonathan Bingham).

41. See committee press release by Chairman Thomas Morgan (D., Pa.), March 5, 1975. The principal documents from the House International Relations Committee are: U.S., Congress, House, Committee on International Relations, 94th Cong., 1st Sess.,

The Vietnam-Cambodia Emergency, 1975; Part I: Vietnam Evacuation and Humanitarian Assistance, April 9, 15, 16, 18, and May 7 and 8, 1975; *Part II, The Cambodia-Vietnam Debate,* March 7, 11, 12, 13, and April 14, 1975; *Part III, Vietnam Evacuation: Testimony of Ambassador Graham Martin,* January 27, 1976; and *Part IV, Cambodia Evacuation: Testimony of Ambassador John Gunther Dean,* May 5, 1976. Other important related documents are: U.S., Congress, House, Committee on International Relations, hearings before the Subcommittee on International Security and Scientific Affairs, May 7 and June 4, 1975, 94th Cong., 1st Sess., *War Powers: A Test of Compliance, Relative to the Danang Sealift, the Evacuation of Phnom Penh, the Evacuation of Saigon, and the Mayaguez Incident;* U.S., Congress, House, Committee on International Relations, *Oversight Report on Assistance to Indochina Evacuation.* H.R. 94-205 (Washington, D.C.: Government Printing Office, May 13, 1975; Comptroller General of the United States, *Executive-Legislative Communications and the Role of the Congress during International Crisis,* report to the Subcommittee on International Political and Military Affairs, September 3, 1976 [Members of Congress were questioned as to the quantity, quality, and timeliness of information available to the Congress during four international crises: the war in Angola, 1975; the evacuation of Vietnam, April 1975; and the Middle East War, October 1973]; *The New Vietnam Crisis,* Special Report no. 94-4, issued by the Democratic Study Group, U.S. House of Representatives, April 13, 1975; Larry Niksch, *South Vietnam: The Question of Continuing U.S. Military Aid,* Issue Brief IB 75011, Congressional Research Service, Library of Congress, originated February 19, 1975, updated February 28, 1975; and Robert Shuey, *Cambodia and U.S. Foreign Assistance,* Issue Brief IB 75022, Congressional Research Service, Library of Congress, originated March 11, 1975, updated April 2, 1975.

42. See, for example, *Washington Post,* January 12, February 2, 1975. See also, Snepp, *Decent Interval,* p. 139: "By the end of the first week of January the North Vietnamese were thus embarked on a strategy of escalation and improvisation whose ultimate objective and potential even they could not forsee."

43. On March 10, for example, CIA Director William Colby told the Hamilton subcommittee he doubted Cambodia could survive, even with more American aid (*Washington Post,* March 10, 1975). Four days later Secretary of Defense Schlesinger told those watching the "CBS Morning News" that the North Vietnamese offensive was "extensive," but still not a countrywide assault like that of 1972. Schlesinger announced his belief that the North Vietnamese probably would wait until 1976 to intensify their attacks, for the administration would find it even harder in an election year to persuade Congress to aid the Saigon government (*Washington Post,* March 14, 1976). On March 18, Thieu began the ill-fated withdrawal from the Central Highlands.

44. Ibid., January 30, 31, 1975.

45. See, for example, Secretary Kissinger's speech on executive-legislative relations on January 24, 1975, *Department of State Bulletin,* February 3, 1975; and his news conference a few days later (*Washington Post,* January 29, 1975). Kissinger liked to color his appeals with dark hints about a "crisis of authority" in the Western democracies. See, for example, the column by Rowland Evans and Robert Novak, *Washington Post,* February 6, 1975. President Ford sang the other note in a meeting with the congressional leaders, saying: "The odds are in favor of disaster if we don't do anything" (*Washington Post,* January 30, 1975).

46. See *Washington Post,* February 5, 1975.

47. Ibid., February 4, 1975.

48. Evans and Novak, ibid., February 6, 1975. They quoted a Republican member of Congress at the meeting as saying: "I was just hoping the President wouldn't pick me to

go." Evans and Novak attributed the idea to send a congressional delegation to Indochina to a "key Pentagon official," who had been favorably impressed by the South Vietnamese on his many trips to their country and who thought they would impress members of Congress in the same way. See their column in the *Washington Post,* February 24, 1975.

49. Snepp, *Decent Interval,* pp. 150–51.

50. Shawcross, *Sideshow,* pp. 348–49.

51. *Washington Post,* February 9, 1975. Awkwardly for the president, Army Chief of Staff General Frederich Weyand had just said he believed major aid would be needed for five to ten years (ibid., February 7, 1975).

52. Ibid., March 4, 1975.

53. Two aides from the Senate Foreign Relations Committee made their own journey in late March (Richard Moose and Charles Miessner), as did two from the House Foreign Affairs Committee (Jack Sullivan and Jack Brady).

54. Representatives Abzug and Fraser refused to support any additional military aid.

55. Letter of President Ford to House Speaker Carl Albert; news conference of Secretary Kissinger, *Washington Post,* February 25, 1975.

56. During testimony to a Foreign Relations Subcommittee, for example, Senator Humphrey warned Assistant Secretary Habib to "give serious consideration" to the possibility that Congress would reject both supplemental requests. "Isn't this a loser?" Humphrey asked (ibid.).

57. Passman's end run was possible because on March 1 the regular foreign aid bill had still not passed the Congress, nine months into the fiscal year it covered. On March 7 yet another Senate-House agreement continued funding until March 25.

58. Ibid., March 5, 1975.

59. Article by Philip McCombs, "U.S. Legislators Reassess Views Following Indochina Aid Tour," Ibid., March 4, 1975.

60. "Dear Colleague" letters serve a number of purposes, not necessarily restricted to their ostensible purpose of persuading others to support a legislative proposal. They help count noses in advance of votes, line up prestigious cosponsors, allow small legislative accounts to be settled, and provide copy for constituent mail.

61. President Ford evoked the dangers to world peace that he believed would result from a refusal to vote money for the Cambodians, observing that the United States would be saying "to all the world that war pays." Aggression would increase, and the United States would have shown that if negotiations are protracted the United States will tire of the struggle and abandon its friends, and force will prevail (*Washington Post,* March 6, 1975). See also his letter to Speaker Carl Albert of February 25 in *WCPD,* March 3, 1975, p. 214.

62. A copy of the department statement is reproduced in the records of the Hamilton subcommittee, U.S., Congress, House, Committee on Foreign Affairs and its Special Subcommittee on Investigations, *The Vietnam-Cambodia Emergency, 1975, Part II: The Cambodia-Vietnam Debate* [hereafter *Cambodia-Vietnam Debate*], pp. 247–48.

63. Ibid., pp. 249–52.

64. On a military stalemate leading to negotiations, see ibid., especially 243, 255–57; on the indefinite term of any assistance, pp. 265–79; on holding until the river rises, pp. 278–79; on the nature of the U.S. commitment to Cambodia, pp. 287–88. About the fear of a Khmer Rouge massacre, Habib's position was moderate and prescient: "If the present government falls, I think the impact within Cambodia . . . would be an unbelievable transformation of that society against the wishes of its general population and through the use of great force. I think that there certainly would be what people freely

call the bloodbath, but in any event great cruelty (ibid., p. 281).

65. Shawcross, *Sideshow,* p. 355; Snepp, *Decent Interval,* pp. 177–82.

66. *New York Times,* March 9, 1975.

67. *CQ,* March 15, 1975, p. 552.

68. *Cambodia-Vietnam Debate,* p. 292.

69. Ibid., p. 293. Fraser said that if Congress refused to give any aid the Cambodian government might run out of ammunition in April and the war would end in an unstructured way. "It ought to be a negotiated end—you might call it a negotiated surrender, if you will, but an orderly transfer of power."

70. Ibid.

71. Ibid., p. 294.

72. Ibid.

73. Ibid, pp. 306–7.

74. Ibid., p. 308.

75. Ibid., p. 337.

76. Ibid., p. 344. At 15 percent of each ceiling, the amounts came very close to McCloskey's recommendation: $123.75 million in military aid and $79.65 million in food.

77. *Military and Economic Situation in Cambodia: Report of a Staff Survey Team to Cambodia,* Confidential Committee print, Committee on Foreign Affairs, 84th Cong. 1st sess., March 13, 1975. The author was given access to the confidential report in the files of the committee.

78. In the committee files are unpublished draft reports by Brady on the military and supply situations in South Vietnam and by Sullivan on political and economic conditions in the country. The report on Vietnam was not published because it was overtaken by the disastrous retreat from the highlands and the fall of Saigon. The author was given access to these manuscripts in the files of the committee. They reflect the judgments of the two senior staff members on the deteriorating situation in Vietnam and are referred to in the discussion of the committee's response to the request for aid to South Vietnam.

79. *Vietnam Aid—The Painful Options,* Report of Senator Sam Nunn to the Committee on Armed Services, United States Senate, February 12, 1975, 94th Cong. 1st sess.

80. *United States Aid to Indochina,* Committee print, Committee on Foreign Affairs, 83rd Cong., 2nd sess., July 1974, p. 19.

81. Ibid.

82. *Military and Economic Situation in Cambodia,* March 13, 1975, p. 2.

83. Ibid.

84. Ibid., p. 14.

85. Ibid.

86. See Shawcross, *Sideshow,* pp. 322–43. My discussion of the "controlled solution" is based on Shawcross's account.

87. Shawcross insists that the United States destroyed any hope of returning Sihanouk to Phnom Penh. However, it would be hard to argue that the French government disagreed with the Ford administration about Cambodia and Sihanouk, whatever the views of its ambassador in Peking. Giscard endorsed the American position on Cambodia during a summit meeting with President Ford in Martinique in mid-December 1974. Ford doesn't even mention Cambodia in his discussion of the summit in his memoirs. See *A Time to Heal: The Autobiography of Gerald R. Ford* (New York: Harper and Row, 1979), pp. 221-23. See also Shawcross, *Sideshow,* pp. 341–42.

88. Personal correspondence with John Sullivan. Ford doesn't mention these considerations in his memoirs, although he refers to the importance of safeguarding U.S. credibility *(A Time to Heal,* p. 250). Snep insists that strategic considerations of credibil-

ity were paramount *(Decent Interval,* pp. 176–77). Shawcross accepts the credibility thesis and adds the administration's wish to blame Congress (*Sideshow,* pp. 350–51).

89. Shawcross, *Sideshow,* pp. 353, 355–57.

90. *Washington Post,* March 11, 1975.

91. *Cambodia-Vietnam Debate,* pp. 342, 348, 352.

92. The compromise appears in ibid., p. 362.

93. *Washington Post,* March 12, 1975.

94. In favor were Gale McGee (D., Wyo.), Jacob Javits (R., N.Y.), Clifford Case (R., N.J.), and Hugh Scott (R., Pa.); opposed were Hubert Humphrey (D., Minn.), Frank Church (D., Idaho), and George McGovern (D., S.Dak.).

95. *Washington Post,* March 12, 1975; *CQ,* March 15, 1975, p. 553.

96. *Cambodia-Vietnam Debate,* pp. 375–76.

97. Chairman Hamilton asked Michael Van Dusen of the committee staff to begin the markup by explaining the major changes in the subcommittee draft. Van Dusen said that the most important change was the direction by Congress that the United States end the Cambodian conflict by June 30, 1975. The money amounts were given, he said, to make certain that the administration used some of the funds for food and didn't put it all into military assistance, as would have been possible under the earlier draft. The reference to the UN was intended to make available UN forces to "monitor the end of the conflict perhaps or to help with the distribution of rice and food" (ibid., pp. 376–77).

98. "This is the understanding," DuPont added, "and I so informed the administration that there will be no support out of my corner for any additional military aid in fiscal year 1976" (ibid., p. 380). Shawcross reported that the administration agreed to stop military aid to Cambodia on July 1 *(Sideshow,* p. 351).

99. Harrington asked Jack Sullivan how one could take as reliable the Cambodian government figures on their ammunition shortage. Sullivan answered that he and Jack Brady had relied on figures supplied by the U.S. military *(Cambodia-Vietnam Debate,* pp. 383–8).

100. Ibid., p. 389.

101. See the chapters on the Foreign Affairs Committee in Richard F. Fenno, Jr., *Congressmen in Committees* (Boston: Little, Brown, 1973).

102. Ibid.

103. *Cambodia-Vietnam Debate,* p. 399.

104. The critical exchange occurred between Ingersoll and Zablocki:

> ZABLOCKI: Mr. Secretary, the executive branch agrees to the compromise. Did I understand you correctly?
> INGERSOLL: Yes, sir.
> ZABLOCKI: Does the executive branch agree to setting a date of June 30, 1975?
> INGERSOLL: No, sir, we don't believe that would be correct, but we do agree to the compromise proposed by the Senate. (Ibid., p. 401)

105. Ibid., pp. 403–4.

106. Ibid., pp. 404–5.

107. Ibid., p. 411.

108. Ibid., p. 413.

109. Ibid., p. 415–16.

110. Ibid., p. 417.

111. The text of the Solarz amendment is in ibid., pp. 421–22. Solarz would have prohibited the use of force in carrying out the evacuation.

4 Vietnam: The Next Step

1. *Washington Post,* March 15, 1975.
2. Frank Snepp, *Decent Interval,* p. 193.
3. Ibid., March 18, 1975. See also *New York Times,* March 18, 1975.
4. Ibid.
5. *New York Times* and *Washington Post,* March 18, 1975; the analysis by Sydney Shanberg, "Confusion over Cambodian Aid"; *New York Times,* March 25, 1975; and *Washington Post,* March 29, 1975.
6. See especially his remarks in the Senate on March 26. *Congressional Record,* S5209–S5212.
7. Quoted in the *New York Times,* March 19, 1975.
8. *Washington Post,* March 19, 1975.
9. Ibid.
10. *New York Times,* March 19, 1975.
11. These amounts were based on Ambassador Martin's recommendations. See Snepp, *Decent Interval,* pp. 153–54.
12. Ibid. "Senior Administration Officials" also told Gelb they regarded the Cambodian aid as "much more urgent, but far less important" than the emergency supplemental aid for Vietnam. See also the long article by Murrey Marder in the *Washington Post,* March 27, 1975. Also involved in the negotiations were the U.S. ambassador to Vietnam, Graham Martin, Assistant Secretary of State Habib, and Assistant Secretary of State Robert McCloskey.
13. Copy of the letter in the author's possession. The letter was signed by many first-termers, but also by several members of the Foreign Affairs Committee, and such prominent representatives as Andrew Young and Phillip Burton.
14. *New York Times,* March 20, 1975.
15. *CQ,* March 22, 1975, p. 605.
16. *Washington Star,* March 20, 1975. On Republican pressure on Mr. Ford to attack Congress, see the Evans and Novak column, *Washington Post,* March 19, 1975.
17. Snepp, *Decent Interval,* pp. 210, 213. See also Gareth Porter, *A Peace Denied: the United States, Vietnam, and the Paris Agreement* (Bloomington, Ind.: Indiana Univ. Press, 1975), p. 273.
18. Snepp, *Decent Interval,* pp. 213–14; *Washington Post,* March 20, 21, 1975.
19. *Washington Post,* March 23, 1975.
20. *New York Times,* March 20, 1975. Copies of the documents are in the author's possession.
21. Snepp, *Decent Interval,* pp. 161–62.
22. See Porter, *Peace Denied,* pp. 272–273.
23. *Washington Post,* March 23, 24, 1975.
24. Drew Middleton writing from Vietnam, *New York Times,* March 25, 1975.
25. Articles by John Finney and Drew Middleton, *New York Times,* April 1, 1975.
26. Text of Press Conference, March 26, 1975, Department of State, Bureau of Public Affairs, PR 172/51, p. 2.
27. Ibid., p. 7.
28. Ibid.
29. Ibid., p. 2.
30. Ibid.

31. *Washington Post,* March 27, 1975.
32. Shawcross, *Sideshow,* p. 358.
33. Washington Post, April 1, 1975. This article included a reference to "a growing belief among White House officials that the South Vietnamese government cannot be saved, although no one has said as much directly."
34. Snepp gives April 6 as the date of the fall of Camranh Bay (*Decent Interval,* p. 275).
35. *Weekly Compilation of Presidential Documents,* April 7, 1975, pp. 328, 332.
36. For the text of a presidential statement about the refugees on March 29 see *WCPD,* April 4, 1975, p. 319.
37. Ibid., p. 331.
38. Ibid., p. 329.
39. For some hints about these discussions see the statements by Defense Secretary Schlesinger that Mr. Ford had ruled out B-52 strikes in *New York Times,* April 7, 1975; and the wish by the administration officials to have the United States make a strong show of strength in an article by John Herber, *New York Times,* April 7, 1975.
40. *Washington Post,* April 4, 1975.
41. *Washington Post,* March 31, 1975.
42. Ibid.
43. Ibid., April 4, 1975.
44. *New York Times,* April 7, 1975.
45. See the commentary by Rod MacLeish, *Washington Post,* April 8, 1975.
46. *New York Times,* April 7, 1975.
47. *Washington Post,* April 4, 1975.
48. These statements are in *Department of State Bulletin,* April 28, 1975, pp. 548, col. 2; 549, col. 1; 551, col. 2.
49. Ibid., pp. 548, col. 1; 549, col. 2; 551, col. 2; 554, col. 1.
50. Ibid., p. 552, col. 1.
51. Ibid., p. 553, col. 1.
52. Ibid., p. 554, col. 1.
53. Ibid., p. 555, col. 1.
54. *New York Times,* April 7, 1975.
55. *Washington Post,* April 7, 1975.
56. Ibid.
57. *New York Times,* April 7, 1975.
58. Snepp, *Decent Interval,* p. 315.
59. *New York Times,* April 9, 1975.
60. For a partial list of those who gave this report, see "New Indochina Aid Strongly Opposed," *Washington Post,* April 8, 1975.
61. Ibid.
62. Ibid.
63. *New York Times,* April 9, 1975.
64. *Washington Post,* April 9, 1975.
65. Quoted in the article by Murrey Marder in *Washington Post,* April 9, 1975. See also the articles by George Wilson, *Washington Post,* April 10, 1975, and John Finney, *New York Times,* April 9, 1975.
66. Quoted in *Washington Post,* April 10, 1975.
67. *Washington Post,* April 10, 1975.
68. Quoted in *Washington Post,* April 10, 1975.

69. From the text of Mr. Ford's address in *WCPD,* April 14, 1975, p. 364. The text of the order to evacuate Cambodia, dated April 12, 1975, is in ibid., p. 373. Mr. Ford also complied with section 4 of the War Powers Act and reported to the Congress that American troops were being used in the evacuation. See House Document 94-105, in *Congressional Record,* April 14, 1975, H2706–H2707.

70. *WCPD,* p. 361. If this seems too strongly stated, one need only examine the text to be assured it is not: "The chances for an enduring peace after the last American fighting man left Vietnam in 1973, rested on two publicly stated premises: first, that if necessary, the United States would help sustain the terms of the Paris accords it signed two years ago, and second, that the United States would provide adequate economic and military assistance to South Vietnam."

71. Ibid.

72. Ibid., pp. 362, 363.

73. Ibid., p. 364. Several other areas had been affected by congressional action from which the president also sought relief: the embargo on arms for Turkey, the provisions of the 1974 Trade Act which restricted trade with members of OPEC and denied most-favored-nation treatment to the USSR, and the oversight of U.S. intelligence agencies and their activities.

74. Quoted in *Los Angeles Times,* April 10, 1975. This statement was drafted under the close supervision of Henry Kissinger, *Washington Post,* April 10, 1975.

75. To avoid confusion I have combined the sums involved. For fiscal year 1975, it will be recalled, the Armed Services Committees had authorized $1 billion in military aid, but only $700 million had been appropriated. This left $300 million already authorized. The proposals actually defeated, in the Armed Services Committee, therefore, were for $215 million, $149 million, $101 million, and $70 million, which would have been added to the unused $300 million.

76. *CQ,* April 19, 1975, p. 775.

77. See *Washington Post,* April 22, 23, 1975.

78. See article by Murrey Marder, ibid., April 12, 1975.

79. Just before the president's address, Richard Moose and Charles Meissner, members of the staff of the Senate Foreign Relations, reported from Saigon that it might already be too late to evacuate all the Americans in Saigon, let alone tens of thousands of South Vietnamese.

80. Personal interviews with Congressmen Hamilton and Fraser, and House Foreign Affairs Committee staff members Sullivan and Brady.

81. *Cambodia-Vietnam Debate,* p. 429.

82. Ibid.

83. Ibid., pp. 430–37. Gardiner also said that several emergency steps had been taken: virtually all remaining foreign aid funds had been allotted for refugee relief; 100,000 tons of rice and food supplements would be given as grants under P.L. 480. The exact request was to authorize only $73 million in new money and to use $177 million in aid funds previously authorized but not appropriated (see pp. 431, 439, 440). The administration bill submitted to the Speaker of the House was given the number H.R. 5961; the text is in ibid., p. 465.

84. Ibid., p. 438.

85. Ibid., p. 441, see also p. 446.

86. Ibid., p. 440.

87. The text of the administration bill, numbered H.R. 5960, is in ibid., p. 441. For the substance of the acts named by the administration, and all others restricting or prohibit-

ing combat by American troops in Indochina, see Marjorie Niehaus, Robert Shuey, *Legislation Restricting Involvement of U.S. Military Forces in Indochina,* Congressional Research Service Issue Brief IB 75022 (Library of Congress, January 21, 1975).

88. See especially ibid., pp. 449–50.

89. Ibid., pp. 465–88.

90. Snepp, *Decent Interval,* p. 284.

91. Quoted in ibid., p. 359.

92. Ibid., p. 360.

93. Letter from John Sullivan, August 10, 1979. Snepp, *Decent Interval,* pp. 295–96, discusses the origin of the figure of one million Vietnamese evacuees. A group of junior bureaucrats with some experience of Vietnam and responsibility for policymaking decided just before the fall of Danang on March 30 to try to speed the evacuation of Americans in order to be able to evacuate the well over a million South Vietnamese they had calculated should be removed from the country.

94. Article by Murrey Marder and Spencer Rich, *Washington Post,* April 15, 1975. See also *New York Times,* April 15, 1975. See also Gerald Ford, *A Time to Heal: The Autobiography of Gerald R. Ford* (New York: Harper and Row, 1979), p. 255.

95. *Washington Post,* April 11, 1975.

96. Ibid. Underlining this concern, the Senate Democratic Caucus on April 14 approved the following statement by Majority Leader Mansfield: "It is one thing to use U.S. force briefly, to safeguard and to remove Americans from a dangerous area . . . It should be quite another matter if the presence of such forces in a danger zone for the removal of non-Americans should produce new U.S. combat casualties and become the basis for reinvolvement in the military conflict in Vietnam in any way, shape or form" (quoted in *CQ,* April 19, 1975, p. 776).

97. The actions of the committee during this period and the provisions of H.R. 6096 are described in the House Report no. 94–155. See also Appendix 4.

98. In the opinion of the Legislative Counsel to the Senate, the president has no legal authority to use force to evacuate South Vietnamese citizens from Vietnam. Counsel was prepared to admit that the president *may* have a "limited constitutional power" to use force to rescue Americans from danger abroad. See Appendix to Senate Report no. 94-88.

99. P.L. 91-171, Department of Defense Appropriation Act, 1970, December 29, 1969, Section 643; repeated in P.L. 91-668, Department of Defense Appropriations FY 1971, January 11, 1971, Section 843; P.L. 92-204, Department of Defense Appropriations, FY 1972, December 18, 1971, Section 742; and P.L. 92-570, Department of Defense Appropriations, FY 1973, October 26, 1972, Section 741.

100. P.L. 91-652, Supplemental Foreign Assistance Authorization 1970, January 5, 1971, Section 7.

101. P.L. 91—672, Foreign Military Sales Act, January 12, 1971, Section 12. See the informative discussion of the Nixon administration's response to the repeal of the Tonkin Gulf Resolution in John Lehman, *The Executive, Congress, and Foreign Policy: Studies of the Nixon Administration* (New York: Praeger, 1976), pp. 61–66, 73.

102. P.L. 92-129, Military Selective Services Act, September 28, 1971, Section 401; P.L. 92-156, Military Procurement Authorization Act, FY 1972, November 17, 1971, Section 601.

103. P.L. 92-226, Substitute Foreign Military and Related Assistance Authorization, February 7, 1972, Section 656; and P.L. 93-559, Foreign Assistance Act of 1974, December 30, 1974, Section 38.

104. P.L. 93-50, Second Supplemental Appropriation Act, FY 1973, July 1, 1973,

Section 307; and repeated in P.L. 93-52, Section 108; P.L. 93-118, Continuing Appropriations, FY 1974, October 4, 1973; P.L. 93-124, Continuing Appropriations, FY 1974, October 16, 1973; P.L. 93-126, Department of State Appropriations Authorization Act of 1973, October 18, 1973, Section 13; P.L. 93-155, Military Procurement Authorization Act, FY 1974, November 16, 1973, Section 808; P.L. 93-189, Foreign Assistance Act of 1973, December 17, 1973, Section 30; P.L. 93-228, Department of Defense Appropriation Act, FY 1974, January 2, 1974, Section 741; P.L. 93-305, Second Supplemental Appropriation Act, FY 1974, June 8, 1974, Section 405; P.L. 93-324, Continuing Appropriation Act, FY 1975, June 30, 1975, Section 110; P.L. 93-437, Department of Defense Appropriation Act, FY 1975, October 8, 1974, Section 839.

105. P.L. 93-148, War Powers Resolution, November 7, 1973, Section 26.

106. Ibid., Sections 3–6.

107. Letter from Assistant Secretary of State for Congressional Relations Marshall Wright to Senator Thomas F. Eagleton, November 30, 1973, quoted in Niehaus and Shuey,*Legislation Restricting Involvement of U.S. Military Forces in Indochina.*

108. Testimony of Monroe Leigh, legal adviser to the Department of State. U.S., Congress, Hearings before the Subcommittee on International Security and Scientific Affairs, Committee on International Relations, May 7 and June 4, 1975, *War Powers: A Test of Compliance,* 94th Congress, 1st sess., (Washington, 1975), p. 90, quoted in Pious, *The American Presidency,* p. 404.

109. See the colloquy between the legal adviser to the Department of State, Herbert J. Hansell, and Senator Dick Clark quoted in Richard M. Pious, *The American Presidency,* (New York: Basic Books, 1979), pp. 414–15.

110. Snepp, *Decent Interval,* p. 371.

111. *Washington Post,* April 20, 1975.

112. Ibid., April 22, 1975.

113. Snepp, *Decent Interval,* p. 371.

114. *WCPD,* April 21, 1975, p. 390.

115. Ibid.

116. Ibid., p. 393.

117. Ibid., April 28, 1975, p. 417.

118. Ibid., p. 416.

119. Ibid., p. 417.

120. Ibid.

121. "Strength through Adversity," *Department of State Bulletin,* May 5, 1975, p. 558.

122. Ibid.

123. Ibid., p. 560. These thoughts could have been lifted almost word for word from Kissinger's scholarly writing. See especially "The Nature of Statesmanship," the concluding chapter in Kissinger's *A World Restored* (New York: Grosset & Dunlap, 1964), particularly at pp. 326 and 329.

124. Kissinger, *A World Restored,* p. 329.

125. "Strength through Adversity," p. 560.

126. Ibid., p. 561. Ambassador Martin saw the failure to submit the Paris Agreements to Congress as one of the greatest tragedies of the cease-fire period. (Snepp, *Decent Interval,* p. 579).

127. "Strength through Adversity," p. 562.

128. Ibid.

129. Ibid.

130. Ibid., p. 563.

5 Last Act

1. Snepp, *Decent Interval,* p. 372. See also p. 364.
2. The stenographic record of the "markup" of H. R. 6096 has not been published. The author was given access to the record in the committee files. Since the record is unpublished I do not quote from it, but give page references in order to make it possible to verify the accuracy of my summaries and paraphrases of statements by committee members.
3. Stenographic record of the session of the full House International Relations Committee to consider H. R. 6096, 17 April 1975, unpublished document in committee files, pp. 1–4; [hereafter cited as Markup, H. R. 6096].
4. The decision to accept Chairman Morgan's proposal appears in ibid., p. 31; the exchange on the question of presidential authority occurs during the preceding twenty-five pages.
5. Text of amendment in ibid., pp. 35, 75.
6. Ibid., pp. 52–55. Nine members were absent.
7. Ibid., p. 87. There were not even the five votes needed to have a roll call vote.
8. Ibid., pp. 65–68. Those voting in favor were: Hays, Hamilton, Bingham, Harrington, Riegle, Solarz, Meyner. Ten members were absent.
9. Ibid., p. 92.
10. Ibid., p. 105–8. Those in favor of the Whalen amendment were: Wolff, Harrington, Riegle, Collins, Mayner, Bonker, Whalen. Nine members were absent.
11. Ibid., pp. 108–9.
12. Ibid., pp. 118–21.
13. Ibid. Those in favor were: Fountain, Bingham, Harrington, Riegle, Meyner, Bonker, Whalen. Eight members were absent.
14. Ibid., p. 145.
15. By voice vote, ibid., p. 158.
16. The votes were as follows: Meyner amendment: defeated 7 to 17; voting in favor were Bingham, Harrington, Riegle, Collins, Solarz, Meyner, Bonker; ten members were absent (ibid., pp. 171–74). DuPont-Biester fifteen-day amendment: defeated 8 to 14. Voting in favor were Wolfe, Bingham, Riegle, Solarz, Meyner, DuPont, Biester, Whalen; twelve members were absent. Solarz amendment to allow thirty days for evacuation was defeated by voice vote (ibid., pp. 188–192). DuPont-Biester substitute: defeated 7 to 16. Voting in favor were Hamilton, Wolff, DuPont, Biester, Lagomarsino, Meyner, Bonker (ibid., p. 204–7).
17. House Report 94-155, April 18, 1975, pp. 3–4.
18. The laws named were section 839 of Public Law 93-437; section 30 of Public Law 93-189; section 806 of Public Law 93-155; section 13 of Public Law 93-126; and section 108 of Public Law 93-52.
19. The precise wording authorized the use of force to evacuate the four categories of individuals "Provided, that United States Armed Forces necssary to carry out their evacuation do not exceed those necessary to carry out the evacuation of (a), (b), and (c) above. The authority granted by this section shall not permit or extend to any action or conduct not essential to effectuate and protect the evacuation referred in this section."
20. Ibid., pp. 9, 10.
21. Executive Branch Position Paper, in author's possession.

22. In section 7, the Senate Committee struck boldly at the administration's policy. The United States indeed should help relieve the suffering in South Vietnam and Cambodia, they stated, and they authorized the appropriation of an additional $100 million specifically for that purpose. Although the restrictions on the use of force were more stringent in the Senate than House bill, the Senate provided more new funds—$200 million rather than $150 million.

23. Section 7 of S. 1484, particularly 7 (b) (2): "Funds made available under this section shall be furnished under the direction and control of the United Nations or its Specialized Agencies or under the auspices of other international organizations, international agreements, or voluntary relied agencies." The text of the committee bill may be found in the *Congressional Record,* 94th Cong., 1st sess., vol. 121, no. 61, April 21, 1975, S6398–6399.

24. The president was required to describe "fully and completely" the amount of each type of aid, the expected recipients, the names of the organizations distributing the aid, and the means of distribution.

25. Section 4a of the War Powers Resolution requires the president when introducing American combat forces into hostilities—or into a foreign country without a declaration of war—to report to the Speaker of the House and the president pro tempore of the Senate giving the circumstances necessitating the introduction of the troops, the constitutional and legislative authority for such action, and the estimated scope and duration of the conflict. The president, under section 4b must provide all information requested by Congress and under 4c must submit periodic reports until the troops are withdrawn. The text of the War Powers Resolution, Public Law 93-148, 93rd Congress, H. J. Res. 542, may be found in the Senate Foreign Relations Committee Report on the Vietnam Contingency Act of 1975, Senate Report no. 94-88, April 18, 1975, appendix B, pp. 17–22.

26. These are described in the section-by-section analysis of the bill in ibid., pp. 9–10.

27. Senate Report 94-88, p. 3.

28. Ibid., pp. 4, 5.

29. Ibid., p. 3.

30. See Senate Majority Leader Mansfield's comments to Senator Jacob Javits (R., N.Y.) in *Congressional Record,* April 22, 1975, S. 6500. See ibid., April 23, 1975, S. 6640–6641 for the record vote and the text of the amended bill.

31. April 21, 1975, S6403–6405. See also ibid., April 22, 1975, S6503.

32. Ibid., April 21, 1975, S6406. See also ibid., April 22, 1975, S6504.

33. Ibid., April 22, 1975, S6501.

34. Ibid.

35. Ibid.

36. Ibid. S6502–6503.

37. Ibid., S6503.

38. Ibid.

39. Ibid., April 21, 1975, S6405–6406.

40. Ibid., April 22, 1975, S6500.

41. Ibid., S6399.

42. Ibid., S6500.

43. See ibid., S6519–6523.

44. See ibid., April 23, 1975, S6631–6632.

45. Ibid., April 23, 1975. Hatfield's amendment, cosponsored by Biden and Edward Kennedy (D., Mass.), is at S6623–6625. Brooke's amendment is at S6525.

46. For the first, see ibid., S6606. The amendments requiring the president to give

daily reports made formal a practice that Mr. Ford had been following. See Senator Sparkman's comments, S6606. For the increase in aid, see ibid., S6624–6625. Senators Kennedy and Biden were cosponsors of the change.

47. Ibid., S6620–6624.

48. Ibid., S6608.

49. Both the Clark and Case amendments are in ibid., S6634. In its final form the Clark amendment required the president to report to the chairmen of the Judiciary and Armed Services in the Senate, in addition to the chairman of Foreign Relations and the Speaker of the House.

50. Ibid., S6626. For Cranston's amendment and arguments in favor, see ibid., S6625–S6628.

51. Ibid., S6628.

52. See Michael Barone, Grant Ujifusa, Douglas Matthews, *The Almanac of American Politics, 1976* (New York: E. P. Dutton, 1975), p. 128.

53. *Congressional Record,* April 23, 1975, S6612.

54. Ibid., S6613.

55. Ibid., S6615.

56. Ibid., S6616. Voting Yea were: Abourezk, Biden, Burdick, Gravel, Haskell, McGovern, McIntyre, Metcalf, Schweiker, Weicker.

57. Ibid., S6630. Those voting Yea were: Abourezk, Biden, Burdick, Robert C. Byrd, Hartke, Haskell, Helms, Laxalt, McClure, Schweiker, William L. Scott, Weicker.

58. Ibid., S6628, 6630.

59. Ibid., S6630. See also the remarks of Senator Roth critical of the reluctance to aid South Vietnam: "What European, Israeli, or Japanese will trust us in the future if we fail to carry out our remaining moral obligations?" S6633–6634.

60. The text of this Clark amendment is at ibid., S6616.

61. Ibid., S6617.

62. Ibid.

63. Ibid., S6618–6619.

64. Ibid., S6619.

65. The vote is given in ibid., S6623–6624. Voting for were: Abourezk, Biden, Brooke, Burdick, Clark, Cranston, Ford, Gravel, Gary Hart, Philip Hart, Hartke, Haskell, Hathaway, Leahy, Magnuson, Mansfield, McClelland, McGovern, McIntyre, Metcalf, Mondale, Nelson, Packwood, Proxmire, Ribicoff, Schweiker, Stevenson, Talmadge, Tunney, Weicker, Williams.

66. The vote is given in ibid., S6640. Voting against were: Abourezk, Bellmon, Biden, Burdick, Clark, Cranston, Gravel, Hartke, Haskell, Helms, Mansfield, McClure, Schweiker, William L. Scott, Stevenson, Tunney, Weicker. Though not present, Hatfield announced a "nay" vote. Pell and Johnston, who were also absent, announced "yea" votes.

67. See the statements by Senators Biden (S6636–6637), Haskell (S6638), and Abourezk (S6639).

68. Text of Edgar substitute is in *Congressional Record,* April 23, 1975, H3144.

69. Ibid., p. H3152.

70. Text is in ibid. For the other amendments by Burton, Ottinger, Carney, and Solarz see ibid., H3152, H3154, and 3155.

71. See ibid., H3153–3154.

72. Text is in ibid., H3160. The Eckhardt substitute omitted the committee amendments proposed during the markup by Fountain and Solarz and approved to the original

bill and instead of the limitations in section 4 added the following to the original section 5: "Nothing in this Act is intended to grant, extend, or delegate to the President any of the war powers of Congress which cannot be exercised by the President unless granted, extended, or delegated by Congress. It is the intent of Congress in passing this Act to provide only an authorization for the use of funds for the purposes and under the conditions herein stated."

73. These proposals and the votes on them are to be found in ibid., H3161–3163.

74. These amendments and votes may be found in ibid., H3160, H3163–3165.

75. Ibid., H3165.

76. The parliamentary situation was complex. The rule under which H.R. 6096 was considered waived points of order against sections 3 and 6 (the money sections), but did not waive points of order against amendments. On this technicality the chairman ruled that under clause 5 of rule XXI of the 94th Congress the Edgar and Eckhardt substitutes with their various amendments were out of order. See the discussion in ibid., H3166.

77. Ibid., H3167.

78. These were introduced respectively by Rousselot, Ashbrook, and Ashbrook: ibid., H3196; H3198.

79. Ibid., H3185.

80. The Collins amendment repeated the bill's limit on the evacuation of South Vietnamese to those whose lives were directly and imminently threatened and then specified the kinds of military activities that could be used for their rescue ("combat activity, any involvement in hostilities, or any military or paramilitary operation") provided these actions were needed for the rescue of Americans and their dependents (ibid., H3193–3194).

81. Ibid., H3201, H3202.

82. All amendments and votes may be found in ibid., H3186–3205.

83. Ibid., H3211–3212.

84. Interview with Jack Sullivan, May 1975.

85. The Senate bill allowed only $100 million for evacuation and humanitarian aid, and provided $100 million for humanitarian purposes. For the conference report see U.S. House of Representatives, Report no. 94-176, 94th Cong., 1st sess.

86. Ibid., p. 2.

87. Ibid., pp. 2–3.

88. Ibid., p. 3. Powers Resolution.

89. Ibid., pp. 3–4.

90. Letter from Gerald R. Ford to the author, August 31, 1979, author's files.

91. See the reports in the *Washington Post,* April 30, 1975.

92. Ibid., May 2, 1975.

93. Pious in his *American Presidency* concludes that the failure to pass the evacuation authorization left Congress looking "ridiculous." This seems to be an exaggeration. Moreover, it overlooks the impact on the president of the evident reluctance in Congress in regard to any use of force or any actions that would have reengaged the United States in a war in Vietnam.

94. John Brady, now Chief of Staff of the Foreign Affairs Committee, views the decision to pull the conference report in a somewhat different way: "The conference report did not come to a vote in late April of 1975 because the Leadership did not consult with the Chairman of the Foreign Affairs Committee and succumbed to the pressure of Bella Abzug and others who objected to giving the President any flexibility whatsoever with respect to the use of force during the evacuation" (letter from John J. Brady to the

author, October 5, 1979, author's files).

95. The appropriations bill, H.R. 6894, had already been approved. See *CQ*, May 24, 1975, p. 1075, and July 5, 1975, p. 1420.

6 The Lessons of Failure

1. Interview of General Brent Scowcroft, 10 January 1979, Washington, D.C., by the author. Peter Rodman, a close assistant of Secretary Kissinger, also confirmed that aid became rescue in April (interview with the author, 10 January 1979, Washington, D.C.).

2. Interview with General Scowcroft. Peter Rodman described U.S. objectives in April as the evacuation of Americans and as many South Vietnamese as possible "with a minimum of disaster." The point was to stabilize the military and political situation and "to get out in an orderly way over a couple of weeks" (interview with Peter Rodman).

3. Interviews with Peter Rodman and General Scowcroft.

4. The sensitivity of the South Vietnamese government and military to U.S. policy emerges clearly in a series of interviews of former South Vietnamese officials conducted by the Rand Corporation in 1975 and published in December 1978. The South Vietnamese who were interviewed believed that after the Paris Agreements were signed the United States callously and incomprehensibly abandoned South Vietnam, and this abandonment, in their view, caused the defeat of 1975. It was not just the reductions in aid that ruined their hopes: "the physical side of it—the withdrawal of troops, the loss of U.S. airpower, declining aid—was no more disastrous than the concomitant psychological effects of no longer being regarded by the United States as worth saving. They regarded the decline in aid, particularly in the face of the ever-growing might of their enemy and the support that the enemy received from *his* allies, as irrefutable proof [of abandonment]." Stephen T. Hosmer, Konrad Kellen, Brian M. Jenkins, *The Fall of South Vietnam: Statements by Vietnamese Military and Civilian Leaders,* A Report prepared for Historian, Office of the Secretary of Defense, R-2208-OSD (HIST), December 1978, (Santa Monica, Calif.: Rand Corporation), p. v. See also pp. 5–13, 127, 129.

5. Executive Branch Position Paper, in the author's possession.

6. Ibid., p. 1.

7. Ibid., p. 8.

8. Ibid., p. 11.

9. Kissinger, *A World Restored,* p. 326.

10. See *New York Times,* May 1, 1975.

11. *Washington Post,* May 1, 1975. In his memoirs Mr. Ford said nothing at all about the Nixon-Thieu correspondence. He asserted that the United States had agreed at Paris "to back up the terms of the Paris Peace accords," but declined to say that Congress had been told of the promise to use force (*A Time to Heal,* pp. 248–57). Thieu's name is mentioned only once, in the discussion of the fall of Vietnam, when his resignation is noted. His name does not appear in the book's index.

12. *Washington Post,* May 1, 1975.

13. Henry Kissinger, *White House Years* (Boston: Little, Brown, 1979), p. 1446.

14. Ibid., p. 1448.

15. Ibid., pp. 1451, 1459.

16. Text in ibid., p. 1462.

17. Ibid., p. 1469.
18. Ibid., p. 1470.
19. *Washington Post,* May 2, 1975.
20. Ibid., May 2, 3, 1975.
21. Ibid., May 28, 1975.
22. U.S., Congress, Senate, Hearings before the Subcommittee on Separation of Powers of the Senate Committee on the Judiciary on Congressional Oversight of Executive Agreements, 94th Cong., 1st sess., 1975, p. 318.
23. Ibid., p 27.
24. Ibid., pp. 26, 29. Asked to explain why President Nixon would have chosen to obey the law, even though it was inconsistent with the commitment to South Vietnam, Admiral Zumwalt answered: "The way I reconciled the confusion in my own mind was to decide that a political decision had been made by the President, in view of the difficulties he found himself in over Watergate, not to bring out for public debate the commitments that had been made (ibid, p. 29).
25. News Conference of January 24, 1973, *State Department Bulletin,* February 12, 1973, pp. 116.
26. U.S., Congress, House, Hearings Before the Committee on Foreign Affairs, 93rd Cong., 1st sess., February 8, 1973, p. 83.
27. *Washington Post,* May 6, 1975.
28. Ron Nessen, *It Sure Looks Different from the Inside* (Chicago: Playboy Press, 1978), p. 107.
29. Kissinger, *White House Years,* p. 1470.
30. "But for the collapse of executive authority," Kissinger wrote, "as a result of Watergate, I believe we would have succeeded" (ibid.).
31. See Stanley Hoffmann, *Contemporary Theory and International Relations* (Englewood Cliffs, N.J.: Prentice-Hall, 1960), *The State of War: Essays on the Theory and Practice of International Politics* (New York: Praeger, 1965), *Gulliver's Troubles: Or The Setting of American Foreign Policy* (New York: McGraw-Hill, 1968), and numerous articles, particularly those already cited on the Kissinger foreign policy.
32. Stanley Hoffman, *Primacy or World Order: American Foreign Policy since the Cold War* (New York: McGraw-Hill, 1978), pp. 24–30, 38–39, 40–52, 70–72.
33. Robert O. Keohane, Joseph S. Nye, *Power and Interdependence: World Politics in Transition* (Boston: Little, Brown, 1977); Edward L. Morse, *Modernization and the Transformation of International Relations* (New York: Free Press, 1976); Seyom Brown, *New Forces in World Politics* (Washington, D.C.: Brookings Institution, 1974).
34. Hoffmann, *Primacy or World Order,* p. 118.
35. Ibid., p. 160.
36. Ibid., p. 163.
37. Ibid., p. 162.
38. Ibid., Chap. 4, passim.
39. Ibid., p. 184.
40. Ibid., pp. 190–93.
41. *Washington Post,* October 11, 12, 1979.
42. Holbert N. Carroll, *The House of Representatives and Foreign Affairs* (Pittsburgh, Pa.: Univ. of Pittsburgh, 1958), p. 73.
43. Larry M. Schwab, *Changing Patterns of Congressional Politics* (New York: Van Nostrand, 1980), pp. 102–3.
44. Bayless Manning, "The Congress, the Executive, and Intermestic Affairs: Three Proposals," *Foreign Affairs* 55, no. 2 (January 1977):311.

45. Carroll, *The House of Representatives and Foreign Affairs,* p. 215.
46. Ibid., p. 216.
47. Ibid., p. 217.
48. Ibid., pp. 220–21.
49. See Carroll's account of the activities of the Select Committee on Communist Aggression, previously the Select Committee to Investigate Soviet Seizure of the Baltic States, ibid., pp. 213–14.
50. J. William Fulbright, "The Legislator as Educator," *Foreign Affairs* 57 (Spring 1979):731.
51. Ibid., pp. 731–32.
52. Douglas J. Bennett, Jr., "Congress in Foreign Policy: Who Needs It?" *Foreign Affairs* 57, no. 1 (Fall 1978):46.
53. Louis Fisher, *Presidential Spending Power* (Princeton, N.J.: Princeton Univ. Press, 1975), p. 201.
54. Hoffmann, *Primacy or World Order,* p. 228.
55. Joseph S. Nye, Jr., "Independence and Interdependence," *Foreign Policy* (Spring 1976), p. 153.
56. Manning, ". . . Three Proposals," pp. 311–14.
57. Graham Allison, Peter Szanton, *Remaking Foreign Policy: The Organizational Connection* (New York: Basic Books, 1976), chap. 5; I. M. Destler, "National Security Advice to U.S. Presidents: Some Lessons from Thirty Years," *World Politics* 2 (January 1977):143–76. See also notes 2 and 3 above.
58. Hoffmann, *Primacy or World Order,* p. 219.
59. Carroll, *The House of Representatives and Foreign Affairs,* p. 337.
60. Ibid., p. 233.
61. For a timeless discussion of the difficulties of such a proposal see ibid., pp. 224–30.
62. Ibid., p. 313.
63. The term "networks of continuing relations" is borrowed from Carroll, ibid., p. 335.
64. Lee H. Hamilton and Michael H. Van Dusen, "Making the Separation of Powers Work," *Foreign Affairs,* 57, no. 1 (Fall 1978):33.
65. Ibid., p. 39.
66. Ernest R. May, *"Lessons" of the Past: The Use and Misuse of History in American Foreign Policy* (London: Oxford Univ. Press, 1973), p. xi.
67. Ibid. About American policy in Vietnam, May said: "Here one can see men who would have been scandalized by an inelegant economic model or a poorly prepared legal brief making significant use of historical parallels, analogies, and trends with utter disregard for expertise or even the inherent logic of their assertions. No example illustrates better both the importance of history for men in government and the carelessness and lack of system with which they characteristically use it." (ibid., p. 121).
68. Ibid., p. xii.
69. On the unsuitability of the Vietnamese military organization and its dependence on American advisers and an extremely high level of military aid, see the interviews of Vietnamese officials in Hosmer, Kellen, and Jenkins, *The Fall of South Vietnam,* particularly the sections on Vietnamization, reliance on U.S. help, disagreements on force structure, pp. 9–15, 38–42; and chapters 5, "Strategy and Tactics," and 7, "The Balance of Forces before the 1975 Offensive."

Sources Consulted

Interviews

Interviews with decision makers in Congress and the executive branch are of critical importance to a study of this kind. In all, I conducted more than fifty separate interviews with individuals in both branches over a period of nine months. Most of the interviews were semistructured—that is, the questions were systematically formulated but posed in a way intended to draw the greatest spontaneous response possible—and I seldom took notes in the presence of the person I was interviewing. Some interviews, those with committee staff, for example, could be repeated; others, with General Scowcroft or Peter Rodman, were brief, directed at specific points, and conducted by telephone. Information gathered in interviews with the following individuals was of significant help to me in my research: Congressmen Pete DuPont, Donald Fraser and Lee Hamilton; Foreign Affairs Committee staff members John Brady, John Sullivan, and Michael Van Dusen; and National Security Council staff members General Brent Scowcroft, Les Janka, and Peter Rodman.

U.S. Government Documents

There are several standard sources that are used so frequently in research that a general citation is appropriate. These are the *Congressional Record,* the *Weekly Compilation of Presidential Documents,* and the *Department of State Bulletin*. In addition, there are hearings and reports by committees, members of Congress, and committee staff, and studies by the Congressional Research Service. Although many others were consulted, those most important to my research were:

U.S., Congress, Congressional Research Service. *Cambodia and U.S. Foreign Assistance*. By Robert Shuey. Issue Brief IB 75022. Washington, D.C.: Library of Congress, originated March 11, 1975; updated April 2, 1975.

———. *Legislation Restricting Involvement of U.S. Military Forces in Indochina.* By Marjorie Niehaus and Robert Shuey. Washington, D.C.: Library of Congress, January 21, 1975.

———. *South Vietnam: The Question of Continuing U.S. Military Aid.* By Larry Niksch. Issue Brief IB 75011. Washington, D.C.: Library of Congress, originated February 19, 1975; updated February 28, 1975.

U.S., Congress, House, Committee on Foreign Affairs. *Chronologies of Major Developments in Selected Areas of International Relations.* Cumulative edition, Jan.–Dec. 1974. Committee Print. Washington, D.C.: Government Printing Office, 1975.

U.S., Congress, House, Committee on International Relations.*Chronologies of Major Developments in Selected Areas of International Relations.* Jan.–June 1975. Committee Print. Washington, D.C.: Government Printing Office, 1975.

———. *Congress and Foreign Policy: 1974.* Committee Print. Washington, D.C.: Government Printing Office, 1975.

———. *Executive-Legislative Communications and the Role of the Congress during International Crisis.* A Report by the Comptroller General of the United States to the Subcommittee on International Political and Military Affairs. 94th Cong., 1st sess., 1976.

———. Hearings. *The Vietnam-Cambodia Emergency, 1975. Part I: Vietnam Evacuation and Humanitarian Assistance,* April 9, 15, 16, 18, and May 7 and 8, 1975; *Part II: The Cambodia-Vietnam Debate,* March 7, 11, 12, 13, and April 14, 1975; *Part III: Vietnam Evacuation: Testimony of Ambassador Graham Martin,* January 27, 1976; and *Part IV: Cambodia Evacuation: Testimony of Ambassador John Gunther Dean,* May 5, 1976. 94th Cong., 1st sess., 1976.

———. *Military and Economic Situation in Cambodia: Report of a Staff Survey Team to Cambodia.* Confidential Committee print. Washington, D.C.: Government Printing Office, March 13, 1975.

———. *Oversight Report on Assistance to Indochina Evacuation.* H.R. 94-205, 94th Cong., 1st sess., 1975.

———. *Survey of Activities.* Committee Print. Washington, D.C.: Government Printing Office, 1975.

———. *War Powers: A Test of Compliance, Relative to the Danang Sealift, the Evacuation of Phnom Penh, the Evacuation of Saigon, and the Mayaquez Incident.* Hearings before the Subcommittee on International Security and Scientific Affairs, May 7 and June 4, 1975. 94th Cong., 1st sess., 1975.

U.S., Congress, House. *Committee Reform Amendments of 1974: Explanation of H.Res.988 as Adopted by the House of Representatives, October 8, 1974.* Staff Report of the Select Committee on Committees, 93rd Cong., 2nd sess. Committee Print. Washington, D.C.: Government Printing Office, 1974.

U.S., Congress, House, Democratic Study Group. *The New Vietnam*

Crisis. Special Report no. 94-4. Washington: photocopied, April 13, 1975.

U.S., Congress, Senate, Committee on Armed Services. *Vietnam Aid—the Painful Options*. Report of Senator Sam Nunn. 94th Cong., 1st sess., 1975.

Books and Articles

Acheson, Dean. *Present at the Creation*. New York: Norton, 1969.

———. *This Vast External Realm*. New York: Norton, 1973.

Allison, Graham, and Szanton, Peter. *Remaking Foreign Policy: The Organizational Connection*. New York: Basic Books, 1976

Barone, Michael; Ujifusa, Grant; and Matthews, Douglas. *The Almanac of American Politics 1976*. New York: E.P. Dutton, 1975.

Bennett, Douglas J., Jr. "Congress in Foreign Policy: Who Needs It?" *Foreign Affairs* 57, no. 1 (Fall 1978):40–50.

Brandon, Henry. *The Retreat of American Power*. Garden City, N.Y.: Doubleday, 1973.

Brown, Seyom. *New Forces in World Politics*. Washington, D.C.: Brookings Institution, 1974.

Burns, James MacGregor. *Presidential Government: The Crucible of Leadership*. Boston: Houghton Mifflin, 1965.

———. *Uncommon Sense*. New York: Harper and Row, 1972.

Campbell, John. *The Foreign Affairs Fudge Factory*. New York: Basic Books, 1971.

Carroll, Holbert N. *The House of Representatives and Foreign Affairs*. Pittsburgh, Pa.: University of Pittsburgh, 1958.

Davis, Nathaniel. "The Angola Decision of 1975: A Personal Memoir." *Foreign Affairs* 57, no. 1 (Fall 1978):109–24.

Dodd, Larry. "Emergence of Party Government in the House of Representatives." *DEA News Supplement*, Summer 1976.

Fenno, Richard F., Jr. "The Internal Distribution of Influence: The House." In *Readings on Congress*, edited by Raymond Wolfinger. Englewood Cliffs, N.J.: Prentice-Hall, 1971.

Fisher, Louis. *Presidential Spending Power*. Princeton, N.J.: Princeton University Press, 1975.

Ford, Gerald R. *A Time to Heal: The Autobiography of Gerald R. Ford*. New York: Harper and Row, 1979.

Frye, Alton. *A Responsible Congress: The Politics of National Security*. New York: McGraw-Hill, 1975.

Fullbright, J. William. "The Legislator as Educator." *Foreign Affairs* 57, no. 4 (Spring 1979):719–32.

Goldwin, Robert A., and Clor, Harry M., eds. *Readings in American Foreign Policy,* 2nd ed. New York: Oxford University Press, 1971.

Graubard, Stephen R. *Kissinger: Portrait of a Mind.* New York: Norton, 1973.

Halberstam, David. *The Best and the Brightest.* New York: Random House, 1972.

Hamilton, Lee H., and Van Dusen, Michael H. "Making the Separation of Powers Work." *Foreign Affairs* 57, no. 1 (Fall 1978):17–39.

Hartley, Anthony. "American Foreign Policy in the Nixon Era." *Adelphi Papers* no. 110 (Winter 1974–75). London: International Institute for Strategic Studies, 1975.

Hoffmann, Stanley. *Contemporary Theory and International Relations.* Englewood Cliffs, N.J.: Prentice-Hall, 1960.

———. *Gulliver's Troubles: or, The Setting of American Foreign Policy.* New York: Published for the Council on Foreign Relations by McGraw-Hill, 1968.

———. *Primacy or World Order: American Foreign Policy since the Cold War.* New York: McGraw-Hill, 1978.

———. *The State of War: Essays on the Theory and Practice of International Politics.* New York: Praeger, 1965.

———. "Weighing the Balance of Power." *Foreign Affairs* 50, no. 4 (July 1972):618–643.

———. "Will the Balance Balance at Home?" *Foreign Policy,* no. 7 (Summer 1972), pp. 60–86.

Hook, Sidney. *The Hero in History: A Study in Limitation and Possibility.* New York: John Day, 1943.

Hosmer, Stephen T.; Kellen, Konrad; and Jenkins, Brian M. *The Fall of South Vietnam: Statements by Vietnamese Military and Civilian Leaders.* Santa Monica, Calif.: The Rand Corporation, 1978.

Hughes, Emmet John. *The Living Presidency: The Resources and Dilemmas of the American Presidential Office.* New York: Coward, McCann & Geoghegan, 1972.

Jones, Joseph Marion. *Fifteen Weeks.* New York: Harcourt, Brace, Jovanovich, 1965.

Kalb, Marvin, and Kalb, Bernard. *Kissinger.* Boston: Little, Brown, 1974.

Kennan, George F. *Memoirs, 1925–1950.* Boston: Little, Brown, 1967.

Keohane, Robert O., and Nye, Joseph S. *Power and Interdependence: World Politics in Transition.* Boston: Little, Brown, 1977.

Kissinger, Henry. "Domestic Structure and Foreign Policy." *Daedalus* 95 (Spring 1966):503–29.

———. *White House Years.* Boston: Little, Brown, 1979.

Kolko, Gabriel. *The Roots of American Foreign Policy.* Boston: Beacon Press, 1969.

Kolko, Gabriel, and Kolko, Joyce. *The Limits of Power: The World and United States Foreign Policy, 1945–1954*. New York: Harper and Row, 1972.

Landau, David. *Kissinger: The Uses of Power*. Boston: Houghton Mifflin, 1972.

Lehman, John. *The Executive, Congress, and Foreign Policy: Studies of the Nixon Administration*. New York: Praeger, 1976.

Manning, Bayless. "The Congress, the Executive, and Intermestic Affairs: Three Proposals." *Foreign Affairs* 55, no. 2 (January 1977):306–24.

May, Ernest R. *"Lessons" of the Past: The Use and Misuse of History in American Foreign Policy*. London: Oxford University Press, 1973.

Morse, Edward L. *Modernization and the Transformation of International Relations*. New York: Free Press, 1976.

Nessen, Ron. *It Sure Looks Different from the Inside*. Chicago: Playboy Press, 1978.

Neustadt, Richard. *Presidential Power: The Politics of Leadership from FDR to Carter*. New York: Wiley, 1979.

Ornstein, Norman J., and Rhode, David. "Congressional Reform and Political Parties in the U.S. House of Representatives." In *Parties and Elections in an Anti-Party Age: American Politics and the Crisis of Confidence*, ed. by Jeff Fishel and David Braden. Bloomington, Ind.: University of Indiana Press, 1978.

Pious, Richard M. *The American Presidency*. New York: Basic Books, 1979.

Porter, Gareth. *A Peace Denied: The United States, Vietnam, and the Paris Agreement*. Bloomington, Ind.: University of Indiana Press, 1975.

Pusey, Merlo J. *The Way We Go to War*. Boston: Houghton Mifflin, 1969.

Rapoport, Daniel. *Inside the House*. Chicago: Follett, 1975.

Ripon Society, and Brown, Clifford W. *Jaws of Victory: The Game-Plan Politics of 1972, the Crisis of the Republican Party, and the Future of the Constitution*. Boston: Little, Brown, 1974.

Schlesinger, Arthur M., Jr. *The Age of Roosevelt: The Coming of the New Deal*. Boston: Houghton Mifflin, 1959.

———. *The Age of Roosevelt: The Crisis of the Old Order*. Boston: Houghton Mifflin, 1957.

———. *The Imperial Presidency*. Boston: Houghton Mifflin, 1973.

Schwab, Larry M. *Changing Patterns of Congressional Politics*. New York: Van Nostrand, 1980.

Shawcross, William. *Sideshow: Kissinger, Nixon, and the Destruction of Cambodia*. New York: Simon and Schuster, 1979.

Snepp, Frank. *Decent Interval: An Insider's Account of Saigon's Indecent End Told by the CIA's Chief Strategy Analyst in Vietnam*. New York: Random House, 1978.

Stockwell, John. *In Search of Enemies: A CIA Story*. New York: Norton, 1978.

White, Theodore H. *Breach of Faith: The Fall of Richard Nixon*. New York: Atheneum, 1975.

Wildavsky, Aaron., ed. *Perspectives on the Presidency*. Boston: Little, Brown, 1975.

Index

THE LIBRARY
ST. MARY'S COLLEGE OF MARYLAND
ST. MARY'S CITY, MARYLAND 20686